DONNA TIERNAN MAHONEY, a
cut, received her BA in Psychology
the Sacred Heart in 1969. Twenty ye
of Theology *summa cum laude* from
Seminary.

Recently elected Second Vice-President of the National Council of Catholic Women, Donna has served in various national and diocesan positions. She was the first president of Catholic Charities of the Diocese of Palm Beach and was appointed as diocesan representative to the 1986 NCCB Convening for the Synod on the Laity, the 1989 NCCB National Convening on 'Women's Concerns in the Local Church', and the 1990 NCCB 'The Wisdom of Women' Conference.

Programmes in social ministry, women's concerns, collaboration, ecumenism, lay ministry, education and empowerment have benefited from Donna's energy and expertise. Highlights of her many national interests are Future of the American Church, Campaign for Human Development, Pax Christi, International Conference of Consulting and Residential Centres, and Network. Diocesan boards include Maurawood Home for Unwed Mothers, Cursillo Movement, Diocesan Parish Social Ministry Task Force, Middle Income Project, and Ecumenical Committee.

Business partners, Donna and her husband John, own and operate restaurants in North Carolina and Florida. As their children were growing, Donna's community activities included school advisory boards, Junior League and coaching children's sports. The Mahoneys reside in West Palm Beach with their four children.

TOUCHING THE FACE OF GOD

Intimacy and Celibacy in Priestly Life

By

Donna Tiernan Mahoney

THE MERCIER PRESS

The Mercier Press
P.O. Box 5, 5 French Church Street, Cork
24 Lower Abbey Street Dublin 1

ISBN 1 85635 019 3

First published in the United States of America by Jeremiah Press

Dedicated to
Mom
teacher of faith and love
Dad
teacher of kindness and gentleness
and
John
teacher of courage and strength

Printed in Ireland by Colour Books Ltd.

CONTENTS

ACKNOWLEDGEMENTS

With each passing day, I become more powerfully aware of the existential reality of the Body of Christ; the idea that each of us in the Body needs all the rest of us so that we can more fully become who we are called to be. Many whose names may or may not appear below have encouraged, affirmed, directed and challenged me during the preparation of this book, first as my Master's thesis at St Vincent De Paul Regional Seminary, and more recently, in its present context.

John, my love and life-sharer, has been ever-present with his strength and encouragement, especially when life got tough. Our children – John, Patrick, Shannon and Erin – as well as my parents, Ellen and Arthur Tiernan have covered all the home bases on innumerable occasions. I thank all of them for their love, humour and patience and for the time sacrificed so that I may do this work.

A very special priest of my childhood, Fr Jack Skehan, provided an image of a priest as gentle, loving and approachable. This image has travelled with me for many years. Thank you!!!

I am most grateful for the many close friendships of students and professors at St Vincent's, and I particularly wish to thank Fr Michael Scanlon, who in my first course of 'Fundamental Moral Thelology' encouraged first year theologians to become 'critical lovers of the Church'. Fr Orlando Espin, my thesis director, encouraged me in my topic and helped give structure and form to my initial understandings, while Fr James McCartney, Fr Tom Foudy, Fr Josef Fuchs, Fr Felipe Estevez, Dr Sixto Garcia and Fr John Morrissey complemented my understandings of moral theology. Fr

Gerald Grace, Fr Steve Bosso and Fr Robert Gibbons were of tremendous aid in filling in the gaps of their respective disciplines of systematic theology, scripture, and canon law. I wish to give a special thank you to Fr Foudy for his insightful pastoral understandings of ecclesiology and time shared in friendship and discussion.

Many friendships made at St Vincent's have continued over the last few years. I am especially thankful for the depth of friendship and frequent interactions especially with Frs Jeff McGowan, Bob Napier and Jerry Kaywell, all of whom are now partners in ministry in neighbouring dioceses. Their presence in my life has been, as Jerry would say, 'less than a miracle, more than a coincidence'!

The support of Dr Hilda Montalvo, Joan Hauser, Anne Skowronek and Mary Maguire, all co-mentors who make up my Wednesday morning discipling group, 'The Open Circle', has been essential and invaluable. I especially wish to thank Joan for her endless patience in editing and her 'turns of phrase ' which have added both interest and humour. I am also most grateful to Hilda and Fr Bill Sheehan directors of my lay ministry formation.

The support and interest of many women locally and especially my sisters across the country on all levels of the National Council of Catholic Women has been most refreshing and beneficial. I am strengthened by the boundless energy of our own diocesan moderator, Msgr Irvine Nugent, who tirelessly encourages us to 'go for it' in all of our endeavours.

Lenore Read has been my faithful companion at the word processor and has added both depth and lightheartedness to this project; Ann Kolak Edleman did the very same labour of love and added her ministerial expertise during the thesis preparation of this work, and Jeanne Hullihan generously offered and gave her gifts and skills in editing my original manuscript. To all of them, I wish to extend my sincerest thanks.

My dear friend and pastor, Fr Frank O'Loughlin, has been available whenever I pushed the 'panic button'. His constant challenge in all areas of my life has been most growth-producing. My fellow 'ENFP', Fr Marty Devereaux, has constantly been there for support, discernment and strength. I wish to acknowledge Marty's doctoral work in this area which has been most helpful.

Marnie Ritchie Poncy, nurse-lawyer, has changed her schedule, moved patients and clients, and has been available for sharing and listening at any hour of the day or night. She shares a part of my soul.

Finally to my everyday partners in ministry and life-long friends, Fr Frank Flynn and Fr Tim Lynch, affectionately dubbed 'the Flynch boys' by my family – thank you for the many times you have affirmed me, fought with me, challenged me, shared with me, stood by me, and helped me to 'Touch the Face of God'.

FOREWORD

'Do not be afraid!
Open, indeed, open wide the doors to Christ!'
Pope John Paul II, 22 October, 1978

I would like to invite you on a journey of healing, healing of hearts and minds, attitudes and perceptions, expectations and laws.

For the past eight years, I have criss-crossed the United States and Canada, presenting Isaiah Parish Missions, teaching evangelisation courses in parishes, seminaries and continuing education programmes, and consulting with various diocesan or religious order councils, commissions and staffs.

In the course of my travels, I have been trapped in burning buildings (the 28th floor restaurant of a hotel on fire!), have experienced a precautionary landing of an aeroplane with no landing gear, have been in an aeroplane hit by lightning, have been whisked off the altar by a bomb squad, and have been caught in the middle of a guns-drawn drug bust. None of these situations is as frightening to me as the large number of lonely, sad, alienated, isolated, or angry priests whom I have found along the way.

To be honest, I must exclude the pastors and my other 'hosts', for they are usually a 'breed apart', simply by virtue of their invitations of collaborative ministry to a lay woman in the first place! These psychologically healthy men are open, empathic, sensitive, and, self-admittedly, 'still in process'. They are secure in themselves and in their relationship with God. They are creative, challenging, and 'fully alive'. They are not perfect. They struggle, they cry, they scheme, they dream ... and, they laugh a lot!

The singular common factor I have found in these men is

that nearly every single one is involved in at least one close, personal, intimate relationship, either with other priest friends, lay men, or religious or lay women. They share openly that these 'significant other' relationships are life-giving, challenging, energising, sanity-producing, and serve to 'keep them honest!'

My alarm comes when I observe with sadness the 'walking dead' among us – the controllers, the legalists, the sexists, the rigid, the authoritarians, the addicted, the disillusioned, the disenchanted, the burnt out, and the exhausted! Particular friendships are anathema to them!

When I first read Donna Mahoney's original thesis, I felt as if a door had truly opened for all priests, encouraging intimacy, trust, affection, and, yes, even love. Her thesis, simply stated, is that like *all* human beings, priests also have an enormous need and capacity for intimacy and love. Her final conclusion is both logical and compelling: a call for reconsideration of optional celibacy, remembering that the word *optional* is critical and operative here.

With many others who read her original thesis, I encouraged her to revise and publish it in its present form, with the hope that all priests and those who love them – their families, friends and parishioners – would read and benefit from this authoritative but compassionate survey. *Touching the Face of God* is neither scandalous nor sensational; instead it is sensitive, positive, realistic, and reasoned. It offers permission, protection and empowerment, the three necessary ingredients which promote positive change, personal development, and transformation. Indeed, open wide the doors to Christ, who came to bring fullness of life to all of us, including priests!

Susan W. Blum, Ed.D.
Director, Isaiah Ministries

PREFACE

Our thirtieth grammar school reunion took place this summer. We had the time of our lives! All weekend long, many of the hundred or so classmates from seventh and eighth grades reminisced about those carefree years of our lives. After thirty years, some long-kept secrets were finally revealed, like who stole the mascot, which eighth grade 'friend' thought it would be funny to put a match to my dress (with me in it!), who was the phantom poet, and who regularly replaced my turkey sandwich with peanut butter and jelly.

All weekend long we sang and danced, relaxed and talked. We cried a little too. Every once in a while his name would pop up. He was pictured frequently in the video that had been prepared by the organisers ... Michael.

From the viewpoint of a thirteen-year-old girl, Michael was the eighth grade sweetheart. From the viewpoint of a 'now mother-of-four', Michael was the ideal eighth-grade son. He was loved by all: bright and full of life. It was at Michael's birthday party that our class first played the tempestuous game of spin-the-bottle!

At our eighth grade graduation, Michael announced, much to the dismay of his family, that he was entering the seminary. He wanted this so badly. We were all happy for him, but a little saddened, too, knowing we would miss him in the high school years to follow.

Every once in a while, I'd hear about him. Life went on, however, and we lost contact over the years. Then, in 1968, I heard that Michael had decided to leave the seminary because of too many personal demands. He did not think he could commit to the priestly life. Knowing Michael, I fully understood.

In the Fall of 1970, a few weeks before our second son was born, Sister Martha called. 'Michael,' she said, 'took his life by overdose. I know he was special to you, Donna, so I wanted you to know that Michael's funeral is on Thursday.'

One of my special childhood friends was dead. How would I ever make meaning out of this senseless death?

This book is for all the Michaels who have tried so hard to find meaning within the celibate reality.

Donna Tiernan Mahoney
West Palm Beach, Florida
27 September, 1991
Feast of St Vincent de Paul

INTRODUCTION

Hermeneutical methods have shown the necessity of getting behind the text and asking why the author feels the urgency to write. The motivation of the writer is essential for the understanding of biblical literature. Similarly, I believe the motivation for this writing is important for its understanding. Some will question why a Catholic laywoman would choose to write on 'Intimacy and Celibacy in Priestly Life', even though few would question the reasoning or credibility of a celibate's writing on marriage. There is a need for an explanation, even if limited.

Ever since I was very young, my family has had many very close friends who were priests. Because we were in the restaurant business, these close priest friends would often gather together at my family's business for food and companionship. Often times they would end the evening in our living room with songs, stories and laughter. These childhood experiences, which were enhanced by my life experiences at Catholic schools, our family's active involvement in Church, and my years of sharing as a seminary student have enabled me to see a side of priesthood not visible to many. Since my husband and I have continued our family business, we too have found ourselves involved in the lives of numerous priest friends. We have made many warm and wonderful friendships. In addition, however, we have also been put in touch with the tremendous pain, loneliness and isolation of many priests.

Having been in ministry for as long as I can remember, first informally and then formally, has also brought me in contact with many priests. Over the years I have found many loving men who reflect the life of Jesus in their encounters with others. But I have also encountered many who were cold, indifferent, fearful, and had difficulties in dealing with the humanity of their lives. Over the years, I have asked myself many times: 'What makes the difference?'

Our American Church has certainly not put its head in the sand with regard to this topic. Even though much diagnosis has taken place, as witnessed by the volumes of literature (for example, see Footnote 29, Chapter 4), the heart of the matter has never been substantially resolved.

Experientially, I have observed that the difference seems to lie in the relationships that these men have or have not found with 'significant' others. The common human experiences that have to be dealt with in close human relationships enable priests to accept themselves, first of all as human beings and then as priests. Those values, sometimes painful, sometimes joyful, that must be dealt with in close friendships are values that can be transferred into ministerial relationships which reflect God's love to others. Having been loved, the priest is free to show God's love to others to whom he ministers. He is unafraid to do this because he has come to realise that love dispels fear. Often those priests who lack the experience that human relationships bring turn to the use of power, control, rigid religious forms, or abusive and irresponsible habits in order to compensate for a lack of fulfilment of their affective needs. These men have an inability to relate to the average struggling person; they have an inability to show love and compassion.

One of the national organisations to which I belong is primarily composed of people who work with dysfunctional priests and religious. During the presentations at the annual meetings, I often find myself asking why we in the Church are reactive rather than proactive; why we spend so much time, effort and money treating pathological situations rather than teaching mature development in formation that results in healthy ministerial lives. Certainly, this book is one effort to do this.

Having given the brief explanation above, I can state two explicit reasons why this book is important to me.

The first is related to my involvement as an active Catholic lay minister. In that role I have observed how desperately the Church **needs** psychologically healthy priests. The Church and her priests have a tremendous impact on society. Priests, by virtue of their ministry of preaching, have the ability to influence large groups of people. If they send out messages which are not reflective of holistic gospel values they will do one of two things: They will either negatively influence society (since many still consider the word of the priest to be absolute truth), or they will turn people away from the Church (since many of the more educated will reject a theology that is not holistic). In either case, these priests will not be promoting the reign of God.

The second reason for my writing this book is more personal. I have observed that the pain, frustration, isolation, and loneliness of many priests has been caused by past training which has left them with the conviction that 'particular friendships' are inappropriate. As a young woman, I lost a very dear friend who I felt had struggled with the lack of intimacy in seminary life, until he finally took his own life. This, I feel, was an unnecessary loss of life. Having experienced what close friendships can do in the lives of priests, I reject the inhumane idea that particular friendships are inappropriate. Having shared that friendship with many, I am convinced of its goodness, its creativity, and its ability to bring people 'to touch the face of God'.

The challenge in this book is to take the intuitions that

have been experientially felt and to ground them in an understanding that has its basis in both theological and psychological truths. This is necessary in order to show that there is a need for intimacy in the life and ministry of a priest, whether that be in the existing celibate structure, or in some future structure where celibacy may be optional.

The purpose of this work is to show that this 'bias' against 'particular friendships' is not reflective of biblical thinking, and, in fact, is opposed to the gospel dictates. In addition, evidence of much psychological work which has shown intimacy to be an absolute need for authentic adult living will be presented. One cannot love the whole world without loving at least one person in particular. The work of both the fields of psychology and theology will be combined to show that intimacy is not only compatible (psychologically) with celibacy but that it is also necessary (theologically); that it is, in fact, responsive to true gospel values. It also will be shown that celibacy, although much affirmed in our tradition, is not essential for priesthood and should not be considered the only viable path for priesthood of the future.

Intimacy can be achieved by some within the existing celibate structure. When this intimacy is integrated with a celibate lifestyle, it gives witness to a very powerful love of God and people. Throughout the ages, within and outside of the Church, we have evidence of this.

However, many who are or who desire to be priests have not been given this charism of celibacy. We are certainly at a pivotal point in Church history. This book is a call to re-examine some of the historical realities and some of the reasons for which celibacy was originally enforced and to ask ourselves if these reasons are still valid today. In particular, we will look at our theology of sexuality as well as the issue of women's equality and ask if there is some connection between them and the Church's refusal to consider optional celibacy.

We have long passed the stage of an *either/or* dualism in our theology (at least consciously). We are becoming comfortable with a *both/and* mentality in our religious endeavours. *Both* a life of celibacy *and* a life of married sexuality are valid styles of serving God and each other. We must encourage the Church to continue efforts to pursue this line of thinking, as many today cannot reflect the intimate love of God to others within the existing framework.

The method that we will use is to integrate the fields of theology, psychology, and storytelling. Christian theology today has emphasised the use of human experience as a valid locus for theologising. The faith experiences of believing people are indeed the basis for theological reflection, and these experiences, as interpreted by the social sciences, have contributed a vast amount of research which is indispensable to contemporary theology.

Karl Rahner tells us that theology's most significant dialogical partner today may not be philosophy. Rather, psychology and the natural and social sciences may be the partners of theology because they shape human self-understanding today.[1] Psychology, in particular, has been called a valid partner because it is an essential tool for understanding human experience.

The dialogical and integrative approach is essential for looking at moral theology in terms of what has been given to a graced and sinful humanity. This approach must include a whole new theology of sexuality. Such a theology (which is still in the process of development) would stress the dignity of each individual and look at 'human sexuality in the context of intimacy, spirituality, and interpersonal growth'.[2]

The text will begin with some real life vignettes which I have composed from my years of sharing meals, hospitality, and ministry with many priests and of being a lay student in our seminary. These stories are all essentially true although I have changed the names, places, situations, and have at times merged two or three people into one for the sake of anonymity. In addition, out of respect for the confidences of priests who have shared with me or priests I have known, I have asked for and received permission to use any story based primarily on one character. My intent in Chapter One is not to show anyone in bad light (in fact, I have omitted stories which might be considered scandalous). My intent is, however, to reflect some of the pain and distortion caused by a lack of intimacy or an inability to let oneself be known on a close personal level. The stories which are in Chapter One and interspersed throughout the book point to the difficulties of a lifestyle which has particular strains and stresses that could be overcome if one were to have at least one or a few intimate friends. The stories are not shocking but are simply stories reflective of the lives of many priests known to all of us. The reader is left to make his/her own conclusions.

Chapter Two will include necessary theological background in order to show that the love that we Christians are called to is not 'removed and far away' but must be 'up close and personal' if we are ever to find out anything about God, ourselves, and one another. Too frequently, love in our tradition has been thought of as idealistic and untouchable rather than intimate and bodily. This we will see is not necessarily our reality.

Chapter Three will give basic psychological theory which will ground all the work that will follow. The integration of Chapters Two and Three provide the essential background showing that psychological intimacy and theological love name the same reality.

Chapters Four and Five will speak of the need for intimacy within the existing celibate reality in the Church today. Many of the ideas contained in these chapters are also valid and valuable even if celibacy becomes an option for priests in the near future. Each one of us may be called to intimacy with more than one person, although not necessarily genital intimacy. Therefore, the insights presented in these two chapters are valuable for all who minister or who are desirous of leading a full Christian life.

The possibilities of intimacy and optional celibacy will be explored in Chapter Six. The presentation of a true life story will cause us to question the intricate historical weaving of the realities of how and why celibacy has come to be so important.

The short historical sketch on celibacy in Chapter Seven will enable us to ask ourselves whether mandated celibacy is still a valid form of discipline within the Church today.

Chapter Eight will speak for itself in light of recent events in the Church. We can no longer put our hreads in the sand with regard to the issue of celibacy.

We seem to be undergoing a transition within priesthood for which there is only one sensible answer. We are moving from the 'experience of religious authority to the authority of religious experience'.[3] Authenticity is critical in religious experience today. Our priests, walking hand in hand with laypersons, are rewriting our theology of priesthood. We can do this only if we are full of faith and trusting in the Spirit of God.

1

INTIMACY AND CELIBACY:
SOME PORTRAYALS OF PRIESTHOOD TODAY

Oh Priest of God

To live in the midst of the world without desiring its pleasures,
To be a member of every family without belonging to any,
To share in all sufferings, to penetrate into all secrets, to heal all wounds,
To go from men to God, to offer Him their prayers,
To return from God to men, to bring pardon and hope,
To have a heart of bronze for chastity, and a heart of gold for charity,
To console and to pardon, to bless and to love.
What a life!
And it is yours, Oh priest of God.

Lacordaire

This lovely, idealistic, and traditional poem can often be found in the homes of many of our priests' families. It shows a captivating understanding of the priest of thirty years ago, or at least it gives an idealistic understanding of what was expected of the priest of that era.

The priest of the 1990s, or at least many with whom I have been in contact, has at least some difficulty in relating to the above portrayal. The priest of our day is involved with most of the same life struggles as we are. If he has tried to be an effective man of God, he has been out in the marketplace and has been affected by the same secularisation, computerisation, automation, and degradation as all of the rest of us struggling men and women. He has had little chance to be a man set apart unless, of course, he has spent his time hiding in his rectory and afraid of life. He may have aspired to the idealism presented in the above poem, but the psychological realities of the human person, with or without the imposition of hands and the ontological change, do not permit perfection.

The stories which follow will, I hope, provide a basic understanding of the lives of priests today. They will speak indirectly of the power and effects of positive and negative relationships in one's life: the power of having an intimate friend with whom to share life's journey or the pain produced when, for some reason, an intimate friend is not permitted in one's life. The portrayals are all of men who have stayed in priesthood many years. The stories of those who have left would require many more volumes.

Again, the stories are essentially true, although names, places and situations have been changed to avoid identification, and permission has been granted to use any of the stories based primarily on one character. Because similar characteristics may exist in many priests, the reader will undoubtedly identify personality traits here and there. These stories are not outrageous or scandalous. They are intended to portray the realities existing in priesthood today and to give some idea of the difficulties and struggles of men who are at different levels of acceptance of intimacy in their lives.

These stories will be referred to throughout the book and will be compared to other life stories as they are presented.

Fr Matthew: It was the summer when John and I were engaged to be married. How can I ever forget that summer! Everything was more passionate; everything was more painful. Bobby Kennedy, Martin Luther King and Fr Matthew; they all died within a few months of one another.

My family had known Fr Matthew since he had come to Florida. He was one of the good old boys from the 'FBI's' or foreign born Irish, as Dad affectionately called them.

He did most of the things that Irish priests did back in the 1950s and 1960s; golf every Wednesday, dinner at a local restaurant (usually ours) every Sunday night, an occasional drinking party, and whatever else in between. He was, as we would have said back then, 'a good priest'. He spoke in a whisper with a gentle Irish brogue. He was a quiet man, or so it appeared to me at the innocent age of twenty.

Mom and Dad got to know him pretty well in the early sixties, and I remember that before I went away to college he used to be a frequent patron at their South Florida restaurant. I'd seen him a lot for dinner. During the summer when I was out of school and working at the restaurant, I'd seen him frequently for lunch as well. He'd arrive a little later than most lunch customers, and he'd always sit and drink his two double martinis while he ate alone and read for two or three hours. He did this, I recall, two or three times a week.

Frequently, I would try to talk to him. Being brought up in the hospitality business, I was taught that most customers will return not only because of the food, but also because they liked to be known, to be talked to, to be listened to. Although I had grown up among many priests and was comfortable with them, it was always a little difficult to maintain a conversation with Fr Matthew. More than being introverted, he seemed to be a man lost within himself. But that was just my perception at a young age, and I could have been wrong.

Seldom did Fr Matthew bring anyone with him. I have only a few recollections of seeing him with other people during all those years. Usually they were business acquaintances: an architect, a fund-raiser, or someone who was going to install an organ in his church.

One summer when I was home from Manhattanville, my north-eastern college, I remember asking Dad about him – about why he always looked so alone and lonely. Dad probably knew him as well as anyone; not that he knew him terribly well at all, but then Fr Matthew did not encourage people to get close to him. Dad told me Fr Matthew's history.

It was said that at one time Fr Matthew had the Church world on a string. He was, as we say, 'moving up' in our diocese and becoming quite competent and well-known as an administrator. I remember this for, when I was a little girl, he would come bursting through the restaurant door with bright eyes emanating from his slight but energetic Irish frame. There was always a small group tagging along behind him. I actually remember that at one of my parents' parties he did an Irish jig! But those memories are dimmed now and are replaced in my mind by thoughts of a quiet, sad, solitary man.

Along the way Fr Matthew had encountered a power-play, Dad said. The 'higher ups' turned against him, and from this he never recovered. His self-concept had been shattered, and he spent the rest of his days doing routine things. Mostly, he got lost in his own world which was fogged by too much drink and too few, if any, close friends. He dropped his Wednesday golf games; he even dropped Sunday night with the guys.

Toward the end, during the summer of 1968, we would see him more frequently, as he came to eat and drink several times a week and stayed longer each time. Perhaps it was a way for him to hide from the pressure. I think he felt safe with my parents, as they would just let him be. They learned to read his body language well. Although they tried to converse with him and draw him out a little, he had made it clear what he wanted: a brief hello and to be left alone with his book, his drink and his meal. He was not going to be hurt again by anyone. That was blatantly obvious, even to a young girl of twenty. His demeanour spoke loudly and clearly.

It was a Thursday night, two weeks before our wedding, when my parents became concerned about his condition. We were at a small private party, mostly Irish priests and a few lay people. The small middle-aged man was already 'gone', as they say. He had been drinking, but it was more than just that. It was almost as if he had been overtaken by other spirits. It was one of the eeriest things I have ever experienced, even to this day. He spoke as if he were in another orbit, and his face had a strange look which, in the fifteen years of knowing him, I had never seen before. At the beginning of the evening he remained in the group. Later he became reclusive and retired to a corner alone. Had I known what was going to happen, I would have kept him company, but I was younger then and rather afraid that he would reject me.

My father drove Fr Matthew home that night in the priest's big black car. Mom picked up Dad and brought him home. Much to our amazement, he appeared the next day, Friday, for lunch. We saw him only briefly as it was a hectic Friday with hurried customers trying to get an early start on the weekend. I had remembered the eerie feeling that he gave me the night before, and I felt both pained for him and frightened by him. He stayed for his usual few hours and then left.

It did not come as a great shock to arrive home that evening with John, my husband-to-be, and have Mom and Dad tell us of Fr Matthew's death. The autopsy said he died of a heart attack ... Mom said he died of a broken heart.

Fr Jack: Fr Jack was about my age, but he looked much older than his forty plus years. When I first met him, my impressions were of a man who was searching for God in all the wrong places: in bars, in instant intimate relationships, and in a series of parish activities which never allowed him to spend any quality time alone, with God, or with significant others.

Fr Jack had ministered in a nearby diocese for almost twenty years, and, although we worked on many similar projects, we had never met. We were finally introduced at a party given by a mutual priest friend. Immediately, when his name was mentioned, the many ludicrous stories I had heard about him flashed through my mind.

His quick and gregarious manner was open and friendly, almost too friendly, and I knew that he was well on his way to becoming drunk. This concerned me although I knew that he'd be spending the night at the rectory where the party was being held; I knew he would not be driving himself home.

He was the type of priest who incessantly told jokes. He was the life of the party. This I interpreted as wanting to reveal himself but not in a very private way. He wanted to let go, and, at the same time, he was afraid of doing so. He was petrified but so desirous of letting himself be known.

I explained to him how I was trying, along with a priest-friend, to establish an affirmation house for priests in our area. This seemed to fascinate him, and he asked many questions and began to open up. The night passed quickly. I was beginning to feel the depth of his sharing when, unfortunately, the conversation began to deteriorate due to his drinking. At that point, I felt it best to leave. I found out later that Jack had kept the host up talking until 3 am.

The next morning, much to my surprise, Fr Jack called at work and asked if we could 'do lunch', as the preppies were prone to say. I laughed to myself, wondering where someone who lived in the 'boonies' would ever pick up that expression but quickly regained my thoughts and agreed to meet him for a late lunch.

When I walked into the lobby of the restaurant, I was delighted to find him freshly dressed, wearing a casual sport shirt, and seemingly sober. (Having four teenagers has provided many opportunities for doing quick 'breathalysing'). Although his face was flushed and puffy, he had not yet started his daily drinking. I was relieved, as I figured I'd get at least a good forty-five minutes of straight talk from him before he might be affected by the alcohol.

He began with many jokes and off-colour stories, which were making me uncomfortable and were also attracting glances from nearby diners. After about ten minutes of showing my displeasure, he gave me an opening during which I zapped him: 'Jack, what are you running from?'

He gave me one of those looks I've occasionally encountered which say, 'How dare you, a laywoman, talk to me like this?' His look was not enough, or so he thought, and he protested vehemently with a few expletives to make it all the more convincing. I gently reminded him of our in-depth conversation the night before and then put my question to him again in a way that let him know that I was not going to be put off and, in fact, that I had done this type of thing many times before.

'Jack,' I said, 'I deal with many priests every day of my life. They are my friends, my family, and in a few cases, my intimate friends. There is nothing you can tell me which I have not heard in many different variations. Nothing! So why don't you tell me why you're afraid of getting close to anyone; why are you afraid of intimacy?'

This time, I seemed to have phrased my words more to his liking, and I think he felt my sincerity and honesty. Slowly, he began to open up and share his world with me.

It seems that ever since he was a young man, Jack passionately wanted to be a priest. In addition he was powerfully attracted to women, one in particular. All through strict seminary training Jack lived a double life, persevering in studies and religious training, yet still womanising whenever possible. He figured that when he was ordained to the deaconate, it would be time enough to separate from the women in his life and it would no longer be a particular problem.

Deaconal ordination came and Jack's vow of celibacy was soon forgotten. He took up with many and various women whenever possible. Usually he did not tell them that he was a priest. Weekend stands were enough for him. If a relationship lasted longer, he feared emotional entanglements because, after all, he was a priest and couldn't get involved.

There was one time in particular in which he became powerfully attracted in an emotional way to a young woman who lived nearby. She did know he was a priest. They had a very close celibate relationship for about six months. Finally he encouraged her to move away because he couldn't stand it any longer. Since their relationship, he told me, no one had ever come close to being intimate with him in an emotional way. He mentioned that he thinks of her often and wonders if he did the right thing by sending her away. He felt he was happiest when she was around as he really had a friend and companion to share his life. He finds it difficult without her, especially on long Sunday evenings.

Jack, as we know, is on a life-long quest, this mysterious journey called priesthood. In his journey, he has never perceived his calling as a celibate as compatible with a committed intimate relationship. More than anything in the world, Jack wants to remain a priest – no matter what.

Jack will not permit an emotional attachment with a woman in his life. As soon as he sees it coming, he backs away and runs from what may be the one thing that will save him from destroying himself.

Therefore, Jack drinks, tells dirty jokes, and abuses his body. He has short-term sexual encounters, busies himself with activities, and runs away from himself. But his 'saving grace' is that he will not get emotionally involved. Ironically, in the long run, his 'saving grace', in itself, might prevent him from ever achieving his life-long quest.

Fr Smith: The vigorous young man entered the room across the hall where he greeted the shy, middle-aged woman. 'Hello,' he said. 'I'm Fr Smith. You're here to become a Catholic?' With that the woman nodded quickly and looked him in the eye with a meek, 'Yes, Father'.

'Well, that's fine,' said Fr Smith. 'I have a tape here for you to listen to, and I'll be back in an hour and a half to see if you have any questions on the tape. Then I'll set you up with the nuns.' The middle-aged woman looked overcome with the quick, brisk manner of Fr Smith, as she had hoped that her first meeting with a Catholic priest might be a dialogue and that she could talk to him about the difficulties of being a single parent. She tried to disguise her dismay and said, 'All right, Father', as he turned on the recorder and swiftly left the room.

With that, I watched from the office as Fr Smith ran to answer the door. It was two little girl scouts who had come on this early March morning with their cookies to sell. Being one who would kill for their chocolate mints, I was practically out of the office, on the way to the door, when I heard him say, 'Look, little girls, this is a rectory, not a real home. We don't buy girl scout cookies, so tell all your friends not to come here.' He closed the door, and, much to my amazement, he came in grinning and said, 'Little rascals! They drive me crazy. With all the important things I do, I certainly can't be taking time out to buy girl scout's cookies all day long.'

Fr Smith, a Roman-trained priest appeared to be a typical 'keeper of the establishment'. It was rumoured that he, even though quite young, would soon be made a monsignor, even though the practice was rapidly losing its appeal. He was new and, I was told, that he had been sent there to 'get the place in shape', after the previous pastor had retired.

I had come on behalf of a diocesan parish social ministry project, trying to solicit his help in getting some pilot projects going. I was somewhat put-off by his brisk mannerisms, as I had expected someone extremely pastoral in this position. His behaviour in the two situations I had observed did not elicit my admiration. I was determined, however, to remain open-minded about the man.

I took a deep breath and began. Gently, but persistently, I explained our pilot programme to him, every once in a while throwing in how important this was to the bishop. I had found this to be successful several times before but, try as I may, I did not have a good feeling about this presentation with Fr Smith. From the beginning, I had an intuitive feeling that Fr Smith had never taken any courses in active listening and that, in fact, his mind was in a hundred other places. My mind flashed back to a similar feeling a previous bishop used to give me.

After about seven or eight minutes he said to me, 'Look, Mrs ummm – what did you say your name was?'

'Mahoney,' I answered, 'Donna Mahoney.'

'Look, Mrs Mahoney,' he said, 'I admire your zeal and dedication in doing this, but I want you to understand my position here. I was sent here by the bishop to get this place in shape. I don't intend to be here for long. It's a small, disorganised, poor parish. The people here are uneducated and it would take too much effort to start this programme here. All I want to do is get this place on its feet. I have no time to do this sharing or community building or whatever you call it. And besides, it's not my thing. I am an administrator. I'm not one of these 'huggy-feely' priests. Priests get in trouble that way you know. Why you know all about Fr Larry – everyone does. Poor guy got in trouble just because he got close to the wife of the wrong man. Nope. I wish you luck but I cannot see this programme starting here.'

Looking back, I'm sure my mouth must have been wide open in astonishment as I tried to regain my composure. I thanked him as graciously as possible for his time as he quickly whisked me to the door. In my months of doing this ministry, I had never been dismissed in one paragraph without a chance for further explanation.

I remember terrible feelings of anger as I went through the door. I was fiercely mad at this pompous young fool. I was angry at our Church that someone like him was in a pastoral position. I thought back to my ecclesiology classes at the seminary and wondered what my dear friend Fr Tom would have to say about this man. Was this cold and distant manner due to the way they trained them in Rome?

As I was going down the steps, I passed a timid little eleven-year-old girl on her way to the door asking if she could see her mother, obviously the woman listening to the tape. As I opened the door to my car, I heard Fr Smith say, 'Look, little girl, your mom is busy and so am I. Wait here on the steps. She'll be out when she's finished.'

The outrage was welling up inside of me. I felt pain for the little child who didn't understand the structure of the Church her mother and she were joining.

Eight months later, I read that Fr Smith was made a monsignor.

Fr Bill: A propensity for ending up sitting next to priests seems to follow me wherever I go. It happens to me on planes, in restaurants, and last week it even happened to me at our local dinner theatre. A few years ago, as fate would have it, I spent my seven-hour trip to Ireland seated next to an auxiliary bishop from New York! I cannot escape this feeling that, like it or not, I am supposed to work with priests.

Last summer, as I was returning from my visit to Ireland, it happened again! As I was boarding the plane at Shannon, I ran into a priest I had known, but not too well. He had spent winters in Florida and was a seasonal customer at our restaurant. I had seen him a lot over the years, but had never shared too much with him.

Before leaving Shannon, we arranged to sit next to each other on our flight back. As he sat next to me drinking his bourbon and water, he reminisced of times past. He was getting on in years and was questioning if he had made the right choices. His pain was evident. To come to the end of one's life and never to have recognised and accepted love had to be the most tragic of all life's hurts. Kierkegaard was right: 'To cheat oneself out of love ... is an eternal loss for which there is no reparation either in time or in eternity'.[1]

He spoke quite openly to me. Perhaps it was the drink and the long flight which loosened him up since I did not really know him that well. He knew I was heavily involved in the Church and maybe that was the reason for this seemingly 'instant intimacy'. It did not make me uncomfortable. His openness put me right at ease.

He told me many stories, all of women whom he had warded off over the years because he was, after all, a good priest and did not want to violate his celibacy. There was one story however which I would not easily forget, and a sharp pain literally hit my heart as he told it. The tears dribbling down his face did not make the pain subside very quickly.

She was his childhood sweetheart who had returned to his home parish for a reunion. She had married soon after he entered the seminary and had four children by a man who treated her well. She had come to love her husband over the years and together they built a good life. Now, however, she was widowed.

She remained in town for a few days after the reunion. After all, she had no reason to rush home, and autumn in New England had always been her favourite time of the year. In addition, she still had some old friends she wanted to visit.

Before Sunday evening of the reunion was over, Fr Bill asked her if it would be all right to have lunch together on Tuesday. After all, he was in his mid-sixties and occasionally took a woman parishioner to lunch for counselling purposes. He did not think that it would create any scandal in the still-Victorian New England town. This was 1988 and people had finally adjusted to the fact that having lunch in public was not necessarily to be looked on with suspicion. In addition, he always wore his clerics and carried his briefcase.

The lunch was a wonderful get-together. She spoke of her children, her grandchildren, her volunteer job at the hospital, and her involvements with Church. He spoke of ministry, of his several assignments, of tough times he had had with some of his pastors and especially of the pastor he had when he was in his early thirties who kept a lock on the refrigerator door so that the young priests would not go over his food budget. One day, a young priest (not him) in frustration blew the lock off with a shotgun.

They laughed 'til they cried. She drank her wine. He had his bourbon but only one since one could never be sure of what others might say, especially in this small Massachusetts community. They talked on for three hours until it became embarrassing when the waitress tried to fill their coffee cups for the fourth time. He realised that he must leave as this was not going to sound too good if it got around the small suburb. He took her back to the rectory where they sat in the office with the door open. They talked of old times when they were young. They reminisced about friends, some of whom had died and with almost all of whom they had lost contact.

Finally her daughter, who had accompanied her on the trip, came to pick her up. She waited in the outer office as they said their last farewell. After a hug and very tender kiss on the cheek, he looked her in the eyes and said shyly, 'Mary, in my heart, I have never left you'. She looked at him longingly, searchingly and painfully and replied, 'Why, Bill, why did you leave me forty-five years ago?' She quickly turned and ran out of the door as tears streamed down her rosy cheeks.

As he was telling me this story, he became sadly introspective and his mind wandered. He had had a few drinks, and, perhaps, when the plane landed, he wouldn't even remember that he had shared this with me. But the things he said and the way he said them convinced me that my newly-made priest friend, way past mid-life, was questioning his choices, his decisions. Logic, discipline and 'holy order' can be maintained for just so long. Eventually, the heart will break through.

Fr Mike: I had just come out of the swimming pool with my hair dripping and my body exhausted when Fr Mike showed up on our back porch. I could see that he was excited so I quickly gave the children some juice and cookies and sent them inside.

He was like a little child who had just found the Holy Grail. He stood with it clutched in his hands. Not a young man, Fr Mike was approaching the age when most would soon retire. He was of small frame and lively with a twinkle in his eye. He had confided in me many times, mostly of his hurts and anger. He knew I was safe and that I would not betray his confidences. I was honoured and beginning to recognise that I had a gift for being 'safe' for priests. Perhaps it was easy to be safe since our ages were thirty years apart. Perhaps he would not feel as comfortable with someone his own age. But then again, maybe he would.

As he pushed through the patio door, he said in a hurried and excited voice, 'Donna, you must listen to these right away.' He clasped at the box of tapes which he had brought back from a workshop he had attended in Chicago.

The workshop, he explained, had been given by a psychiatrist who was somehow involved in a ministry-to-priests programme.

Because I had never before seen him so excited, I questioned him about the nature of the tapes. He told me that they were about the need that we all, priests included, had to love and be loved. I listened, somewhat amazed, as this was not a topic that we'd ever discussed before and, for some strange reason, it never crossed my mind that this was so important to him.

I had known Fr Mike for several years. He was an order priest who had often expressed that he found the order less than satisfying, but, regardless, he remained and had a powerful life of service. He was, what we would have called, back in those days, a good holy priest which meant he strove to serve others and to be faithful to his vows. He had a need to be needed and a need to be loved. Today, we would recognise him as a 'two' on the Enneagram.

It later occurred to me why he had brought me the tapes. As I mentioned, love and intimacy were topics we had never discussed. The tapes said all the things that he couldn't say in person. They spoke of the human need for love and that being a priest did not make one transcend this need. They spoke of power and control in the priesthood and how we, as Catholics, would put up with all kinds of deviations from priests whether they be stealing, manipulating people, drinking, abusive language, or abusive deeds. Yet, we Catholics would not forgive their sexual sins. The psychiatrist's tapes candidly said that all of the other sins were just as bad or even worse and that we must redefine our morality to address more than just sex.

What my friend Fr Mike was trying to find out was what I thought about the tapes. Did I approve or disapprove?

What did I, a decent enough young woman with a lot of religious training and a little common sense, think about these tapes? Quite frankly, I told him I heartily agreed and that many people had a very distorted view of morality and sexuality. Sexuality was good and holy and was, in fact, one of the greatest gifts of God to create and unify. Yes, Fr Mike, I agreed.

The next week was my birthday. He sent me balloons and came by to take pictures of me with the balloons. He later blew these pictures up and sent them to me. Now that he has passed away, I keep one of these pictures on my desk.

He never spoke to me of his love(s) ... He didn't have to.

Fr Peter: I arrived the day before she did. I picked her up at the airport, this fine looking woman in her early sixties. She was obviously accomplished in her field which was writing. She stood straight, tall and was strikingly beautiful for a woman of her age. She could have been an ambassador, a business women, a college professor, or a doctor. She was lovely and had a gentle warmth. In her early years she had been a nun.

We had come to celebrate his dream, the opening of his first of many homes for the homeless. He, Fr Peter, had been a social activist all his life and was loved by many. He was one of those priests who seemed to be the self-sufficient, independent type, but I never really bought the role he played. He had a depth of compassion and love for all, especially the underdog. His love for poor children was overwhelming. At one stage he tried to adopt two of them, but his bishop absolutely refused to allow this arrangement and threatened to release Fr Peter if he insisted on going through with this plan. His eyes were tender and telling. This man, for all his strength and independence, was deeply loved and he loved deeply as well.

I had followed his career from afar for a long time. He had gone from being an average young priest to being a defender of the rights of prisoners, immigrants and anyone whom he thought had been oppressed by the capitalist system, for which he had great disdain. He spoke out against oppression wherever he went and in whatever he did. He got himself in a lot of trouble with the wealthy in his parish, and letters to the bishop regarding him were frequent.

He was, in my estimation, the most convicted person I had ever met. In fact he had almost given his life many times for the sake of the gospel of Jesus – the real gospel of Jesus – not the 'sweet Jesus stuff' preached in many churches on Sundays. Many called him a prophet ... I did.

When he telephoned and told me that she too was coming, he made light of it. He said she was some 'whacko' ex-nun whom he met years ago. He neglected to tell me she was tall, lovely, intelligent, and madly in love with him. He also neglected to tell me that he had any warm feelings for her.

I watched them, the two of them, from afar during the activities of the next few days. They were hectic days but I watched their interaction. He was dependent on her for many decisions. He trusted her – completely. I had been told by a dear priest friend a few months prior that trust is the same as love. When I saw their interaction, I knew the secret of this great prophet: a secret which he denied and tried to conceal over the years, a secret which he would never consciously admit to, or maybe one he never even recognised.

This wonderfully convicted, prophetic man of God was empowered by this woman. Their years of relationship, their years of trust and unconditional love, had enabled him to become who he was. He would never admit it – not even today. Frequently I tease him and call it one of his 'unredemptions'. But, admit it or not, she has helped him become who he is. She has challenged him, encouraged him, been there for him, admired him, and powerfully loved him. Together, consciously or not, they have touched the face of God.

Bishop Jim: Every book of this type must include at least one story about a bishop. I write the following story with great delight, as this one bishop gives much hope for the future of our Church.

We were attending a Catholic Charities Convention in the Midwest. There were three of us from Palm Beach. Since this was a yearly event, we had gotten to know several of the participants well over the years. On one of the evenings my friend Mike, a priest, invited me to go out afterwards with his group. Since I knew most of them fairly well, I readily agreed.

There were eight of us who ended up, after searching many places, in a downtown hotel lounge. It was rather quiet which was fine with us as we were all raging extroverts and wanted to talk. The group consisted of a married couple, a woman religious, another laywoman, two priests, a bishop, and myself. The bishop preferred to be called Bishop Jim.

I had known Bishop Jim but not that well. Most of what I heard was from his seminarians with whom I studied. They were crazy about their bishop and spoke about him with gracious and exultant remarks. This was very unusual as most of the seminarians I knew had already formed passive-aggressive attitudes regarding their bishops long before they were ordained. Bishop Jim's men were different, and it was obvious from their performance and their willingness to serve. Somehow he had the gift of empowering them, of making them feel comfortable.

I was delighted to be sharing an evening with this man because I had already formed very positive feelings for him. As we sat around in a group, you could tell how very comfortable he was. Dressed in a sports-jacket and slacks, he could have been a businessman, a teacher or an attorney. Not many people would have pegged him for a bishop.

The conversation was light-hearted, flowing back and forth from Church to family life to the day's business. After a long wait, the cocktail waitress finally came to take our order. Bishop Jim saw her approaching our table from across the room. Seeing her dressed scantily in a brief outfit, he looked around the table and said to us: 'If any one of you dares call me "Bishop" you've had it!' He looked at all of us and said, 'My name for the rest of the evening is Jim'. We all laughed, gave our orders to the waitress, and the night rolled on.

We all shared our many Church experiences. The bishop spoke of his trip to Africa and India and his horror at some of the living conditions. He spoke of his concerns for the Church and his feelings about certain institutional practices. His honesty and warmth were glaringly apparent and refreshing as was the compassion in his eyes. As he spoke he very naturally would reach out and pat someone on the hand or knee. After one funny story, told by Sister Joan, he hugged her with delight as his face crackled with laughter. This was an intimate man.

Since that night a few years ago with Bishop Jim, I have come to know him much better. Our paths cross a few times a year at different functions. He is always warm and unafraid to be the affectionate man that he is.

There is no doubt in my mind that he is a man who loves and is loved by many and, I'm sure, a few in particular. My friend Mike has confirmed this reality. Whoever they are, wherever they are, they are gifts from God to Bishop Jim and to the Church.

Fr Steve: He walked into the room with a gentle confidence aided by his cane which gave support to his left leg. The years of life in a religious order were good to him. I thought to myself how kindly he looked and remembered back a couple of months ago when he had changed my life so drastically by his words. But I knew that there was a depth about this man and a history, a long history of life and love which had given him such compassion.

Fr Steve had come along with two other elderly Jesuits to spend a month at our home while we were away on vacation. The home was on the lake, with swimming pool and surrounded by an abundance of flora and fauna. There would be space for the three of them to spread out, relax and enjoy their time, both alone and with each other. It would be a nice reprieve from the other eleven months of the year when he and the others lived in a converted trailer which had been previously used for parish offices.

Accompanying him were Fr Wally, a dear old friend whom my family had known for years, and another priest whom I had just met. Fr Wally was one of those priests who needed people so badly. He was a frequent visitor at our home and was rather like a grandfather to many of the families in our parish. He was especially close to my husband and me. When his order pulled out of our local parish, he stayed around and continued his ministry at a local hospital. Although he was past the traditional retirement age, that didn't keep him down. He had years of life and ministry to be shared until God called him home.

I gave the three of them a light dinner. We were leaving

with our four children early the next morning, and there were still many chores to be done.

The evening moved along and the three Jesuits got settled in while we packed the car. We were close to finishing when all of a sudden I heard some exquisite piano music and a deep, resonant voice coming from our living room. I remained in the garage, sitting on the cold floor so that the priest with the cane wouldn't feel like he was on stage. For ten or fifteen minutes I heard all those songs from the 1920s, 1930s and 1940s. Most of them I knew from my mother who, when I was young, would wake me in the early morning with her whistling and singing. They were love songs, songs like 'Moon Over Miami', 'I'm In The Mood For Love', 'Tea For Two', 'Moonglow'. Eventually the cold hard floor got to me and I tip-toed into the living room and sat in a corner rocking chair. Fr Steve didn't know I was there. I watched his face; I saw his gentle expression and keyed in on his soft grey-blue eyes as he sang.

All of a sudden, it all made sense. It was an 'aha' moment. From a few months ago, his words of comfort came thundering back to me. 'Love,' he had said, 'is always of God. You must work with your gift of love. Do not deny it. It is the greatest of all of God's gifts'. I mulled these words over in my mind. He would never know it but years later when I would think back on my life's journey, his advice would have earth-shaping effects on the direction of my path.

As I rocked back and forth, I wondered about his life, his experience in ministry and the people who had formed him. Mostly, however, I wondered about her.

After many beautiful love songs, he stopped and took notice of my presence. Tenderly, he smiled a long and knowing smile. I didn't really have to say it because my intuition knew it. But I felt that I needed to verbally let him know. I leaned in toward him and asked softly, 'Fr Steve, was she beautiful?' He nodded, looked directly in my eyes and replied, 'She was the most powerful person who ever entered my life.'

The stories written here are meant to be an introspective aid in helping us gain some recognition of the difficulties of a life without intimacy and the blessing of a life shared with a loved one.

The priests in these stories all differ in their acceptance of intimacy. Fr Matthew, hurt and fearful, died rather than risk it again. Fr Jack had tremendous fear of an emotional entanglement that might divert him from the quest to fulfil his childhood dream. Fr Smith was a cold and calculating man who had no intention of letting anyone come close to him in his striving to get to the top. Fr Bill, at an elderly age, is beginning to question if he made the right decision in not letting anyone get close to him. Fr Mike apparently had some intimate relationship(s) for which he needed approval. Fr Peter, had a very close friend whom he couldn't even consciously admit to himself, even though he had a deep love for her. Bishop Jim had apparently integrated intimacy into his priestly life, and thus became a role model for many who looked to him for direction. The elderly Jesuit, Fr Steve, lived with the memories of a very powerful woman who apparently transformed his life. Each priest, in his own way, had to struggle in determining whether or not intimacy was compatible with celibacy for him.

These are just a few of the many scenarios we find today and perhaps they are some of the milder ones. One only has to pick up the newspaper any day to find priests involved in distorted sexual practices such as pedophilia, in manipulative power plays, in addictions, in projecting their own guilt-ridden Jansenistic theology onto their congregations, in 'hiding out' in their rectories, or in leading lives that are anything but service-oriented. Those offences, it seems to me, are far more serious offences than finding intimacy (an absolute necessity for adult living) and possibly, but not necessarily, risking the parameters of one's celibacy. For many years, however, the Church has not agreed and, in fact, has made intimate relationships (celibate or sexual) a cause for suspicion of priests.

We will turn now to take a look at some theological underpinnings to see if this attitude is in any way reflective of gospel teaching or of our tradition.

2

THE THEOLOGICAL DIMENSIONS OF LOVE

'I give you a new commandment:
Love one another.
Such as my love has been for you,
so must your love be for each other.
This is how all will know you for my disciples:
by your love for one another'
(John13:34-35).

As a person God gives personal life, he makes us as persons become capable of meeting with him and with one other. But no limitation can come upon him as the absolute Person, either from us or from our relations with one another; in fact we can dedicate to him not merely our persons but also our relations to one another. The man who turns to him therefore need not turn away from any other *I–thou* relation; but he properly brings them to him, and lets them be fulfilled 'in the face of God'.[1]

Martin Buber
I and Thou

Perhaps it may seem somewhat unusual that a work involving theology would need to ground itself in the command to love and give contemporary meaning to Jesus' words in John 13:34-35. In one sense, this approach may seem as wrought with futility as standing in the evening glow of a harvest moon and trying to prove theoretically to six-year-olds that the moon is round!

Despite what may seem obvious to some, the necessary task of this chapter is to give an interpretation of what, theologically, is meant by 'love'. This chapter will attempt to take the words of John 13:34-35 (above) along with other pericopes and show that the love required by Jesus is not only a universal and 'willed' type of love, but that it is also a love that can address the notions of friendship and intimacy – values which have for so long been denied in the life of a priest. Having made that connection, we will be able to appreciate the words of Martin Buber who, along with many other philosophers and theologians, believes that a personalistic (intimate) love is very much within our theistic tradition.

Faithful Christian persons believe that Jesus has called us to love one another as He has loved us. That call is an imperative given to us in several places in both Testaments. However, for some persons there are many problematic questions as to just what 'loving one another' means. Not all would agree that this love can or should be too close or too personal. Many would point to this word 'love' as more comfortably defined by the word 'esteem' or by 'honouring of one's neighbour', or would define it with a more universal approach where one can love a group of people without loving any one person in particular. As a result of the confusion which results, some would make this love so sterile and universal that it cannot be equated to personal loving. Others would point to this love as an ideal which simply cannot be maintained in our cultural and historical situation.

More specifically then, the **problem** of relating biblical love to personal (intimate) love seems to have two dimensions which make the relationship a difficult one. The first dimension points to the idea that biblical love, and love as expressed in our Christian tradition, were idealistic and removed forms of loving that did not allow for deep emotional friendships between persons. This idea will be addressed here. The second dimension lies in the unfortunate fact that in our twentieth-century cultural situation, intimacy has too often been equated with genital sexuality. As a result of this uncritical connection, relationships of intimacy often did not fall within the moral norms for persons not married to each other (this will be more fully addressed in Chapter Three). As a result of these two problematic dimensions, contemporary love has often been equated with values that are somewhat removed from biblical love and theological intimacy because, at the extremes, some notions of theological love made it acceptable and desirable to profess love for another or others without ever becoming psychologically close to another human being. At the same time, some notions of psychological love made it possible to become genitally involved without ever really loving in a committed way. In addition, popular notions of love have ranged from one-time uncommitted sexual encounters to different degrees of commitment in temporary relationships to life-long faithful *hesed*.[2]

To begin, we must describe what is meant by biblical love, and, as we move forward, our analysis must question whether or not there is a type of biblical love which can be equated to psychological intimacy or a more personal love. This chapter will look at some linguistic and biblical understandings of love as well as writings which reflect how spiritual masters, Christian theologians as well as theistic philosophers, have interpreted the biblical notion of love and how they have integrated it into their lives. An attempt will be made to connect types of biblical love to that type of love which we call psychological intimacy. This connection will provide the background for Chapter Three where we will closely examine the psychological intimacy that we claim is most appropriate and necessary in the life and ministry of a priest.

An Overview of the Biblical Notions of Love

We begin by stating that the word 'intimacy', admittedly, is a psychological term and is not specifically found with any degree of frequency in biblical literature. This finding is true even though intimate friendships and relationships do seem to be evidenced in Scripture, as will be noted later. The word 'love', however, is a theological term and is most frequently found in the New Testament with words like *agape* or *philia*. More precise definitions will be given subsequently, but at this stage it would be important to know that, of the two words for biblical love, *agape* is more frequently used (especially in Johannine writings) and denotes the type of active and faithful love of the God of Abraham, Isaac, Jacob, and others in the rich Hebrew love-vocabulary of the Old Testament. *Philia* is more descriptive of friendship and denotes a more intimate way of interaction. [3]

Biblical literature reverberates with love of God, love of self, and love of one another. The command to love is found in the Old Testament and reiterated many times in the New Testament.

Many volumes have been written on the Old Testament version of love. We mention a few passages only as background. In the Old Testament, God's loving character was recognised, most especially by Hosea.[4] The command 'to love' was based on the self-revelation and the self-giving of God to His/Her people in Deuteronomy 6:5. The emotional depth of this passage emphasises loving God with one's heart, soul and strength and also emphasises the mutuality of both partners in the relationship. This command, which reaches its depth in the *Shema* (Dt 6:4-9)[5] is used again in the New Testament (Mt 22:37). In the book of Leviticus, we find that loving one's neighbour is as important as loving one's self (Lv 19:18). These two passages from Deuteronomy and Leviticus are seen as the summation of the whole law and the prophets, as mentioned in Matthew 22:40.[6]

Love as expressed in friendship between women is beautifully portrayed in the faithful relationship between Ruth and Naomi (entire book of Ruth);[7] it is found in the strength of love between men in the story of David and Jonathan (1 Sm 18:28-29a; 19:17; 20:1-21:1; 2 Sm 1:26).[8] In the book of Genesis, we see the power of love between man and woman in the story of the love of Jacob and Rachel (Gn 29:4-30).[9] The strength of committed love, despite all obstacles, is powerfully affirmed in the book of Hosea, where God's faithful love is displayed in the person of Hosea, who always remains faithful despite a faithless spouse.[10] Most certainly the Song of Songs, whether taken literally or symbolically, displays the physicality of a deep love relationship.[11]

The New Testament is filled with passages which describe and command love and with the presentation of a compassionate Jesus whose life epitomises love. Certainly, the tradition that we receive from the Johannine community is one of the most valuable and incontestable biblical works that we possess on the love command. 'Love' is the epitome of the Christian life as expressed in 1 John 3:18; 4:7-8,19.[12] In the Johannine tradition, the only explicitly given mandate, Raymond Brown tells us, is called the 'new commandment'.[13] This new commandment will come to be the mark of identification for a Christian.

Loving one's neighbour as oneself is, for the Synoptic

tradition, one of the two greatest commandments (Mk 12:28-31; Mt 22:34-40) and is one of the two requirements which are given if we want eternal life (Lk 10:25-28).[14] Paul sees love of neighbour as fulfilling the Law and as a summation of all the other commandments (Rom 13:8-10).[15] Paul also extols love as the greatest of the spiritual gifts: 'There are in the end three things that last: faith, hope and love, and the greatest of these is love' (1 Cor 13:13).

In the New Testament, Jesus' love is expressed in warm effusive relationships. The gospels testify boldly to this fact. However, we often have translated love so completely as an act of will that we have lost the sense of warmth and wholeness which loving human persons emit to each other. Jesus is always seen as a relational person. His love was natural and instinctive and reflective of His whole Person. The love which Jesus gave and requested was most reflective of intimacy (with God, self, and others).

Some Descriptions and Biblical Meanings of the Notions of Love

A definition of love is almost impossible, for it is far too encompassing a reality to define. Rather, we can describe love in many ways and, more specifically, Christian love can be put into perspective. Karl Rahner boldly states that 'the original relationship to God is the love of neighbour'. He adds that love is:

> the only categorial and original act in which man reaches the whole categorically given reality and thus experiences God directly, transcendentally and through grace.[16]

We use Rahner's description at the initial stages of this

work because it is reflective of current theological, philosophical, and psychological interpretations of love. However, before we can equate his description with biblical love, we must sift back into other interpretations, including very short linguistic definitions as well as a study of traditional theologians.

Xavier Léon-Dufour gives us some initial insights into the biblical search for the meanings of the word 'love'. He states:

> The Hebrew word *ahaba* was translated in the Bible by the Greek *agape*. The noun was practically unknown in secular language, but not so the verb *agapao* – 'to welcome with affection', particularly a child, a guest. This term tended to tell of the deliberate character of a tender 'inclination towards' someone (Gk. *philio, philia*). One never finds the term *eros* ('passionate love').[17]

Further:

> The verb *philio* designates more of an inclination towards someone or something. It was rarely used to mean God's love, but rather was used to manifest the love of friendship which Jesus showed and which he demanded of the faithful. Sometimes it served to indicate love for God or for Jesus, without being able to detect in this a nuance different from that found in the verb *agapao*. Above all, it served to designate that brotherly love which we might call charity.[18]

Léon-Dufour gives us a basic introduction to the word 'love' but, to discover if there is a type of biblical love that could be equated with intimacy, we look back further to all the origins of the Greek words for love. Unlike the English language, Greek has four words that express types of love.

We refer to William Barclay for these definitions:

1. *Eran* (Εραν) is used to express sexual love or love between the sexes. It can be and is sometimes used for patriotic love or to express the passion of ambition, but primarily it is used for the expression of physical love. In the New Testament the form does not appear at all.[19]

2. *Stergein* (Στεργειν) is most properly used when speaking of family affection. It can also be used when speaking of the love of a nation for its ruler, but, most frequently, it describes love between children and parents.[20]

3. The most common word for love in Greek is *philein* (φιλειν) which denotes a sense of warmth or looking on someone with deep affection. It is used for the love of one's friends as well as for the love of husband and wife. According to Barclay, its best translation is 'to cherish'. It includes physical love but it also encompasses much more than physical love. It can also mean to kiss. It is used in the New Testament to describe love of family as well as Jesus' love of his friends. The word typifies a beautiful relationship between people and is a word that well describes the type of intimacy that we will be discussing.[21]

4. The New Testament words that are most commonly used for love are the noun a*gape* (αγαπη) and the verb *agapan* (αγαπαν). It is somewhat dubious whether *agape* is a classical word at all. It is used fourteen times in the Septuagint (LXX) in describing sexual love (e.g. Jer 2:2). We find the word *agape* in the Book of Wisdom for the love of God (Wis 3:9) as well as the love of wisdom (Wis 6:18). We see thus that it has a very wide background.[22] The verb *agapan*, however, occurs more frequently in classical Greek than the noun. It has the connotation of greeting affectionately but can also be used for the type of love one may have for money or gems.[23]

In Greek, then, the difference between *philein* and *agapan* is that *agapan* does not generally carry with it all the warmth that is described by *philein*. One may have *agapan* for a gracious benefactor, while having *philein* for the love of a father. Despite the difference between the two in classical Greek, it is well to keep in mind that, in the LXX, *agape* is even used to describe total sexual love.[24] It is therefore somewhat ambiguous, as sexual love usually includes great emotion.

It seems that a study of these words from their non-biblical origins through New Testament development indicates how they were sometimes used synonymously so that even *agape* did sometimes denote affection. It is also clear that a special type of affective love, *philein,* is spoken about in the New Testament, and that it denoted a sense of closeness and warmth which can be equated to the psychological intimacy which we will study.[25]

We can say at this point that: 1) there is in biblical writings a very special kind of love that can be related to intimacy, and that love of friendship, or *philia,* bespeaks a close emotional relationship between at least two people; 2) even *agape,* although generally thought to be a more 'willed love', which includes sacrifice and obedience, can have within it traces of emotion; 3) often the distinction between the two is negligible for, as we see, especially in John, they are sometimes used interchangeably.[26]

The Tradition

By today's standards many of the Fathers, the mystics and saints had a very impoverished view of human sexuality, due to the Greek dualism of body and soul. In addition, many had an extremely negative view of women, considering them to be 'misbegotten males'.[27] Sexism was present in much traditional literature. To add to this situation, there was an extremely high value placed on celibacy. Because of the above, many well-respected writers on the notion of love and friendship are difficult to interpret without an indepth study of their cultural and historical context. Since that is not our intent, perhaps a more encompassing idea of their views of love and friendship could be gleaned by looking at their lives. We do this with the understanding that often there is somewhat of a dichotomy between mind-sets and life practices which may be difficult for us to understand. An example of that dichotomy is given by Clark who tells us, in *Jerome, Chrysostom and Friends* that:

> For Jerome and Chrysostom ... the living reality of their friendships with women was in the vanguard of the theoretical baggage they dragged with them in their journey from the ancient world to the new age of larger opportunity and higher esteem for the female sex.[28]

Many of the Fathers, as well as highly respected male and female spiritual writers and saints, have had close friendships and loving relationships with members of the same or opposite sex. Some of these were priests while others were not. Some were nuns while others were 'non-religious' laywomen. But in any event, the Church has looked up to and venerated many of these people for centuries, as it has been obvious that they integrated a full Christian love into their lives. Among those who have had close loving friendships have been: Martin de Porres and Rose of Lima, John Chrysostom and Olympias, Jerome and Paula, Vincent de Paul and Louise de Marillae, Bernard of

Clairvaux and the Duchess of Lorraine, Philip Neri and Catherine of Reici, Boniface and Lioba, Jordan of Saxony and Diana d'Andalo,[29] Augustine of Hippo and his unnamed male friends, Teresa of Avila and John of the Cross, Francis de Sales and Jane de Chantal, and Francis and Clare of Assisi.

Although any one of these relationships alone would provide valuable insights for our study, we will try to concentrate on only a few of them, in order to see if their writings and their lives envisioned this love to be of a type we might call 'intimacy'.

In *Celibate Passion*, Janie Gustafson relates that St Jerome, a Father and doctor of the Church, had a lifelong relationship with St Paula. His relationship with Paula (as well as others) remains somewhat of a puzzle to this day because he frequently confesses his love for her and yet he warns others that they should be careful of their close associations. In any event Jerome, despite his condemnation of syneisaktism (a non-coital relationship of male – female intimacy), and Paula had an extremely close relationship which, despite scandal and malicious gossip, lasted for their lifetimes. Paula, a wealthy widow, and Jerome were inseparable dur-ing the later portions of their lives. She left her children and friends and abandoned everything to follow him to Egypt and Palestine and to work with him translating the Bible. When she died, he went into a deep depression, and it is thought by historians that they were buried together or next to each other.[30]

Another intimate friendship that we often hear about was that of St Augustine and his unnamed male friend. When death took his friend, Augustine was left inconsolable. He writes:

> My heart was black with grief. Whatever I looked upon had the air of death. My native place was a prison-house and my home a strange unhappiness ... I hated all the places because he was not in them ... I wondered that other mortals should live when he was dead whom I had loved as if he would never die; and I marvelled still more that he should be dead and I his other self living still. Rightly has a friend been called 'the half of my soul'. For I thought of my soul and his soul as one in two bodies; and my life was a horror to me because I would not live halved.[31]

Augustine, who in many respects had mastered certain aspects of life, shows himself to be completely distraught when it came to his affections for his friend. To think of no less a great theologian than Augustine describing his feeling in this way gives great credibility to the value of friendship and love. In his writings he also speaks of how he resorts to stealing pears as a result of his need and desire for companionship *(Conf* II, 8-9). He even sympathises with Adam in journeying into sin with Eve, because he could not stand the loss of his companion (*De civ D.* XIV, 11). His lifelong struggle with concupiscence is well-documented, and much of his writing reflects his struggle.[32] Friendship was the means by which he related to God while all the time knowing 'our hearts are restless until the time they can find peace in you'.[33] For Augustine, love of persons and love of God are integrated.

A thirteenth century Dominican, Jordan of Saxony, and Diana D'Andalo are well known to Christian writers in this field. Theirs was a strong heterosexual relationship of intimacy, even though they both were strongly committed to celibacy. The passion of his letters to her, however, bespeak that they shared a very deep emotional level:

> You are so deeply engraven on my heart that the more I realise how truly you love me from the depths of your soul, the more incapable I am of forgetting you and the more constantly you are in my thoughts; for your love of me moves me deeply and makes my love for you burn more strongly.[34]

Teresa of Avila and John of the Cross were two consecrated celibates, both ardent and sensual as we know from their writing, the *Interior Castle*[35] and the *Spiritual Canticle.*[36] Although there was a tremendous age difference between them, she being twenty-seven years older than he, they had a fierce and independent love. So great was the love that when his superiors demanded that he leave her convent at Avila after being there six years, he refused and force was used to carry him away.[37]

Another couple, Francis de Sales, the Bishop of Geneva, and Jane de Chantal, lived nearby and were in constant communication. Their love for each other was well-documented. Francis felt strongly that earthly love was not in competition with divine love, but that divine love was encountered by searching through earthly love.[38] Jane, a wealthy widow, left everything she had to follow Francis, who was her spiritual director. They are buried side by side.[39]

Finally, Francis of Assisi and Clare are acclaimed by many spiritual writers of our time, and many even assert that it was their great love for each other that was the basis of their sainthood. Although they lived in separate domiciles, they were in constant communication with each other. Francis, a deacon, wrote the 'Canticle of Brother Sun' while visiting at San Damiano with Clare. She in turn, in her own writing, tells of the depth of her love and passion for both Francis and God as she sees the love of both as inseparable.[40]

The above is just a brief exhibit of some of the very

strong friendships and love relationships which have existed in our Christian heritage. In these friendships, not only is God present, but God is revealed to one person through the love of another.

These men and women who have found God in strong bonds of friendship and love have attempted by means of their lives to actually put flesh and blood in the gospel call to love one another in a manner befitting Christians. They have related their faith to their lives and their praxis. They have extolled the value of love and the necessity to love by their lives.

Recent Philosophical and Theological Thought: Marcel and Rahner

Not only have Scripture and Tradition taught us the value of love and the necessity to love, but also recent philosophical and theological study has emphasised that relationships of love are essential in an effort to come to know God. Since it is impossible for us to discuss here a number of contemporary authors, we have chosen a philosopher and a theologian who have marked modern Christian reflection in major ways.

Philosophy, since it has traditionally been foundational for theology, has tremendous power to make connections between the existential situation and the life of faith.

Gabriel Marcel was a Christian philosopher whose theological convictions were absolutely essential for his life's work. Well-known for his philosophy of communion and dialogue, he has deep theological underpinnings for the I–thou relationship. Marcel relates that the creation of self takes place by the emergence to a 'thou' level of reality. In response to a call from a 'thou', I am created.[41] Fidelity is the active perpetuation of presence and so, when Marcel speaks of creative fidelity, he literally means that fidelity creates the self as something which is in no sense an object but, rather, is extremely personal.[42]

Marcel utterly rejects dualism, claiming that we cannot objectify the relationship between our body and our soul. Furthermore, he insists that we are no more detachable from the world than we are from our bodies. 'Even God had to choose Incarnation – in body and world – and its subsequent total availability as the only means of being Man'.[43] Incarnation is positive proof of the integral connection between body and soul.

Sensation, for Marcel, means immediate participation in being. It is not an objective reception. Therefore, our senses are the part of us which actualise our incarnation into the world.[44] We cannot make pronouncements on ultimate reality as detached and universalised subjects by means of pure thought.[45] We cannot detach ourselves from the reality in which we live. Marcel's beliefs encourage us to look sceptically at definitions of love which are not at least open to intimacy for, when we try to sterilise and categorise love, we do not leave it open to the transcendent. Kenneth Gallagher, commenting on Marcel, adds to our holistic understanding of love by relating:

> If, per impossible, I had **never** been present to others, (had even skipped the stages of community), my 'self' would be an amorphous possibility, not an actuality at all. He who, having been shaped as an actual person by the presence of others, withdraws from the loving tissue of communion, to that extent ceases to be an actual person.
>
> To live and think habitually without reference to the dimension of being which communion reveals would be to approach

> asymptotically the condition of a merely epistemological subject.[46]

Marcel's notion of communion is related to the French word *disponibilite*, which has been translated as 'availability', but which denotes 'openness; release; abandonment; welcoming; surrender; readiness to respond'.[47] 'The disponible person is hospitable to others; the doors of his soul are ajar'.[48] This attitude is the inner disposition which must be present in order to achieve communion. These descriptions of *disponibilite* are all descriptions of the values found in dialogical interrelatedness. They are also descriptions which seem to be characteristics of the life of Jesus who consecrated his life to this type of openness for intimacy, and as a result made the ultimate sacrifice of giving his life for love of others.

According to Marcel, a person is constituted by his or her relationships with another. A person is his or her relationships. It is the 'we' that is encountered in relationships which truly creates the 'I'. Or, in other words, 'inter-subjective acts found the subject'.[49] Each experience of being is formed in communion. For Marcel *esse est co-esse*[50] ('to be' is 'to be with'). That person who is another or 'thou', is the one who 'discovers me to myself'.[51] Similarly Gallagher says:

> I am literally given to myself by others. Unless I am a self, being will not be present to me; unless I am with others, I will not be a self.[52]

Paul Tillich, in *The Courage To Be*, enhances this stance: 'Only in the continuous encounter with another person does the person become and remain a person'.[53] In the process of relationship, I become myself. This will be discussed more fully in the next chapter.

With regard to love, Gallagher (who gives a superb interpretation of Marcel's Christian philosophy) states that:

> Any experience which opens us to another can be called love, until in the end we may not only say that communion is founded on love, but that communion **is** love.[54]

Marcel relates this communion between persons (inter-subjectivity) to Christian charity thus enriching a biblical version of charity by stating:

> But we cannot fail to see the intersubjectivity, which it is increasingly more evident is the cornerstone of a concrete ontology, is after all nothing but charity itself.[55]

Faithful love, for Marcel, creates the self as well as creating the lover.[56] It is in and through faithful love relationships that we come to know who we are. Moreover, these relationships are only possible because they are based on God. Marcel writes 'to love someone truly is to love him in God'.[57] As a result there is no question about whether we love God or a person more, because the more one loves God the more one loves the person and the reverse is also true. So it is here that we find that the dual command to love God and to love human persons is inextricably connected. Loving one is implicit in loving the other.

This eternal yearning of the human person is, for Marcel, a 'creative pursuit of the eternal'.[58] The opposite of this desired communion is ultimate suffering. In his well-known play, *Les Coeur des Autres*, he states: 'There is only one suffering: to be alone'.[59] And so, for Marcel, the way to the transcendent is accomplished in the same way that one alleviates suffering – by communion with another.

Gallagher completes this understanding of Marcel in this way:

> Human communion itself, insofar as it is communion, is a creative pursuit of the eternal. Even more, since all creation is a mutual birth, communion is the ecstasis of transcendence. The transcendent comes to be in communion, just as it comes to be in any work of art, only that here both the painter and the pigments are free beings – since they are one and the same.[60]

In theistic philosophy, Marcel is often associated with Martin Buber and Søren Kierkegaard. Although we cannot delve into either of these philosophers in detail, a brief understanding of Buber will aid in our task. Buber, like Marcel, has a philosophy of communion and dialogue, although Marcel is Christian and Buber is Jewish. He connects his philosophy to theology in a most natural way:

> We are created along with one another and directed to a life with one another. Creatures are placed in my way so that I, their fellow-creature, by means of them and with them find the way to God. A God reached by their exclusion would not be the God of all lives in whom all life is fulfilled. A God in whom only the parallel lines of single approaches intersect is more akin to the 'God of the philosophers' than to the 'God of Abraham, Isaac and Jacob'. God wants us to come to him by means of the Reginas he has created and not by renunciation of them.[61]

Buber, like Marcel, rejects the dualism of body and soul and focuses on incarnate being in the world. For Buber, God is the 'Absolute Person' who is met at all times – whenever we meet another human being as 'thou'.[62] In relationships of love and trust we come to find truth. 'If you wish to believe, love',[63] says Buber. Deeply meaningful personal encounters bring us into relationships with the ultimate truth of life.[64] Buber speaks of these dialogical relationships as the aim of all his studies. He finds that these relationships bring us to a sphere of authentic existence and mutual trust. Boldly he states: 'There is no salvation save through the renewal of the dialogical relation, and this means, above all, through the overcoming of existential mistrust'.[65] Buber would maintain that it is when we move into these relationships and give the fullness of our being to the world that we find God. In this, he shares many of the ideas of Karl Rahner. As we move, then, into this chapter's final section based on theology, we can bridge the gap between philosopher and theology with Buber's words:

> In mankind's great ages, the divine, in invisible becoming, outgrows old symbolisms and blossoms forth in new ones. The symbol becomes ever more internalised, moves ever closer to the heart, and is ever more deeply submerged in life itself; and the man who five thousand years ago saw it in the stars, sees it today in the eyes of a friend. It is not God who changes, only theophany – the manifestation of the divine in man's symbol-creating mind; until no symbol is adequate any longer, and none is needed, and life itself, in the miracle of man's being with man, becomes a symbol – until God is actually present when one man clasps the hand of another.[66]

Karl Rahner, one of the theological giants of our time, tells us in his transcendental theological anthropology that God is revealed to us through the people and situation in our lives. He found God in the ordinary things of life. Specifically speaking of love, he says:

> When, for example, a concrete human being (and whether he is

> aware of it or not is, in the first instance, immaterial) experiences genuine, personal love for another human being, it always has a validity, an eternal significance and an inexpressible depth which it would not have but that such a love is so constituted as to be a way of actualising the love of God as a human activity springing from God's own act.[67]

To understand how Rahner can make such a strong statement for personal love, it may be helpful to mention two insights that Rahner has on the human person. First, Rahner contends that God offers saving grace to all. This means that God offers redeeming presence throughout one's whole life. This presence touches all of one's personhood and influences all of the inter-connections of mind and heart. The orientation, then, is holistic. Second, with regard to the human person's fundamental orientation, all acts of mind and will, even the most mundane, have a direct orientation to transcendence. This position is the *a priori* unreflective ground of experience for Rahner and is 'an unlimited, unrestricted horizon toward which the human being is drawn'.[68]

Rahner states that there are four avenues by which we experience God, all of them inextricably bound with our experience of other human persons. We experience God through situations of responsibility, love, suffering, and through our hope for the future.[69] Norman King, in interpreting what Rahner means by this tenet, tells us that 'God is that which we touch upon in and through our deepest human experience ...'[70] These experiences are depth experience in two senses: they encounter the deepest dimension of human experience, and they are 'thou' experiences in which our deepest self is at stake and involved.[71] These experiences, then, provide us contact with God.

Perhaps one of the strongest statements that Rahner

makes about love and the connection between love of God and love of a human person can be found in his 'Theology of Freedom'. He writes: 'Love of God is the only total integration of human existence ...'[72] He enfleshes his thought by adding what was stated earlier:

> The original relationship to God is ... love of neighbour ... The act of love of neighbour is the only categorial and original act in which man attains the whole of the concretely given reality and finds the transcendental and supernatural, directly experienced experience of God.[73]

For Rahner, then, the embodiment of that experience and the response to love of God is found in loving another human being. However, Rahner uses the term 'love of neighbour' as a process of discovering, accepting, and trying to bring to an integration all the aspects of one's self.[74] This love is certainly not a removed and uninvolved type of love but, rather, one that is full of many of the implications of intimacy that we shall find in the next chapter. This love is realised in the down-to-earth existence of everyday life. It is experienced holistically with body and soul. There can be no dichotomy when speaking of personal love, for love is all encompassing.

Although differences certainly exist between Rahner and Hans Urs von Balthasar,[75] he also sees the human being as the everyday mediator of love. He claims that this love can only be understood as a miracle; an event which takes place when 'a Thou meets me as an Other'.[76] This event cannot be accounted for empirically or transcendentally. Truly, love is a miraculous gift, and its parameters cannot be logically stated by the person experiencing it. He emphatically states that 'love can only exist between persons – a fact philosophy is inclined to forget'.[77] In this respect he concurs with Rahner. He sees God as 'totally other', and, therefore, God cannot be the immediate means by which we experience love. God appears to us through our brothers and sisters, and he sees the revelation of God in this way as a sacramental event.[78] For Balthasar, there is only one counsel: to vow oneself to a self-sacrificing, 'crucified form of love'.[79] Love cannot be captured, monopolised, or condemned to sterility. 'For if the world is to believe it can only believe in love'.[80] We see then that Balthasar concurs with the philosophical thought presented as well as with Rahner. Experiences with other human beings actualise our love of God.

Perhaps a special mention should be made of Rahner's insistence on love as 'the basic act'[81] of humans because, as we shall discuss in future chapters, this personal type of love was thought for so long as inappropriate for priests. Love of another (or refusal to love) is most expressive of how one views his (priestly) attitude to reality as a whole. This is true for Rahner simply because love of another is 'the basic act' of humans. King interprets this to mean that 'it founds and recapitulates, gives meaning, direction and measure to everything else'.[82] One becomes fully aware of oneself and present to oneself only in and through the awareness of another. Echoing the words of Marcel, Buber, and Balthasar, Rahner states:

> The one moral (or immoral) basic act in which man comes to himself and decides basically about himself is ... the (loving or hating) communication with the concrete Thou.[83]

The 'concrete Thou', or human person, can be found in the relationships of communion espoused by Marcel and Buber. These relationships call us to reveal ourselves. They ask for vulnerability, trust, mutuality, availability, openness, and faithfulness. As a result of these relationships, we come to find ourselves – we come to self-knowledge, self-acceptance, self-esteem, and authenticity. These will be discussed later. Theologically, however, if love of God is, as Rahner tells us, 'the only total integration of human existence', then it is through these human experiences that love provides that we truly come to experience God. These experiences are most necessary in the life of a priest, as it is through close personal relationships that one meets God.

Having placed some parameters on the theological dimensions of love, we now are prepared for the following chapter in which we will look at the human need for intimacy.

3

THE HUMAN NEED FOR INTIMACY

How peaceful life would be without love, ...
How safe!
How tranquil!
How dull!

The Name of the Rose
(Neve Constantin Film Productions, 1986)

Although the theological implications of the previous chapter are interwoven into this chapter, our primary focus now is psychological. However, before discussing the psychological aspects of the human need for intimacy and its relationship to the integrated growth of the human person, it is necessary to define terms. It is also necessary to distinguish among three types of intimacy: affectivity, tactility, and genital intimacy. This distinction is due to the tremendous emphasis placed on genital intimacy in the last twenty-five to thirty years, since the sexual revolution of the 1960s. This emphasis has become so pronounced that, in some circles, intimacy is equated with genital sexuality. The second task of this chapter is to consider current psychological interpretations of the need for intimacy. These interpretations regard intimacy as a prerequisite for becoming a fully alive and totally integrated Christian. The final task is to describe briefly the effects of the lack of intimacy.

Definitions and Descriptions of Intimacy

Intimacy comes from the Latin word *intimus* meaning 'inner' or 'innermost'. Mary Rousseau and Charles Gallagher translate the term to mean 'within' or 'inside'.[1] They explain that although it is difficult to understand how one person can live inside another, there is such a thing as psychological presence when people are close. They can have a distinctive type of closeness, a presence with each other which leaves each one intact physically and in their original identities. It is as if one person becomes so much integrated with another that he/she is present in the other person's mind, thoughts, affections, memories, and hopes. In a very real sense, one person becomes part of another and carries that person within him/herself in all the person's daily activities. Intimacy, so defined, is not only psychological, it is deeply spiritual and leads to many theological questions. In fact, as Rousseau and Gallagher state, 'such intimacy, the psychological presence of one person "in" another is most perfectly found in God'.[2]

Erik Erikson, in his book *Childhood and Society*, defines intimacy as 'the capacity to commit ... to concrete affiliations and partnerships and to develop the ethical strength to abide by such commitments, even though they may call for significant sacrifices and compromises'.[3] Elaine Hatfield, in her article entitled 'The Dangers of Intimacy', defines intimacy as 'a process in which we attempt to get close to another; to explore similarities (and differences) in the ways we both think, feel and behave'.[4] In *Celibacy, Prayer and Friendship*, Christopher Kiesling defines intimacy as the 'mutual sharing of inner selves'.[5]

Harry Stack Sullivan states that 'intimacy is that type of situation involving two people which permits validation of all components of personal worth'.[6] His work purports that we love others to the extent that we love or esteem ourselves. One who cannot love or esteem him/herself, cannot love others.[7] His work echoes and reinforces the biblical exhortation to love our neighbours as ourselves (Lev 19:18).

Evelyn and James Whitehead, who have creatively integrated theology and psychology, explain:

> 'Intimacy' often appears as a synonym for sexual expression or romantic sharing. We use the word in a broader psychological sense to refer to those strengths which enable a person to share deeply with another. These strengths come into play across a range of relationships – friendship, work collaboration, community living. Whenever there is personal disclosure and mutuality, intimacy is involved. A well-developed ability to be intimate enables me to be with different persons in a rich variety of different ways, ways that are appropriate to my own personality and to the demands of different situations. It is upon these intimacy resources that I draw in my attempts to live closely with others, to share my talents and ambitions, to merge my life and hopes with those of some one, some few others.[8]

In *An Experience of Celibacy*, Keith Clark says 'intimacy is a human experience of being mutually transparent to another or with others in such a way that personalities are fused but not obliterated or lost in the other'.[9] He writes:

> Life has moments of intimacy. Sometimes they are accompanied by great affection, sometimes not. Sometimes they are pleasant, sometimes sad. Sometimes they are sexual, sometimes not. Sometimes they are romantic, sometimes not. As often as two or more persons are intentionally transparent to one another in a way which brings their personalities together without obliterating any of them, there is intimacy. The moments come and go; the capacity for intimacy remains. Moments

> of intimacy are always satisfying in some way, but they are always incomplete. Even when they are very satisfying in the joy of the moment, they are incomplete in that the moment ends. Other concerns of life take each sharer of the intimacy into different pursuits with other people. But intimacy **is** one of life's moments.[10]

Clark, a religious celibate, has touched on several important aspects of intimacy which deserve attention. Clark points out that moments of intimacy are always incomplete. This idea is the paradox of intimacy: as much as each one seeks it, wants it, needs it, and pursues it, each knows within his/her heart that what he/she seeks is, at best, temporary. Intimacy is not only experienced in great ecstasy but also in great pain and sacrifice, both of which are well-exemplified in the life of Jesus. Intimacy does not mean 'obliteration' or 'possession' of another person but rather a sharing without possessing. On this topic Kahlil Gibran writes:

> Sing and dance together and be joyous,
> but let each one of you be alone,
> Even as the strings of a lute are alone
> though they quiver with the same music.
> Give your hearts, but not into each other's keeping.
> For only the hand of Life can contain your hearts.
> And stand together yet not too near together:
> For the pillars of the temple stand apart,
> and the oak tree and the cypress
> grow not in each other's shadow.[11]

The longing for intimacy that is so deeply ingrained in every human heart continues to fill us with passionate longing because it is a desire which can be completely satisfied only when we are united with God. Still we seek it, still we pursue it 'because you have made us for yourself, and our hearts are restless until they can find peace in you'.[12] Even the most fulfilling relationships leave us incomplete and wanting. Knowing that, however, we still seek and crave them.

From the above descriptions and definitions, we can make some observations. Intimacy calls for a commitment to another in terms of honesty, trust, and faithfulness. It calls us to be open and vulnerable to another. It calls us to accept another as a gifted equal in terms of mutuality. It calls for a commitment of availability and sacrifice. All of these characteristics of intimacy are also reflective of the 'I–thou' relationships spoken of by Gabriel Marcel and Martin Buber.[13]

Now that the word 'intimacy' has some descriptive parameters, we will begin to use the term 'love' interchangeably for 'intimacy' or 'intimate relationship/friendship'. The connection will be more developed throughout this chapter. However, at this stage, it is necessary to make some observations based on Chapter Two and on the preceding descriptions.

Theologically, as we have seen, *philia* is descriptive of a close emotional bond or friendship between at least two persons. In psychological terms, we call that close bond 'intimacy'. It is the psychological presence of one person in another (Rousseau and Gallagher); the process of exploring differences and similarities in personalities (Hatfield); the inner sharing of selves by personal disclosure and mutuality (Kiesling and the Whiteheads); and a sharing without possessing or obliterating the other (Clark). Biblically, it is evidenced in the relationship that Jesus had with his close friends (eg: Lazarus, Mary Magdalene and Peter). Psychologically, it is the reciprocal relationship with another which brings us to the theological exhortation of Lev 19:18. Intimacy (as will be shown) provides us with the self-knowledge, self-acceptance and self-esteem to love others and ourselves.

We have seen in Chapter Two that there is much support for the idea that no real distinction exists between *agapan* and *philein*. This support is most evidenced in the writings of John. However, even if one does not accept that the two words explain the same reality, we still find support for *agape* as being akin to intimacy.

Theologically, *agape,* although indicating emotion, describes a more 'willed' type of love. The 'willed' love includes elements of sacrifice and obedience. Psychologically, we observe that intimacy calls for development of ethical strength which may call for sacrifice and compromise (Erikson); it requires the essential obedience to love others as we love ourselves (Sullivan), which is reflective of Lev 19:18; and it displays the willed and sacrificial determination to love without possessing (Clark). To add to the above, the existential 'longing for' as well as the 'incompleteness of' intimate relationships is a constant reminder of our desire for God, of which St Augustine so eloquently speaks.

From all the above, we can say that theological love and psychological love have many similarities. In terms of a holistic outlook on the human person, we will speak of the realities interchangeably.

Types of Intimacy

Donald Goergen, a Dominican who is a theologian and psychologist, gives us an integration of both fields in his book *The Sexual Celibate.* He differentiates among three types of intimacy: affectivity (emotional intimacy), tactility (the sense of touch), and genital intimacy. We will draw on Goergen for some of our distinctions.[14]

Affectivity

It is necessary to recognise that most theologians today have a positive theology of sexuality and view human beings as holistic persons – that is, persons who are physical, spiritual, sexual, emotional, and intellectual. By nature, we **are** sexual beings, and if, as St Thomas states, grace works through nature, then we **must** accept ourselves as sexual beings. We must become comfortable with the fact that sexual energy exercises a tremendous impact in directing our lives. The acceptance of ourselves as sexual beings is essential for our human development. Not to accept this very basic fact of creation leads to psychopathological problems and lives of distortion and sin.

Given then that humans are created as sexual beings, we have certain human needs. One of these is the affective need, the need to give and receive loving human responses. We need to give and receive care, nurturing, love. We need to share common experiences in an atmosphere of acceptance and warmth; we need experiences which provide laughter, fun, and ecstasy as well as seriousness, sadness, and pain. We need to share thoughts, feelings, and intellectual pursuits. We need to love and be loved tenderly. We must find ways to satisfy the desire to be close, sharing ourselves and our feelings with others. At the same time, we need to understand and be understood. The need for love, affirmation, and friendship is the same need that Jesus displayed in the exchanges of words between Himself and Peter (e.g. Jn 21:15-21). This is the affective need.

Through the affective capabilities, we come to value ourselves. If we fail to receive positive responses in our interaction with others, then we form poor self-images. We esteem ourselves according to the extent that those we love,

love us in return. For Mary Elizabeth Kenel, in 'A Celibate's Sexuality and Intimacy', a very necessary characteristic of intimacy, one that is important for our purposes, is that one must first begin to develop self-intimacy (Erikson will call it identity) before one can hope for intimacy with others.[15] This self-intimacy requires an appreciation of one's own uniqueness, identity, and value as an individual person. The paradox that is seen here is vital because, although this process of self-intimacy must **begin** before we seek intimacy with others, it is actually **through** affective relationships with others that self-intimacy is achieved. It is through a continual process of interactions with others that we come to know who we are.

The reciprocal relationship between knowing oneself and knowing another is well-expressed in a combination of the thoughts of Sidney Jourard and James Kilgore. Jourard writes: 'I only get to know myself when I am willing to reveal who I am to another',[16] while Kilgore states: 'I can never be intimate with another until I know myself'.[17] These two statements indicate the difficulties involved in intimate relationships. Chantal seems to synthesise both positions by saying: 'You came into my life and loved me and somehow, I became me'.[18]

Self-knowledge, self-esteem, self-acceptance, and authenticity are the ultimate prizes of dialogical relationships.[19] We find these gifts through the satisfaction of our affective needs.

Tactile Intimacy

In addition to our affective needs, we also have a need for tactile intimacy; a need to touch and be touched, to hold and be held. As one of our most powerful senses, this need for touch asks for fulfilment each day.

Everyone needs loving touches. Touch is our most basic and earliest form of communication. It is the method of communication necessary in infancy to convince us that we are loved, needed, and accepted. This need remains throughout our lives. Through touching we attain and maintain a sense of our own self-worth. One need only to visit any nursing home or any child-care unit to see what the deprivation of this need can do. The need for touch in infants has been described as being so strong that they literally cannot survive without having the need fulfilled.[20]

Although modern psychology and medicine affirm the value of touch,[21] there exists in modern American culture great fear and social taboos in regard to touching. These are evidenced, for example, by the father who refuses to hug or kiss his son, even at a celebration or homecoming, because of what others might think, or the Christian who looks askance at a man and woman not married to one another who embrace, or the priest who is afraid to hug little children as a result of the fear of pedophilia. This 'no-touch'[22] attitude is so prevalent in our society that it can certainly be viewed as an American aberration. Ashley Montagu in a lengthy study has stated:

> Perhaps it would be more accurate to say that the taboos on interpersonal tactility grew out of a fear of closely associated with the Christian tradition in its various denominations, the fear of bodily pleasures. One of the great negative achievements of Christianity has been to make a sin of tactual pleasures.[23]

Although Goergen does not blame the Christian Churches exclusively (culture has certainly influenced the situation), he does see evidence of this attitude in the Church and calls us to be a people who understand, endorse, and integrate touching. For Goergen, 'chastity is that virtue concerned with the integration of sexuality in our lives as Christians', and the intent of chastity is not 'to lead one into a "no-touch" style of life'.[24]

One of the paradoxes of the prohibition of touching is that it did not originate in the gospels or the tradition of the great mystics. The gospels' many descriptions of touching include the washing of the feet of the disciples (Jn 13:1-16); Jesus' touching the eyes of the blind man (Mt 20:34); the very sensual scene in which we see the woman kissing and anointing Jesus' feet (Lk 7:36-39); as well as the many calls to greet our brothers (and sisters) with holy kisses. In the lives of the saints, one need only look at St Francis of Assisi, St Catherine of Siena, or our modern-day Mother Teresa to reject such a prohibition against touching. Tactile contact has always been a very genuine form of Christian behaviour for these saints.

There are many signs of intimacy which bespeak deep levels of a sharing of life, which reflect both affective and tactile intimacy, and which are genuine signs of love: the kiss in a moment of happiness and joy; the physical holding of a friend; the smile and embrace which tells another 'I love you'; or the childlike play of pulling a friend down in the snow amid the exhilarating feelings of a first winter snowstorm. These are but a few examples of feelings accompanied by tactile symbols which are most appropriate for intimate friends. They speak a language shared only by the people involved.

Affective and tactile intimacy are related since they are both appropriate to any close relationship and, in fact, are necessary to make a relationship grow and develop. The presence of affective and tactile intimacy is very much within the Christian tradition and should be considered symbolic of the love of God between man and woman, woman and woman, or man and man. They do not necessarily lead to genital intimacy.

Genital Intimacy

Genital intimacy is the third type of intimacy necessary for our discussion. In society today, a good portion of the population erroneously believes that when speaking of 'intimacy' we necessarily and naturally mean 'genital intimacy' or a 'genitally involved sexual relationship'. We need to be specific with terms.

Genital intimacy is the completion of an interpersonal relationship in which two persons have chosen to show their feelings of love for each other in terms of a more complete physical relationship. Although this choice might indicate that the end result would be genital sexual intercourse, it could also imply lesser forms than complete genital experience. True genital intimacy usually implies exclusivity (but not always) and some type of commitment (but not always). In its finest form, genital love existentially calls for time, place, and commitment[25] as could be encountered, for example, in marriage.

However, expressions of genital sexuality in less genuine situations begin, for most persons, in the childhood years with the exploration of one's own and another's body. These expressions may continue throughout life.

Although more could be written about genital intimacy,[26] the distinction required here is that intimacy has forms other than genitality. A person may function as a fully human and a fully alive, authentic being without genital intimacy, as we will see.

In addition, emotional and tactile intimacy can be, and most frequently are, separate from genital intimacy. Most of the people with whom we establish warm bonds of friendship do not become our sexual partners, whether that be for reasons of morality or practicality. Many people today, whether in a committed relationship or not, have more than one intimate relationship.[27] This does not mean that they are genitally sexual with one another. Even in a culture such as ours, where great emphasis is placed on genital sexuality, we can maintain that emotional and tactile intimacy are possible without genital intimacy.

Having discussed the different types of intimacy, it is necessary to clarify further the exact sense in which we will use this term. 'Intimacy' is used in the affective (emotional) and tactile (touching) sense, with the very determined notion that such an intimacy is part of our (necessary) repertoire as Christians. Whenever we discuss genital intimacy, it will be specifically named, for, as shall be seen in some of the work that follows, genital intimacy, although very much affirmed within certain moral norms, is not necessary for everyone who is progressing toward full personhood. In addition, each of us, whether we are single, celibate, or married, are called to be intimate with many others over the course of our lifetime. Most frequently this intimacy does not include genital relationships.

Psychological Interpretations of Intimacy

Abraham Maslow

Abraham Maslow has done a tremendous amount of research on people whom he calls self-actualising. His work is important for us to consider because self-actualising persons have integrated intimacy into their lives.[28] Maslow has studied people whom society considers outstanding examples of what it means to be human. His specific work in humanistic psychology is what he calls a 'positive theory of motivation'.[29]

We cite his work because, as followers of Christ, Christians are called to be outstanding examples of being human. In the fields of theology and psychology, many similarities exist in what it means to be 'outstandingly human'. Although we cannot give a complete description here of the self-actualising personality, several important characteristics should be mentioned.

Self-actualising people are described as having deeper and more profound interpersonal relations than most people. In addition, they have a more efficient perception of reality and are accepting of themselves, others, and nature. They lack defensiveness. They are concerned about humanity and have a sense of community. They are secure and not anxious because they maintain an independence from the culture. This does not mean, however, that they are not involved; quite the contrary. They are very involved. They are strongly ethical and moral; they exhibit spontaneity, simplicity, and naturalness.[30]

We can see many characteristics of Jesus in Maslow's descriptions (loving, just, kind, compassionate, countercultural, ethical, and concerned for humanity). Self-actualising persons are considered by Maslow to be achieving their fullest potential as human beings. Their deep personal relationships help them grow and develop as valuable human beings. The concept of self-actualisation is important for Maslow because it is the goal of his 'human motivation theory'.

Maslow's motivation theory divides the hierarchy of

human needs into five areas. They are briefly mentioned here.

The first of these human needs is the physiological need for food, water, shelter, and sex (the sexual need was not proven to be homeostatic, meaning it is not necessary for the body's automatic efforts to maintain a state of equilibrium in the bloodstream and, therefore, should be considered separately from the need for food and water). The physiological needs which are homeostatic would, of necessity, have to be satisfied before one could consider the next set of needs on the hierarchy.[31]

The next group of human needs are those of safety-security, stability, protection, dependency, freedom from fear and anxiety, need for law and order, etc.[32] If all those needs are basically satisfied then, Maslow says, the third level of needs for love, affection, and 'belongingness' will emerge: the need for friends, mate, children, affectionate relationships, family, or place in a group. Having had all the lower needs met, one 'will want to attain such a place more than anything else in the world and may even forget that once, when he was hungry, he sneered at love as unreal or unnecessary or unimportant.[33] Since it is at this third level that the need for intimacy is observed, it would be worthwhile to focus on Maslow's thoughts.

Maslow attributes the rapid increase in intentional communities and personal growth groups as being motivated in part by 'this unsatisfied hunger for contact, for intimacy, for belongingness, and by the need to overcome the widespread feelings of alienation, aloneness, strangeness and loneliness ... '[34] These problems have been exacerbated by the breakdown of traditional families, American urbanisation, disappearance of base communities, and lack of profundity in friendship. Perhaps, for our purposes, we might add the separateness urged in past seminary training.

Maslow says that 'practically all theorists of psychology have stressed thwarting of the love needs as basic in the picture of maladjustment'.[35] He points out that love and sex (genital sexuality) are not synonymous. 'Ordinarily sexual behaviour is multi-determined, that is to say, determined not only by sexual but also by other needs'.[36] Maslow made a very bold and definite statement with regard to genital sexuality which should be emphasised here and which will be be alluded to in later chapters. His statement, because it relates to intimacy and genital sexuality as well as celibacy, is extremely important for understanding the nature of different needs. He says:

> In self-actualising people the orgasm is simultaneously more important and less important than in average people. It is often a profound and almost mystical experience, and yet the absence of sexuality is more easily tolerated by these people. This is not a paradox or a contradiction. It follows from dynamic motivation theory. Loving at a higher need level makes the lower needs and their frustrations and satisfactions less important, less central, more easily neglected. But it also makes them more wholeheartedly enjoyed when gratified.[37]

Maslow thus indicates that loving at a higher need level (affective intimacy) makes the lack of satisfaction at a lower need level (genital or sexual) tolerable because the emotional satisfaction of the need for intimacy takes place at the higher level.

At the fourth level are the esteem needs which Maslow separates into two areas. First he speaks of the desire for strength, adequacy, achievement, competence and self-confidence, independence and freedom. Secondly he discusses the desire for reputation, prestige, status, attention, importance, dignity, appreciation, etc. He makes a particular point of grounding this need for self-esteem on 'deserved respect' from others rather than any false ideas of external fame or glory that is not due to our basic dignity and achievement.[38]

Finally, after all the above levels of needs are satisfied, one still remains, and that is the need for self-actualisation which can be described as: whatever a person can be, he or she must be.[39]

Maslow's work is important because one of our themes is that intimacy is necessary in the life of any human being in order to move one into a life of fuller growth and development, whether that be in ministry, in relationship to God or in relationship to one's own self. In this respect the esteem need as well as the need for self-actualisation must also be considered with the love needs. This is because one will only move into higher levels (esteem and self-actualisation) and into true generativity, care and integrity (Erikson's terms) if and when the love needs are satisfactorily met. It is in this regard that these psychological theories must be studied in their entirety, since it is important to understand the hierarchical nature of needs if one is to appreciate how we are to move beyond intimacy or love relationships, at a personal or individual level, into the more universal concerns of love for all people (participating in the re-creation of a world of peace, justice and love as the gospels envision).

Erik Erikson

Erik Erikson's well-known 'life stages' are mentioned here in order to review how the movement proceeds from infancy to old age and how the stages correspond to their developmental tasks. The stages and tasks are: (infancy) trust *vs* mistrust; (early childhood) autonomy *vs* shame, doubt;

(childhood) initiative *vs* guilt; (school age) industry *vs* inferiority; (adolescence) identity *vs* identity confusion; (beyond adolescence) intimacy *vs* isolation, generativity *vs* stagnation, and integrity *vs* despair.[40]

Each of the successive stages is a 'crisis' in the sense that it is a turning point, a period in which a person is in a state of increased vulnerability and heightened potential. To move to subsequent stages, one must be willing to reach out and risk being vulnerable in order to achieve whatever potential might be possible.

It is the last three of Erikson's tasks that are a concern for us. All tasks are necessary if we are to grow and develop as mature loving persons. However, it is assumed that the persons about whom we speak have successfully completed the tasks through adolescence, so as to focus on the task of 'intimacy *vs* isolation' and on those that follow. This is necessary in order to look progressively at human development. Working through the task of intimacy is seen as essential to further growth and development.

Erikson begins his explanation of true intimacy by saying that 'it is only when identity function is well on its way that true intimacy – which is really a counterpointing as well as a fusing of identities – is possible'.[41] He is quick to point out that sexual intimacy is distinct from what he has in mind, and he reminds his readers that 'sexual intimacies often precede the capacity to develop a true and mutual psychosocial intimacy with another person ...'[42] Promiscuous intimacy is often reminiscent of one who is not sure of his or her identity and is often a way of hiding out from real intimacy with another. Erikson claims that when one does not find intimate relationships with another person in late adolescence or early adulthood, then he or she may settle for 'highly stereotyped interpersonal relations and come to retain a deep **sense of isolation**'.[43] In particular it is well to note:

> If the times favour an impersonal kind of interpersonal pattern, a man can go far, very far, in life and yet harbour a severe character problem doubly painful because he will never feel really himself, although everyone says he is a 'somebody'.[44]

For Erikson, the counterpoint of this intimacy is 'distantiation', which he describes as 'the readiness to repudiate, isolate, and, if necessary, destroy those forces and people whose essence seems dangerous to one's own'.[45] Such a tendency is often attributed to males who are afraid of coming to terms with intimacy needs. As Erikson mentions, this type of prejudice is often exploited in politics and war, which have stereotypically been male-oriented fields of endeavour. Anyone who has ever worked with a Church structure will immediately recognise the 'power plays' often found among the clergy as reflection of this type of distantiation.

In *Childhood and Society*, Erikson explains:

> The strength acquired at any stage is tested by the necessity to transcend it in such a way that the individual can take chances in the next stage with what was most vulnerably precious in the previous one.[46]

He feels that young adulthood should be a time when one is ready to fuse his/her identity with that of others and thus he/she is ready for intimacy even though that may require significant sacrifices or compromises. One must be able to face ego loss in situations which call for abandoning oneself, so that close relationships and friendships can be solidified. Then one can be inspired by another and fuse identities in order to create intimacy.[47]

Erikson recognises psychoanalysis' claim that genitality is one of the developmental conditions to full maturity (Maslow disagrees), but he adds that it is something that is not fully understood.[48] In *Childhood and Society* he states a position which approaches Maslow's in saying that psychoanalysis has upon occasion gone too far in its emphasis of genitality. Erikson claims that whenever preferences or ideals of duty or loyalty call for restraint in terms of genital sexuality, the human being should be capable of bearing the ensuing frustration.[49]

Love as mutual devotion, says Erikson, is the vital strength of young adulthood. Humankind has developed a selectivity of love which admits to a new stage of identity. The estrangement which is typical at this stage of development is called isolation (the inability to risk one's identity by intimate sharing). Often, as a result of this isolation, fear of the results of intimacy, which he lists as offspring or care, is reinforced.[50] Erikson, in ending his section on intimacy, reminds us how very essential such intimacy is in coming to terms with self-identity questions. As he claims, and we heartily agree, 'We **are** what we love'.[51]

As mentioned, the last two stages of Erikson's developmental tasks, those of generativity and integrity, are certainly values to which we, as holistic Christians, are called in adult life. Generativity is the concern for guiding the following generation, whether that means our own children or more universally, the children of the world. An inability to be generative results in stagnation, dullness, and general interpersonal impoverishment. The final stage for Erikson is that of integrity, the absence of which is disgust and despair of life. His explanation of integrity, because it is so pertinent for Christian moral theology today, is given below exactly as he states it:

> It is the ego's accrued assurance of its proclivity for order and meaning – an emotional integration faithful to the image-bearers of the past and ready to take, and eventually renounce, leadership in the present. It is the acceptance of one's one and only life cycle and of the people who have become significant to it as something that had to be and that, by necessity, permitted of no substitutions. It thus means a new and different love of one's parents, free of the wish that they should have been different, and an acceptance of the fact that one's life is one's own responsibility. It is a sense of the comradeship with men and women of distant times and of different pursuits who have created orders and objects and sayings conveying human dignity and love.[52]

This integrity is important, as it very much relates to what we will discuss in Chapter Five and indeed to one's ability to love all of humanity.

Evelyn and James Whitehead

Evelyn and James Whitehead, in their well-known book *Christian Life Patterns*, are urgently concerned with the questions of adult life which integrate religion and psychology. They ask repeatedly 'Who am I?'; 'Who am I with?'; 'What should I do?' and 'What does it all mean?'[53] These questions, for them, represent the great religious questions of a lifetime and are the perennial questions to which human persons repeatedly address themselves and yet never completely answer in the course of a lifetime. The Whiteheads also consider these questions as central to coming to some type of psychological maturity.[54]

Basing their work on Erikson, the Whiteheads spend

much effort dealing with the challenges which each 'life stage' brings. Each is a critical time in one's life. Decisions must be reached as a result of the challenges, or else stagnation occurs. In addition, the strength of earlier stages of development remains only if it is tested and transformed in later stages. If a transformation does not take place, then each strength atrophies and dies. With regard to intimacy, the Whiteheads feel that the opposing forces of intimacy and isolation can be transformed into a vital capacity for mutual devotion and into consistent strength for love. If this transformation does happen, then one can further develop the qualities of care, wisdom, and integrity that mark a mature life. The values of intimacy, generativity, and integrity are the three psychological issues of adulthood upon which the Whiteheads base their integration of religion and psychology.[55] Intimacy for them is a necessity in the life of anyone growing toward God. They feel that the true psychological test of intimacy is to ask the question, 'Am I sure enough of myself and confident enough of my ability that I can risk being influenced through closeness with someone else?'[56]

As they explain, intimacy implies risk. I must risk that the person with whom I become intimate may change me and may bring me to a different awareness of who I am as a result of our close sharing. Can I risk that? If I am confident enough in myself, I can take the risk, but if I am not confident enough then I will not risk because of my fear. In that case, I will defend my identity in a very rigid interpersonal style so that no other can invade my territory. Whereas a strong identity can move toward intimacy, a weak one cannot; a weak identity will not sustain itself because intimacy implies being open to change. Openness to change means that in an intimate relationship space is shared and that there must be a willingness to be influenced by another.

(Based on the philosophical work in Chapter Two, we can very easily see how one's openness to another human being might parallel one's openness to God.) A weak identity cannot take the chance of accepting another and being influenced by another. Mutuality is an offspring of intimacy. If I know who I am and what I am about, then I have no problem in accepting the other in my life with his or her strengths. If I have little sense of who I am, then I will be overwhelmed.[57]

Six psychological resources, according to the Whiteheads, are developed in the struggle for intimacy. They are:

(1) a supple sense of oneself – basic knowledge and acceptance of self, coexisting with an openness for new information;
(2) empathy for others and awareness of their individuality;
(3) willingness to let the awareness of others influence me and an ability to modify myself when new information to situations becomes available;
(4) the flexibility to take these modifications into my personality so that I am strengthened;
(5) a creativity which enables me to find behaviour patterns and lifestyles which are self-enhancing;
(6) tolerance for the tension that is always necessary in personal relationships and compromise which follows from these relationships.[58]

Needless to say, all of these resources are vitally important for anyone who ministers. It seems that we are moving toward developing these qualities in some of our ministers today. But we only need look back ten or twenty years and question if these resources were required or affirmed in the past.

When intimacy fails, the Whiteheads believe that 'a person may develop a characteristic reserve with others or even seek to avoid many interpersonal situations altogether'.[59] There are three types of avoidance which may occur and which, if continued into adulthood, would be judged as immature. They are: isolation, stereotyped behaviour, and promiscuity. Isolation refers to those who believe they **have to** remain alone and avoid interpersonal relationships which cause psychological strain. This avoidance can take the form of physically isolating oneself or psychological isolation, making oneself present but not open to relationships (e.g., Fr Smith, the cold administrator who later became a monsignor). Stereotyped behaviour means not making oneself vulnerable because of a refusal to let self-disclosure take place (e.g., Fr Matthew, the victim of an internal power-play who later died of a 'broken heart'). This limiting may occur, for example, by hiding behind the public 'priestly' role. Promiscuity involves frantically seeking after intimacy in relationships in which one does not really reveal oneself (e.g., Fr Jack, the life of the party, joke-telling priest with his many short-term sexual encounters). A person can easily give him/herself to someone in an improbable relationship (such as prostitution), which prevents one from sharing his/her whole self with another.[60]

The emphasis placed by the Whiteheads on mutual devotion, as the most highly developed strength of intimacy emerging from early adulthood, characterises their stance that mutual love prepares one for psychological adulthood. This is so because such 'love moves beyond the energising but psychologically passive experience of "falling in love" toward a relationship that is chosen and cultivated'.[61] The mutual care and concern of one for another is most reflective of gospel values. This type of love, according to the Whiteheads, requires 'commitment' and a 'generous self-disregard'.[62]

All the psychologists we have studied include elements of *agape* in their notions of intimacy. Maslow's self-actualising persons have integrated intimacy into their lives. These persons have shown a love that is far more than emotion. Their love has virtues of compassion, justice, and kindness. They take on tasks they feel **they must do** based on unselfish motives and concern for humanity. These qualities are reflective of self-sacrifice, commitment, obedience, and 'willed' love. For Erikson, a definition of intimacy includes an ability to develop ethical strength to abide by commitments, even though they require sacrifices and compromises. These values certainly are reflective of *agape*. The Whiteheads give an initial interpretation of love which may be reflective of *philia*, but they add that love requires commitment and generous self-disregard (*agape*). They consider it essential to integrate the psychological requirements for intimacy with the ability to develop the virtues of *agape* and *diakonia* (service).

None of the psychologists studied here include genital sexuality as a requirement for intimacy. Maslow says that loving at a higher-need level makes the lower needs and their satisfactions less important. Sullivan relates that intimacy can consist of many things without genital contact. Erikson claims that society has placed too much emphasis on genitality. In addition, human beings should be capable of bearing sexual frustrations whenever ideals of duty or loyalty call for restraint, and thus intimacy without genitality is possible. The Whiteheads tell us that intimacy has a broader psychological sense than that implied by genital sexuality, and that the development of intimacy does not always involve sexual expression.

Gerald May as well as Rollo May hold that love can be separated from genital sexuality.[63] For these reasons and others already mentioned, we can state that theological love does have a tremendous likeness to psychological intimacy and, in terms of moral norms, that love is most desirable and essential in the life of any human being.

Effects of the Lack of Intimacy

Maslow, Erikson, and the Whiteheads all point to loneliness as the primary effect of the lack of intimacy. Maslow finds that alienation, aloneness, strangeness, and loneliness occur because of a lack of intimacy. This can cause maladjustment as well as an inability to reach self-esteem and self-actualisation. For Erikson, isolation and stereotypical interpersonal relationships are the result of an inability to form intimate relationships. In addition, one cannot approach the higher needs of generativity and integrity. As a consequence, stagnation and despair occur. The Whiteheads also believe isolation, stereotypical behaviour, and promiscuity are the effects of a lack of intimacy.

Most researchers in this field of intimacy, whether they be in psychology or theology, agree that a lack of intimacy leads to a painful loneliness. Men and women are existentially lonely, and this loneliness can be changed only by overcoming our fear of intimacy. Erich Fromm goes so far as to say that 'the deepest need of man, then, is the need to overcome his separateness, to leave the prison of his aloneness'.[64] The experience of separateness arouses anxiety and is even considered by some as the source of all anxiety. Fromm spends a great deal of time analysing this in *The Art of Loving*, where he most powerfully affirms that we are constantly seeking union with another or others. He states: 'This desire for interpersonal fusion is the most powerful striving in man. It is the most fundamental passion ... '[65]

Edgar Jackson, who has done much work on loneliness, maintains that the end result of quickly seeking intimacy in this technological age is an abandonment of our honour and dignity. It results in feelings of failure rooted in needs so deep that only a religious perspective can interpret them.[66] 'Fast intimacy' is often a term used to describe the behaviour of those who are afraid of real, profound, psychological, and spiritual intimacy and thus seek satisfaction by fulfilling a biological desire without taking the time necessary for a complete relationship.[67] (Again, we are reminded of the promiscuity of Fr Jack.) The last two decades have seen an incredible amount of this type of grasping at intimacy.

Loneliness is produced by a lack of intimacy and estrangement from others and from God. Connected with this loneliness is an inability to trust. This lack of trust is especially prevalent in our society today. This inability to trust pervades our society and institutions. (It seems to me that it is particularly rampant in seminaries where there is a tremendous inability for one to 'be oneself'.) It begins early in families and surfaces repeatedly throughout our lives as an inability to love without defence mechanisms. The lack of trust and the fear which is at the root of our loneliness can be overcome only by reaching out and making ourselves known to others. Sidney Jourard suggests that we should reverse the Delphic oracle's advice, 'know thyself', to re-read 'make thyself known and thou shalt then know thyself'.[68] Every maladjusted or lonely person is one who has not made him/herself known and, as a consequence, does not know him/herself.[69]

In speaking of loneliness as the primary result of a lack of intimacy, it is essential to make a distinction between loneliness and being alone. Paul Tillich in *The Eternal Now* describes 'loneliness' as the pain of being alone while 'solitude' expresses the glory of being alone.[70] This distinction is essential for the affirmation of the need for solitude in intimate relationships both with human persons and with God. This distinction very much relates to the theory of the Whiteheads as described. They speak of the tension between intimacy and isolation as being essential to growth and development. Henri Nouwen tells us:

> Without the solitude of heart, the intimacy of friendship, marriage and community life cannot be creative. Without the solitude of heart our relationships with others easily become needy and greedy, sticky and clinging, dependent and sentimental, exploitative and parasitic, because without the solitude of heart we cannot experience the others as different from ourselves but only as people who can be used for the fulfilment of our own, often hidden, needs.[71]

Nouwen, who has written extensively about the need for intimacy in the human search for God, states repeatedly that the solution for our experience of loneliness is not to be found in togetherness. This concept seems to be affirmed by countless married persons who still find themselves existentially lonely.

The psychological works cited in this chapter have shown that intimacy is a fundamental necessity in the life of healthy human beings. Relationships of love are essential for those who journey through life. Strong human love is natural for people who show signs of having lived and who desire to become real human beings. Love is powerful enough to accompany one through physical, emotional, and spiritual changes of one's life. No one reaches the goal of adult relationships magically or effortlessly. There is no skipping over any of the steps that lead to having a friend or sharing with another. Love often hurts and cannot be possessed without being vulnerable to the pain.[72]

The following story of the *Velveteen Rabbit* is most descriptive of the struggle which intimacy calls us to face. The story is told that one day the young rabbit asks the Skin Horse who has been around the nursery for a long time,

> 'What is real? ... Does it hurt?' asked the Rabbit.
>
> 'Sometimes,' said the Skin Horse, for he was always truthful. 'When you are Real, you don't mind being hurt.'
>
> 'Does it happen all at once, like being wound up,' he asked, 'or bit by bit?'
>
> 'It doesn't happen all at once,' said the Skin Horse. 'You become. It takes a long time. That's why it doesn't often happen to people who break easily, or have sharp edges, or who have to be carefully kept. Generally, by the time you are Real, most of your hair has been loved off, and your eyes drop out and you get loose in the joints, and very shabby. But these things don't matter at all, because once you are Real you can't be ugly, except to people who don't understand.'[73]

Like the velveteen rabbit, people become wrinkled, get grey hair and accumulate many scars. However, such things do not really matter to one who has known love because that love is powerful enough to accompany one through physical, emotional and spiritual imperfections and through the shifting stages of one's life.

So, lest one thinks intimacy is all ecstasy, it must be recognised that intimacy, if it is real, is filled with tension, pain, and sacrifice as well as joy and fulfilment. In that intimacy brings us in touch with our faults and failures, it also creates a capacity to confront death. It constantly brings us in touch with many 'little deaths' in which we are called to let go of our selfishness, wants, and desires and to give to the other. We are called to yield when we want to control. We are called to let go when we want to hold on. 'Suffering is, in fact, guaranteed for anyone who takes on the task of loving. The man who loves will suffer, but he will also find a fullness of life and a personal experience of the Spirit's presence',[74] writes Eugene Kennedy. Intimacy is not for the weak-hearted, but, if we are willing to put up with the pain and sacrifice as well as the joy and ecstasy, we can open ourselves to a very confident intimacy.

In the following chapter, which specifically deals with priesthood, it is important to look at the gospel call to love and to integrate it with the human need to love and be loved. Together, the two fields of theology and psychology speak to all men and women of faith. There are, however, particular implications for ministry and priests, because priesthood is not a call to mediocrity. It is a call to a fullness of life in Christ. 'It seems to me,' Bernard Bush states, 'that to be called to the celibate priesthood means being called to strive toward an extraordinary degree of maturity ...'[75] It is heartily agreed that the call to priesthood is a call to responsible adult living. As the Second Vatican Council's *Decree on the Ministry and Life of Priests* states: '... every priest in his own way assumes the person of Christ ... '[76] Each, therefore, must plunge himself fully into the incarnate world as Christ did.

The people of our times have been called to be critical lovers of the Church, and as critical lovers, we must call priestly leaders to task and to responsibility. An initial task of being a responsible leader is to re-examine our deeply ingrained heritage which reminds us that grace works with nature and to rethink the transcendental precept which dictates that we must 'be human'. No one can magically become human. It is possible only through integrating the mystical process of prayer into our lives. We become human by engaging ourselves in life; by looking at the junk and the joy, the grace and the garbage that fill our lives. We become human by facing the realities of life rather than by unhealthily hiding behind theological axioms. Most of all, we become human by doing what humans are primarily called to do: by loving. For, as William McNamara writes in *Mystical Passion*: '... if religious men and women are not great lovers, what hope is there for Christianity?'[77]

The human need for intimacy and its relationship to theological 'love' now established, let us look at this need in terms of priestly life.

4

INTEGRATING INTIMACY INTO THE LIFE OF THE PRIEST

> To be good priests we must first be good men. This requires that we seek to understand the mystery of our whole humanity. We must make provision for our physical, emotional and psychological health. We cannot hide from life. Our vocation is not a matter of 'easy hours and no heavy lifting'. Only by living life in all its complexity will we be able to serve our people with compassion. Our genuine interest and authenticity should be manifest. If we are truly comfortable with ourselves and have a deep appreciation of our celibate commitment, we should not fear opening ourselves to others in love and lasting friendships. Like everyone else, the priest needs affection.[1]
>
> *Cardinal Joseph L Bernardin*

These words of Cardinal Joseph L Bernardin clearly reflect a healthy and holistic approach to living a priestly life today. Unfortunately, however, neither all priests nor all lay people would agree with Cardinal Bernardin. There is much confusion surrounding the definition of priesthood in today's world. The 4 February, 1988 issue of *Origins* boldly states one of the immanent problems in priesthood today. It reads simply: 'Needed: A Theology of Priesthood'.[2]

This chapter will point to **some** areas that need to be examined in order to develop a theology of priesthood that integrates intimacy into the life of the priest. The chapter will begin with a brief overview of priesthood as it was seen in the past. That model of priesthood often negated one's humanity by frowning on friendships. After examining some of the problems inherent in the negation of one's humanity, we will consider the cultural, historical, social, and ecclesiological demands for a new theology of priesthood. Such a new theology is in the process of emerging. However, as we progress through the 1990s we are in 'transition times' and are still forming a new view of priesthood.

One of the foundational themes of this book is that a new view of priesthood must allow for human intimacy. Intimacy is, as we have seen in preceding chapters, a requirement for living our gospel values and progressing toward full human development. A theology of priesthood that integrates intimacy is a challenge to full adult living. This adulthood is the view of priesthood proposed here.

Priesthood Past

Numquam solus cum sola!
Sit sermo brevis et durus ...[3]

This exhortation, 'Never one (male) alone with one (female)! Let your discourse be brief and tough ... ' succinctly reveals past thinking regarding man-woman friendship and intimacy in the life of a priest. It was, under no circumstances, to be tolerated. Celibacy was often regarded as a negation, a giving up of the married state. Prior to Vatican II, the law on 'particular friendships' was emphatically enforced in seminaries all over the Roman Catholic world. The caution never to go anywhere with just one other person, but rather with at least two people, was rigidly followed in training. 'Particular friendships' were thought to be exclusive and divisive. They were considered to threaten individual growth and development since they fostered overdependence and emotional immaturity. Sometimes such friendships also led to compromise in terms of a life of chastity and availability for pastoral and apostolic duties in the community.

Intimacy in the life of a celibate was outrightly discouraged. A book written in 1949 by the well-respected M Eugene Boylan tells us:

> In regard to those who come to us for direction we should remember that it is a well-known fact that personal attachment often lessens considerably a priest's official power of guidance. He does not seem to have the same grace for his work. And there may be considerable truth in the frequently repeated observation that the bestowal of inordinate affection by a priest on any person brings a blight that is almost a curse.[4]

The prohibition against friendships with women was stated even more strongly. 'Very special circumstances excepted, a new intimate friendship formed with a woman after ordination, should be regarded with great suspicion, if not for what it already is, at least for what it may become'.[5] Although advice of this nature may cause us to shake our heads today, this advice was considered with utmost seriousness until very recently (Vatican II era) in the life of committed priests.

Past prohibitions against intimacy for a celibate priest existed because many could not imagine that loving could be separated from genital sexuality: loving and the celibate lifestyle were thought to be contradictory. Many historical factors led to the prohibitions of intimacy.

Certainly the body/soul dichotomy that we inherited from Greek philosophy and on which much of our theology is based did a tremendous disservice to the idea of intimacy. Platonic philosophy thought of the body and the soul as distinct entities. Intimacy was connected to love, and love was integrally involved with sexuality. Since sexuality belonged to the corporeal nature of the body, it was regarded as suspect. Over the centuries we came to regard the soul as good and the body as evil or as leading to evil.

What followed from the body/soul dichotomy was a very unhealthy situation which gave a negative connotation to sexuality. As we know, a negative view of sexuality was not held in the Old Testament; the Old Testament view was earthy, well-integrated, and whole. The New Testament, too, when read within its specific cultural and social context (especially the writings of Paul),[6] offers a positive view of sexuality. For the most part, however, the Church has based a great deal of its teaching on the Platonic, rather than the Scriptural model. The situation has been further distorted by the Augustinian bias.

This Augustinian bias, itself so influenced by Platonism, attempts to short-circuit the process by which we grow spiritually by identifying sexuality with concupiscence or a creation which is disordered, rather than identifying sexuality with our natural capacity for creative goodness and love. Therefore, we viewed our sexuality and a capacity for intimacy as a major problem rather than a moral virtue. This Augustinian bias has created a consistently negative regard for sexuality (Jansenistic tendencies) and has saddled us with an anthropology which does not properly address the human person who has been redeemed by the death and resurrection of Jesus Christ.[7]

The combination of the body/soul dichotomy and its negative views of sexuality, the Augustinian bias, the 'elevated' view of the priest[8] along with ideas of ritual purity and cultic priesthood[9] and negative views of women,[10] have combined to shape the denial of the basic needs for human friendships for priests. As a result, the view of celibacy which has emerged over the centuries into the mid-sixties (and even, for some, to the present day) clearly discouraged intimate relationships.

Priesthood has been thought by many to be an almost 'supra-human' calling in which the humanity of the priest was superseded by a call to orders.

In *Dare I Love,* McGoey tells us:

> Generations of Christian celibates, unfortunately, had it drummed into them that if they were 'good priests ... ' they were everything. 'Good' was defined with legal negatives so that they could, in some mysterious way, be considered loving without actually loving anyone. They were encouraged to be real men ... while completely ignoring sex and their positive sexuality. They succeeded, all too often, only in eliminating love, which is the one justification for celibacy. Much of the present temporary rejection of celibacy can be explained by this historic development of celibate life into the obligation to love no one but God alone. Such celibacy is as unchristian as it is unloving.[11]

Evidence of such 'unloving' has been abundant within the Church, and complaints are frequently heard about 'cold, indifferent priests', such as we saw with Fr Smith in Chapter One. Fr Smith's inability to be intimate filtered through all of his ministry, even to the little children to whom he showed no patience or tolerance. 'Loveless celibacy produces cantankerous, small-minded people, prone to bickering jealousy, who constantly resent the friendships of others – an indictment of their own unloving'.[12] These men not only fail to see the face of Jesus in their own lives, they also fail to help others find Him.

Generally, the need for intimacy in the life of a priest has not only been ignored, it has been outrightly smothered. This has been the situation in spite of the fact that a great number of well-respected priests, such as Jerome, Augustine, Bernard of Clairvaux, John of the Cross, and Francis de Sales (as well as many others) have had close intimate friendships. We need to keep in mind, however, that several had problems during their lifetimes because of these relationships. Misunderstandings as well as outright accusations of others are not recent by-products of intimate relationships; these difficulties, often spawned by jealousies, have always existed.

Today, however, there is a shift in the way of looking at the need and desire for intimacy. What has caused the shift from celibacy's 'ruggedly individualistic' approach to a vision that sees a possibility of integrating celibacy with intimacy?

A Time of Transition

In coming to an understanding of the multifaceted answer to the above question, it is valuable to offer a view of where we are in our cultural, historical, social, and ecclesiological perspectives in terms of priesthood. One difficulty in speaking on the topic of intimacy in the life of a priest today is that we are caught in the midst of changing structures in all of our lives. This change is true for priesthood as well as marriage, due to a host of reasons. Paramount is the current technological and computer age which has given rise to, and exists along with, the changing roles of men and women and the stability/instability of relationships. Vatican II as well as the feminist movement and recent Church history regarding problems with celibacy have required us to re-examine numerous preconceived notions which affect our views of the celibate male priesthood, marriage, the family, the single life, and many other long-held traditions. In addressing this reality, *Gaudium et Spes* states:

> At all times the Church carries the responsibility of reading the signs of the time and of interpreting them in the light of the Gospel, if it is to carry out its task. In language intelligible to every generation, she should be able to answer the ever recurring questions which men ask about the meaning of this present life and of the life to come, and how one is related to the other. We must be aware of and understand the aspirations, the yearnings, and the often dramatic features of the world in which we live.[13]

What *Gaudium et Spes* calls 'the signs of the time', might be compared to what Thomas Kuhn in his landmark book, *The Structure of Scientific Revolutions*, has called a 'paradigm shift'.[14] A paradigm shift is a distinctively new way of thinking about an old problem. Marilyn Ferguson, commenting on this shift in *The Aquarian Conspiracy*, describes it as including the old as a partial truth or one aspect of how things work while being open to the new. She says it throws open the doors and windows for new exploration. The problem with it, however, is that one cannot embrace the new values unless one is willing to let go of the old.[15] Vatican II was clearly a call for us to do this within the Church. Because of Vatican II we have been called to a new way of listening to the Spirit among us.

Truly, we are in the midst of a paradigm shift in the Church and in the world. Not only our salvation, but also our earthly existence may depend on just how well we choose to adopt new ways of dealing with problems. We are called, then, to look at long-held values, traditions, and established truths and to examine them in new and different ways. *The Spiritual Renewal of the American Priesthood* tells us that 'in this transition period of the Church we are called to move out into uncharted ways'.[16] This is most difficult and most painful, but also most challenging.

Sean Sammon speaks of ours as a transitional age in *Growing Pains in Ministry*:

> The Chinese were right. A transitional age is a curse. Old forms break down and die out. People feel confused, frightened, even overwhelmed. This bad news seems to get worse as a group moves into its critical period. Members make mistakes and sometimes believe that they were better off with what they had before. The period is one of genuine crisis. As such it is also a turning point, a time of decision.[17]

Megatrends' author, John Naisbitt, adds to our understanding by telling us: 'We are living in the **time of the parenthesis**, the time between eras. It is as though we have bracketed off the present from both the past and the future, for we are neither here nor there'.[18]

If we choose to agree with the above authors, as well as with many other social scientists, then we must ask ourselves repeatedly which of the old values must we hold on to and take with us into the future, and which of the values must we discard as no longer meaningful or useful to our lives. Successful marriages are doing this and must continue to do so even more in the future. The impact of the women's movement has been earth-shattering in terms of the re-examination of some of the old structures and of discovering how we need to re-image our lifestyles based on the equality, mutuality and dignity of each human person. Priesthood too is being critically examined as to the value implied in celibacy in today's society. In addition, a married priesthood for both men and women is being openly discussed by many.

In considering how all these structures as well as values are being examined, it is essential to acknowledge the commitments that have been made. Whether the commitment involves marriage or celibacy, it is important to ask the following question: How do those who have made these commitments adjust their lives in order to adapt to the new ways that the Spirit is speaking in this 'time of parenthesis?'

With regard to our topic, a new theology of bodily sexuality and a fresh, new approach to the integration of sexuality into our lives is vital before re-examining intimacy in the lives of celibates. In addition, holistic philosophies and anthropologies must be stressed. Relevant scriptural exegesis and the advances in psychology have underscored the fact that we must take the human path if we are to serve God. A final and important enabler of this awareness can be process theology.

Process theology re-examines the ideas which we have long accepted due to our grounding in Greek philosophy. It makes us aware that the Christian reality of today is not a static perception of ideas but, rather, a dynamic process. Norman Pittenger, in *Process Thought and Christian Faith*, explains that we are all 'in process' of becoming.[19] Humanity, rather than being static, is very much on the move, living, changing and developing. Furthermore, the world is an interrelated society of 'occasions'. Each experience is affected by past experiences as well as present surrounding pressures, in addition to the possibility of the mystique and promise of future events. We are historical, cultural beings and our events are historical, cultural, and future-related. Events in our world are interconnected, interrelated, and effect one another. No person or thing is really and only an island. The ideas of process theology have many implications for moral theology. They are also in keeping with new ideas from science and the study of the environment.

An approach that stresses that we are all 'in process' is important if we are truly going to relate to God who is among us speaking, acting, and working in the world. This approach conforms to one's fundamental option. It views the human person as one who is not only working toward his or her salvation, but who is also dynamically involved with all others who are labouring to see the reign of God in its fullness.

The Committee on Priestly Formation of the National Council of Catholic Bishops acknowledges this view, at least implicitly, in the first two Assertions made in their *Spiritual Formation in the Catholic Seminary*. The first Assertion states:

> As human beings and as believers we live in a number of environments, not simply one. Thus, patterns of growth occur in these various environments. Ministers and programmes of formation must attend to all these various environments.[20]

The second Assertion states:

> The real growth in the spirituality of a person occurs in the realm of personal relationships, that is, the relationship of the person with the mystery of God in Jesus, with oneself, and with other persons. Thus, programmes of formation are designed to serve the process of interpersonal relationships. The level and qualities of fundamental relationships noted above are a gauge and an indication of growth in one's spirituality.[21]

The above statements obviously carry quite a different message from the restricting view of friendship previously mentioned in Boylan's 1949 *The Spiritual Life of a Priest*. Theology has dramatically evolved from a solely vertical mentality of 'God-and-me' to include a horizontal dimension where God's grace is mediated through relationships. In developing a code of behaviour for the priest today, many differences from the code of thirty years ago are occurring due to a changed vision of God, of the person and of the world. In the span of the last thirty years great strides have been made in theology. In developing new views of the priest we must ask who priests ought to be in light of who they say they are.

This concept is indeed a challenge and an adventure. It will not occur without difficulty in the life of every priest. It is not for the weak-hearted or the impatient. But, as Sean Sammon reminds us:

> Every crisis is a time of danger but also of opportunity. Today we can begin anew in the Church, priesthood and religious life. The danger is that we will refuse to pay the necessary price, namely, loss of our old forms and understandings. When the people of God finally reach their new beginning, they will realise that it was indeed a small price to pay.[22]

Specifically in terms of priesthood, many feel that changes in mandatory celibacy are inevitable.[23] We will address these changes in following chapters but, as we are finding out, they will not be happening overnight. A private document issued in 1982 by seminary rectors in this country states:

> We realise that many of the older supports for maintaining celibacy ... have either faded or are being challenged. Some of the contemporary justifications for celibacy, whether hoarded from the past or newly minted, are not authentic for many in formation.[24]

Many issues on priestly life are being realistically examined and will undoubtedly bring about new changes. As we await these changes and perhaps even implement them, what is the priest's stance?

The Human Need for Intimacy in the Life of a Priest

One thing seems to be certain if priests are to live their lives fully and authentically: there will be a very real need to be in relationship with others who can provide trust, support, love, and care. These relationships, characteristic of all healthy human relationships, will be working simultaneously toward autonomy and connection.[25] Although these goals may appear to be contradictory, they provide the constant tension that each person needs in a growing spirituality which leads to wholeness and self-authenticity.

In relationships with valuable others, one must constantly strive to seek those values which our biblical grounding and traditions have taught us are essential. At the same time, experiences, situations, and events of life must be reflected upon to determine what should be re-examined or discarded. We are called to do this reflection by the God who created us and who, by virtue of creation, gave us everything we need to participate in that creation.[26] We are called to belong to a Church, society, and world which we must constantly question if we are to come to any kind of meaningful existence and if we are to come to any realisation of how God is speaking to us today. Generally, we do this questioning by being in interdependent relationships with others. These relationships help us to look deep within and to listen to God who is found there.

Priests, in particular, must be autonomous in determining the parameters of their lives. All priests are ultimately responsible for the creation of their own lives.[27] At the same time, however, they should seek out significant others with whom they can share their intellectual and emotional thoughts in this regard. Bernard Bush states: 'Psychic and apostolic availability in no way precludes the possibility of intense life-enhancing personal friendships. In fact, precisely the opposite is true'.[28] A genuine search for friends who share life's same values is essential.

This search is a tremendously difficult task for all priests today but most especially, or so it would seem, for the youngest ones. The role models of the past are quickly disappearing, and the dwindling number of dedicated, celibate men seems to be taking its toll. The problems of celibate life are perhaps graver than in recent past history. At every turn one encounters a significant percentage of priests struggling with loneliness, alcohol, drugs, sexual integration, power, dominance, lack of control over their lives, low self-esteem, isolation, the inability to relate to people, and the difficulties in relating to change. It may appear that there is nothing sacred, peculiar to priestly life. Scandals of all kinds have taken their toll. The media has placed much emphasis on these scandals; they are no longer hidden away in diocesan files, safe from public viewing. These realities make it somewhat difficult for a dedicated young man to find good role models. The dedicated, mature priest shares the struggle as a result of the lack of identity present among many priests. The 'brotherhood of priests' seems to have fallen apart in many dioceses and has certainly experienced pains not unlike those of the dysfunctional American family. Communication, or a spirit of family trust, seems to be at an all time low and, although some of the older men hang on to what used to be, it is happening with less enthusiasm and more difficulty.[29]

There are, of course, exceptions, just as there are exceptions in families, but much of the 'spirit of brotherhood' has been torn asunder by a lack of trust, jealousy, power, and a desire of some to control or protect their domains. The situation described by Fr Matthew in Chapter One is an example of the seesaw nature of the clerical power struggle. So hurt was he by this power struggle that he decided to retreat into himself, never again to reach out and risk being hurt by those he called his own. The animosities which exist among the different nationalities of priests in many dioceses make the situation even more critical.

A report and study done in 1985 on *The Health of American Catholic Priests* by the Bishop's Committee on Priestly Life and Ministry indicates that 39.8% of those studied in the previous twelve months of their lives had experienced 'severe personal, behavioural, or mental problems'.[30] We find these statistics even more revealing and alarming in light of the fact that:

> Men tend to minimise their needs, failings, physical state and weaknesses ... The mystique of the strong male, free from sickness or difficulty, is the self perception that tends to dominate American men. This, along with the 'be perfect', 'don't feel' messages, makes them likely candidates to over-estimate their personal well being. Priests are no exceptions.[31]

Possibly, priests would be the least likely exceptions due to the impossible 'be perfect' exhortation that they have received over the years which can make their job all the more unbearable.

Another study was begun in 1981 by the Centre for Human Development. This study focused on the Ministry to Priests Programmes in the Archdioceses of Miami and

Newark. Four hundred and fifty men participated in this study.[32] The study substantiated that friendship, trust, and intimacy as well as affirmation, acceptance, and identity were some of the most essential needs of priests.[33] Although 36% of the priests studied felt that they actually had the ability to form warm, lasting bonds of friendship, a majority, 52%, felt that they were having moderate to serious difficulties in terms of these relationships.[34] The statistics in these and other similar studies seem to be characteristic of male intimacy and also of the inability to form relationships with either sex.[35] The study also showed that:

> In addition to the need for fellowship with brother priests, the need for 'close priest friendships and intimate spiritual sharing', 'priest-confidants', and friendship in general was noted by many Miami priests ... These priests spoke repeatedly of the need for true 'friendship' and 'trust' to deal with isolation, loneliness, anger and depression. Specifically, the 'need to be needed' and the need 'to love and be loved', and the need to 'trust and be trusted' vocalised. Related to the need for 'personal friendship' and 'trust in one another', these men spoke of the need for 'intimacy' and a clearer understanding of 'sexuality' and 'celibacy'.[36]

Martin Devereaux, a priest and clinical psychologist who worked on this study as his doctoral dissertation, cites many other studies which display similar needs. These studies, many of which are concerned with self-actualisation in religious people, give a most interesting profile of priests.[37] Notable among these studies is the National Opinion Research Centre's 1971 study which was done under the direction of the National Conference of Catholic Bishops. The study showed two-thirds of the priests in this country to be 'psychologically underdeveloped' as persons.[38] This statistic means that they have not reached a stage of growth which is expected of them at their respective ages.[39]

Another study by Kennedy, Heckler, Kobler and Walker shows 6% to be in the category of 'developed', 29% to be 'developing', 57% to be 'underdeveloped', and 8% to be 'maldeveloped'. As would be expected, the 'developed' 'love one or more persons with an enlightened self-interest,' while the 'underdeveloped', 'have had a few, if any, experiences of intimacy'.[40] The 'developing' priests are:

> intent on liberating themselves from an emotional and social insularism. These developing priests have had their personal growth suspended or delayed and now through circumstances of personal decisions, find themselves challenged anew by the problems of growth.[41]

Studies such as these are extremely valuable. The Archdiocese of Miami is certainly to be commended for its interest in the study undertaken by Devereaux, who was one of Miami's priests. This study in itself is a first step in dealing with difficulties in priestly life.

The above information should encourage us to examine the pressures and the stresses that, in the past, seem to have been unrealistically placed upon our priests, and to determine how priesthood needs to be re-imaged. We must reaffirm the idea that, in order for a priest to function in this reality, he must seek out valuable others who will help support and strengthen him in his commitment.

As discussed, developing meaningful relationships was not an acceptable priestly response within the Church. The elevated status of priests, which existed for years in the Church, tended to underplay the fact that a priest is, first of all, a human being, created as all other human beings with psychological, emotional, physical, social, and sexual dimensions. One of the first notions that must be discarded in reimaging priesthood is that the priest is supra-human. Johannes Metz in *Poverty of Spirit* states that the only answer to God's love is to accept the challenge by obeying the law of our being and accepting the human condition where the response to the love of God takes place.[42] This challenge is fraught with inherent temptation and is a process of trial and error, but it is essential.

Cognizant of the power and poverty of our human condition, Michael J. Brickley, rector of the Jesuit School of Theology at Berkeley, wrote a letter to the ordination class of 1972 about the paradox of this human condition: 'The priest must also be liable to suffering, weak as a man because he must become like what he touches – the body of Christ'. Further on he asserts that 'the strength of our priesthood lies precisely in and through the weakness of our humanity'.[43]

Asserting that the priest is first of all a human being, as mundane a statement as it may be, is essential to our understanding. As a human being, the need for intimate friendships is a need the priest shares with all other men and women on his journey to God. Acknowledging this human need, Mary Elizabeth Kenel firmly states the desires of many celibates who are seeking a realism in their lives:

> The need and desire for intimacy has become one of the major themes of the renewal of religious life and priesthood that has grown out of Vatican II. The pendulum has swung from a position of fear and suspicion regarding interpersonal relationships to one of acceptance of warm, supportive relationships as the norm.[44]

Sandra Schneiders agrees with her and tells us further:

> If consecrated celibacy is to be lived integrally it involves foregoing the normal path to human affective maturity. But to fail to develop affectively means to fail to become fully human and, more importantly, to subvert the possibility of coming to a full experience of the love of God and a full development of ministerial potential. In other words, the stakes are very high. Unless the religious can find an alternate path to human intimacy, the chances are very good that he or she will sabotage the very project for which consecrated celibacy was undertaken. Bypassing the challenge to intimacy is not a viable alternative. It is a resignation from the human adventure, a self-consignment to perpetual childhood. Consequently, the concern with affectivity in the life of the consecrated celibate must not degenerate into strategies for avoiding sexual relations or rigid catalogues of what is and is not permissible. Our task is not to get through life without having sexual intercourse, or to eke out enough human warmth to survive without incurring paralysing guilt. It is to find the authentically celibate way to adult intimacy and therefore to affective maturity.[45]

Schneiders continues her line of thought by telling us that there are two essentials involved in the quest for celibate intimacy: one being friendships with people of both sexes and the other being contemplation.[46] One does not survive without the other. Bernard Bush, director of the House of Affirmation in Montava, California, agrees with Schneiders and claims: 'Even for the celibate, there is still a need for a loving relationship with the opposite sex'. He adds: 'In my experience, successful integration of all the dimensions of personhood requires both close personal relationships and spiritual reflection on inner experiences'.[47] Certainly my friend Father Mike, described in Chapter One, was aware of the value of spiritual reflection regarding his close personal friendship(s). The very fact that he was so enthralled by the tapes he brought back, and his need to share them, showed a depth of interest and concern for some spiritual direction regarding his friendship(s). This 'checking out' of relationships is an essential element of discernment in the lives of all of us.

Frank McNulty, who sensitively and perceptively addressed Pope John Paul II in Miami on his 1987 trip, also affirms this desire and need for intimacy:

> During the past few decades celibate people have been honest in admitting the personal struggles which are part of a celibate lifestyle. We went from agreeing that celibates should have intimate friendships with people of both sexes to admitting that celibates **need** these kind of relationships.[48]

Richard Rohr, a Franciscan who frequently directs retreats for priests, asserts that they must be free to fall in love.[49] His witness is shared today by many men and women in the fields of spirituality and retreat work.

If, as William McNamara intimates, becoming great lovers is compatible with and maybe even essential for becoming great saints, we must work with the great gift of sexuality (which is not necessarily equal to genitality). Whether priests, religious, married, or single, people must find ways to work at being great lovers that are in keeping with the parameters of commitments.

Priesthood Present – A Challenge

Given past views on celibacy which have negated one's sexuality, feelings, emotions, and physical needs, how then do we make the gigantic leap from old views to a view of the priest as one who is fully alive and fully functioning within a priestly commitment?

Perhaps Helen Keller's words, which apply to the lives of all of us, are particularly valuable for the priest: 'Life is either a daring adventure or nothing at all'.[50] Priestly life today is most certainly an adventure which takes one to the unknown. Celibacy today, if it is to be lived in accordance with gospel values of truth, authenticity, genuineness, fidelity to commitment, and love, can only be approached as a tremendous challenge. In this challenge, the priest is brought into contact with all the realities of life and, with the help of God and of close friends, he comes to probe profoundly at the mystery of his very unique call.

In *Celibacy, Prayer and Friendship,* Christopher Kiesling describes this adventure of living:

> The word adventure connotes a positive undertaking, like discovering the source of the Nile River or scaling Mount Everest. It involves struggling to meet challenges: limited human energies, diseases, difficult or dangerous terrain, extremes of heat or cold. In meeting challenges there are advances and reverses, successes and failures. Adventure entails planning ingeniously, mustering courage, attempting, failing, revising strategy, renewing courage, trying again, and persevering through challenge after challenge until the goal is reached. The outcome of adventure is uncertain: challenges to progress along the way may not be overcome; the final attempt at the goal may fail. Adventure means taking risks and requires daring, courage, patience and perseverance. It means achievement, at least the very struggle with opposing forces, but also completion of part of the journey and eventually attaining the goal. Adventure is stimulating and exciting; it gives zest to life and a feeling of satisfaction.
>
> Religious celibacy is an adventure in living humanly. This affirmation may surprise those who see celibacy only or mainly in terms of what is foregone in celibate life – the many-faceted fulfilment of marriage and family. But celibate life has

> all the characteristics of adventure, not merely an adventure inserted into life but an adventure whose enterprise is life itself.[51]

No one who understands the above description can say that the challenge is easy. Living out this mystery is most difficult and often times brings one into full knowledge of his limitations, his sinfulness, and his humanity. 'To grasp a paradox and hold it in tension, requires courage and wisdom'.[52] Priestly celibacy is not for the weak. However, if its challenge is worked through with patience, perseverance, and prayer, the priest may very well touch the mystery of the eschatological reality – the 'yet' but 'not yet' in his life. He may very well touch the face of God.

The call to experience priesthood in this way is perhaps the same exhortation which was heard by the 1987 graduating class of St Vincent de Paul Regional Seminary. Professor Michael Scanlon, in addressing this group, re-worked the words of Socrates, the 'unexamined life is not worth living', and re-formulated them to say that the 'unlived life is not worth examining'.[53] Looking at priesthood as an experience of totally involving oneself in life seems to be most essential for a priest today.

Today's celibate priest cannot hide from himself; neither can he hide from others, or ultimately from God. In order to live out this dynamic and mysterious call, one must continually experience the self-emptying of which St Paul speaks (e.g. Ph 2:5-8). This self-emptying speaks to the priest of God and enables him to love, with a tremendous intensity, all the people who are in his life. This view of celibacy, although calling for much sacrifice, does not mean a 'total deprivation in the sphere of love'.[54]

Loving in this way is not contrary to a celibate commitment; rather, it is the most powerful way of truly living that commitment since it involves entering into the unknown where God truly expresses Godself to us. It is loving with a passion so powerful that, paradoxically, the sublimation of that passion for the Reign of God puts all of one's reality in perspective. It means working **with** what John of the Cross calls 'the warmth and strength and temper and passion of love'.[55] The fact that this adventure requires full participation into life, fully exposing oneself to the realities of life is unquestionable. Celibacy, thus seen, refers to much more than a negative command of what not to do. Instead, it should enlarge a person's vision of the true goal of Christian life – the necessity to love all, rather than to narrow that vision to a forbidden realm of sexual acts.

Marc Oraison in *The Celibate Condition and Sex* writes:

> There seems to be room for a kind of celibacy which is not negative but instead expresses the need to find fulfilment and self-realisation beyond or aside from that represented by socially adjusted sexual union. By definition such individuals would have to possess real psychological capacity for such a personal sexual commitment.[56]

Sexuality is our way of being human. We are male and female embodied persons. Honestly facing this sexuality is vital for spirituality. There can be no pseudo-innocence about sexuality and, as Kenneth Leech bluntly explains, religion which does not face sexuality becomes twisted and imbalanced. The history of religion contains volumes of examples of false spiritualities and harmful attitudes on sex which have distorted our heritage and obstructed the wholeness of the human person.[57] Karl Rahner emphasises that 'true celibacy ... has nothing in common with the sexlessness of the eunuch but is possible only in a sound relationship between the sexes, where one recognises oneself as a man and a woman as a woman'.[58] He adds:

> Something should be said about many a ridiculous statement in our usual textbooks of moral theology. How often those books go on and on in legalistic verbiage, miles from reality, encumbering real, serious celibacy with unnecessary and senseless difficulties by manoeuvring the man in the priest into a really superstitious terror of sex. I ought to mention the purpose, nature and limits of a very special kind of love, a real spiritual friendship between a priest and a woman – a thing that can be spoken of only with the utmost discretion. Whatever it should be called – it occurs too often in the history of the saints – it can perfectly well exist in many degrees. I need not explain to you that this is not to be grossly misinterpreted as a 'loophole'.[59]

If Rahner's 'serious celibacy' can be viewed as an adventure which is open to all of life and if it can be admitted that the priest is first of all a human being with the same developmental patterns as were discussed earlier, then, indeed, it is possible to look at some of the characteristics of a sexually integrated priest. Oraison describes these characteristics as being found in mature and sexually integrated married persons as well as celibates. He describes these persons as being agreeable, but not eccentric; human but not perfect; spontaneous and at ease in most situations. These persons also have 'satisfactory sexually based emotional attitudes'; they are ready to reverse their positions and are capable of admitting their errors. These persons are young at any age because they have a determination not to control and not to become entrapped in philosophical, political, and national policies that are immutable. They have a natural respect for others and a desire to spend themselves for them. They are interdependent, but they will not be manipulated. They are often taken on as spiritual directors, mentors, or counsellors. There is a comfort with sexuality and even an ability to risk in some situations. These persons have a good sense of humour and are sure of themselves, but not in a pejorative manner. Finally, these persons are comfortable to be with and have a definite degree of emotional maturity.[60]

In observing Oraison's above descriptions of one who reflects a positive celibacy in his life, it is most interesting and important to notice how compatible they are with those proposed by Abraham Maslow for a self-actualising personality.

At this point it is important to reiterate that 'to choose celibacy, then, is an act of radical doubt about the link between sexual experience and development of humanness'.[61] With regard to genital sexuality and celibacy, it is important to re-emphasise the material explained earlier: that living on a higher need level (that of affectivity) makes the absence of the lower needs (genitality) tolerable because the emotional satisfaction of the need for intimacy is at a higher plane than that of genital sex. Maslow adds:

> It is now well known that many cases are found in which celibacy has no psychopathological effects. In other cases, however, it has many bad effects. What factor determines which shall be the result? Clinical work with non-neurotic people gives the clear answer that sexual deprivation becomes pathogenic in a severe sense only when it is felt by the individual to represent rejection by the opposite sex, inferiority, lack of worth, lack of respect, isolation, or other thwarting of basic needs. Sexual deprivation can be borne with relative ease by individuals for whom it has no such implications.[62]

In other words, the very things that make sexual deprivation bearable, those values found in intimacy, have been the very things that have been denied (for centuries) as valid celibate experiences. This insight indeed should be the crucible for much further study in terms of seminary formation and ministry to priests! Although many, it would seem, would question Maslow's use of the words 'relative ease', nevertheless, his theory tells us that not only are celibacy and intimacy compatible but that intimacy is essential for growth of a celibate priest.

Martin Pable claims that celibates who do not find the type of affirmation resulting from good relationships often exhibit 'low-key hostility'.[63] Henri Nouwen, in referring to this same group calls these the 'grumpy children of God',[64] and one need not go far to find them abounding in rectories and institutions. Those who exhibit such behaviour see religion as a 'form of protection against life and experience'.[65]

For these people, religion tends to become an end in itself: that is, God is not at the end. Forms and ceremonies are obsessive, and religion can be an obstacle to spiritual growth. This type of formal, ritual religiosity breeds and prolongs immaturity and is reflective of the man described by Erikson as ready to repudiate, isolate, and destroy others. Jung, although he strongly defends religion (against Freud), condemns the religion clung to by men of this nature, which he calls false.[66] Men who cling to this type of religion and hide out from life do little service to the message of Jesus.

Celibacy integrated with intimacy is a contradiction for those who have not been idealistic and realistic enough, as well as vulnerable enough, to see that love can be separated from genital sexuality. In addition, as an institution, the Church has been unwilling to risk the possibility of what is seen as imperfection in the lives of priests. Today too much is known in terms of theology, psychology, and in the realities of the lives of too many unfulfilled priests to hold to this inhumane idea any longer. Deeply affectionate yet non-genital relationships are definitely possible as long as people are committed to setting limits.

'The Church ... ' says Desmond McGoldrick in *Living the Celibate Life*, 'needs men who have accepted their manliness and women who are alive in their womanliness ... There must be no denying of one's sexuality under any false pretext of "preserving chastity".'[67] Perhaps, too, the Church and society should re-examine what we mean by morality as we may have lost the ability to speak on wider moral issues. Rather than adopting an act-centred morality, we must look at the whole and find out what we, as a Church, are proclaiming to the world. John McGoey tells us:

> Honest errors in chastity are surely less of a scandal than power struggles between religious orders or the ambitions of inflated churchmen daring to stand, without trembling, in the place of God for others.[68]

Although our focus is on intimacy, there are certainly many gospel values which are most reflective of a celibate commitment to this life of adventure. We could mention, among those to be integrated with intimacy, the values of truth, authenticity, genuineness, and fidelity to commitment.

Being truthful about one's life involves an ongoing process of purification and requires one to **be** true as well as to speak, think, and act truthfully. Honest and deep introspection with ourselves, as well as reflectively sharing with others, aids in the process of purification in which a person tries to assess honestly the truthfulness of his/her life.

Authenticity means being oneself and being honest in

relationships with others. It means that often one must drop pretences, defences, and phoniness, and put an end to the 'caginess' which is sometimes found in priests. Authenticity is essential in the lives of priests if they are to proclaim the value of honesty to the world. The days of hiding **from** relationships with others (in community or ministry) should be ending.[69] In addition, the days of **hiding** relationships from others (in community or ministry) should be ending. Honesty is most definitely the best insurance policy in making those relationships work and in integrating them into priestly lives. Only truly authentic men can handle this intimacy in their lives and make it creative, holistic and integrative.

Genuineness is related to authenticity and truth; it is the opposite of hypocrisy and is described as 'being the person you say you are'. Although possibly idealistic, since none of us is exactly the person we say we are, the challenge to become real or genuine is perhaps the task of a lifetime. One does not become a perfect celibate overnight, and perhaps 'two steps forward and one step back' is the norm. Becoming genuine is a life-long task for the priest.

Finally, fidelity to commitment is essential in the life of a priest. This means one must strive to do the very best he can to remain faithful. At the same time, he must remember that he is human with all the desires, longings, dreams, and fantasies of any other human being. When failings in celibacy occur, he must honestly relook at the situation and try to begin again. Fidelity to commitment has a mysterious element, the essence of which even a brilliant theologian such as Karl Rahner cannot appropriately describe. In an open letter to priests he writes:

> I myself am dissatisfied with this letter. It does not make clear what the mystery of renouncing marriage out of faith, hope and love for God (who is more to man than a stabilising factor) **and** for man really means. But perhaps after all you will see what lies behind words that are at once too simple and too complicated. Perhaps when one would speak of the elemental, abysmal things of life – especially things 'hidden' in Christ – all one can do is work round the edges of mystery, stammering in this way.[70]

Most certainly, to be a fully loving person, without genitally expressing that love, is a call to be stammering around the edges of mystery. This call makes sense only in the eschatological plan of God. Trying to explain this reality to someone who is not also fully convinced of its power and dynamism is not only futile, but also a waste of time. Therefore, it is especially important that the celibate priest establish friendships with those who have similar values and visions with regard to fidelity and with those who will see the power of God in this very dynamic, creative, life-giving yet mysterious way of life. As noted in Chapter Two, many of the saints felt that this was an essential prerequisite for Christian friendship. One comes to a fuller appreciation of the eschatological dimension of celibate priesthood in both the support and the tension that relationships provide. The characteristics of truthfulness, authenticity, genuiness, and fidelity to commitment were all characteristics found to be present in Father Steve described in Chapter One. These were the characteristics that made him an excellent confessor, spiritual director, teacher, and priest. These were the characteristics which were encouraged and fostered by that 'most powerful person who ever entered' his life. It seems that she showed him 'the goodness of all creation and the blessedness of all human love which finds its true source and end in God'.[71]

Having looked at some of the possibilities of integrating intimacy in the life of the priest, let us now look at some of the practical implications of these relationships for the priest as a person and as a minister.

5

PASTORAL IMPLICATIONS OF PRIESTLY INTIMACY

> The best Christians are those who love well, whether celibate or married. People, not states of life, have the potential to love. But great love is not only within the potential of celibates, it is their professed goal ... Their God-centred, people-centred love is a delusion if their sexuality is not incorporated into their loving relationships. Unloving celibates have absolutely nothing to offer to so much of the world, that is living unfulfilled simply because it has not learned to love.[1]
>
> *John H McGoey in* ***Dare I Love***

We have stated that in order to become a more loving and integrated person and priest, intimacy is essential in life. This chapter will examine the difficulties of intimacy in the lives of all men, and more specifically priests. It will also address the special problems that have existed because of an inability for some priests to live out their adolescence. But the main task of the chapter is to deal with the implications of intimate relationships with others. While it will discuss intimate relationships with other men as valid and authentic forms of intimacy, it will deal more fully with relationships between priests and women and draw some conclusions as to the special requirements, parameters, concerns, and joys of those relationships. Finally, it will suggest that intimacy, if successfully integrated into a priest's life, gives him the ability to be open to a very powerful and mystical love of God, humanity, and all of creation.

The Problem of Male Intimacy

There are problems in becoming intimate men. Sociologically, the intimate friendships of priests share some of the same characteristics and problems as those of other males. Intimacy is difficult for most men, celibate or not. Many consider intimacy a woman's domain.

Same-sex intimacy is often especially difficult for men. Most men feel more comfortable drawing their close friends from women, as they are usually better listeners, more understanding, less competitive, less judgmental, more loving and trustworthy.[2] Michael McGill, in his report on *Male Intimacy* asserts:

> To say that men have no intimate friends seems on the surface too harsh, and it raises quick objections from most men. But the data indicate that it is not far from the truth. Even the most intimate of male friendships (of which there are very few) rarely approach the depth of disclosure a woman commonly has with many other women. We know that very few men reveal anything of their private and personal selves even to their spouses; fewer still make these intimate disclosures to other men. One man in ten has a friend with whom he discusses work, money, marriage; only one in more than **twenty** has a friendship where he discloses his feelings about himself or his sexual feelings.[3]

McGill also tells us that 'the relationship between a mentor and a protege is one of the very few instances in which we regularly see a degree of intimacy between men'.[4] Generally men choose men as their beer buddies, golfing partners, tennis friends, fishing companions and similar types of relationships which seem to be characteristic of their adolescence. These relationships do not require intimacy, but only companionship. Most men have difficulty trusting other men, and the general feeling of competitiveness between men does not allow them to 'show their cards' to each other because one is never sure when another will turn against you.[5]

This terrible indictment of the ability to form close relationships is also associated with the fear of society's difficulties in dealing with homosexual relationships. Feelings of warmth toward other men are particularly difficult to cope with because of the fear of what others will think of these same-sex relationships. This will be discussed later with regard to priests.

Daniel Levinson, who is well-known for his intensive study of American men in different life stages, convincingly states in *The Seasons of a Man's Life* that friendship in the American male is most noticeable by its absence.

> As a tentative generalisation we would say that close friendship with a man or woman is rarely experienced by American men ... The distinctions between friend and acquaintance is often blurred. A man may have a wide social network in which he has amicable, 'friendly' relationships with many men and perhaps a few women. In general, however, most men do not have an intimate male friend of the kind that they recall fondly from boyhood or youth ... most men have not had an intimate, non-sexual friendship with a woman.[6]

This deprivation, it seems, is a tragic situation and has widespread consequences in terms of deprivation in adult life. It also has tremendous implications for the priest who is called to minister as Jesus did, because, if he falls into the categories of most American men, he does not know **how** to be intimate. Levinson does, however, give some hope for this situation by asserting that at mid-life, when most men's lives are enriched, the quality of love relationships improve as men strive to integrate the tender 'feminine' aspects of their personalities.[7] This union of the masculine and feminine principles, often known as Yang and Yin, are essential to work towards full humanity. Thus, the ability to become a more responsive friend to both men and women is enhanced.

Studies like McGill's, Levinson's, and others'[8] are awakening men to a whole new way of looking at intimacy needs in their lives.

Adolescent Development in Intimacy

Intimate relationships have been made more difficult in the life of a priest because of the type of past seminary training which has been discussed. Many of the problems with intimacy discussed in Chapter One were due, in large part, to seminary training which forbade relationships. In addition, the inability to live through one's adolescence has been a major problem in establishing intimate relationships in the life of a priest. The fact that, for many decades, most priests entered the seminary at a very young age required the repression of sexual and emotional feelings. This has contributed to present day difficulties ... If we follow Erikson's life stages, we see that the identity function must be well on its way before one can begin to work on intimate relationships. But often, finding out who one was was not permitted in seminary formation because a life of celibacy (which did not address sexual feelings) was embraced by young men before sexual development and identity were understood and integrated. Even though vows of celibacy were taken toward the end of formation, a celibate lifestyle was always presumed. (This is not necessarily the case today, as sexual mores of the times have made enforcement of this extremely difficult.)

Kenneth Mitchell tells us that 'most priests report that in past seminary training their **effective** choice for the priesthood was made between the ages of twelve and twenty'.[9] He argues that, from a developmental point of view, this age-span is an appropriate time of life for such a choice but, in terms of a vocation, not all can capably make this decision at this time. He contends:

> One possible meaning of the age-specific difference between the choice of a vocation and the choice for celibacy is that the vocational choice may be used by the adolescent boy to protect himself from, or prematurely to foreclose, intimacy struggles. Although intimacy struggles, as I have just said, are appropriate to the young adult period of life, they are fore-shadowed in adolescence, particularly in the area of sexual identity.
>
> The fifteen-year-old who is confused or upset about his sexual identity or his sexual feelings may opt for the priesthood precisely because a celibate life is involved, unconsciously hoping that this early choice not to express his sexuality in marriage will exempt him from the tough problems in intimacy and sexuality which lie ahead. It is exactly the temporary and unresolved quality of his current feelings about his sexual self which makes him emotionally incompetent to make such a decision.[10]

Work like Mitchell's has been acknowledged by those concerned with seminary formation today because he affirms what many theologians and developmental psychologists have taught us. Grace does not work against nature. Many formation programmes in seminaries today should be commended for their more realistic way of handling developmental and vocational questions. But programmes today are in no way ideal. It also must be acknowledged that, for many, the identity and intimacy struggles follow them to mid-life and, therefore, time and patience are needed in dealing with these struggles, not only in the seminary but in the priesthood.

The *Spiritual Renewal of the American Priesthood* has poignantly described these struggles:

> As every man, the priest can yearn to love and be loved, to give freely without imposing and receive freely without demanding. It takes little experience, however, to know that this beautiful ideal is seldom fully realised ...
>
> In some cases the priest may grope through certain adolescent experiences of human love which are more self-seeking than Christ-like. This is to seek unhealthy fulfilment. If, however, he submits such immature self-seeking masquerading in the guise of adult love to the demands of the paschal mystery, he may begin to know that true love is unselfish giving as well as being loved. He may then turn these false steps into the search for Christian fulfilment. But he may have to experience some of the pain of betrayal, self-denial and rejection before he realises that Christ and the purifying role of the Cross must be central in all his human relationships.
>
> Certainly negative aspects of one's experience with friends can be a true stimulus to growth in Christ. But it is a great loss spiritually if the suffering and the pitfalls of these friendships are not recognised as such, and instead alienate a priest and drive him into isolation.[11]

The *Spiritual Renewal of the American Priesthood* calls for patience, perseverance, understanding, and compassion in dealing with the problems of human growth and in handling the difficulties encountered in relationships. It represents a healthy shift in the theology of priesthood.

Relationships with Men

Although most of the work in the balance of this chapter will deal with opposite-sex relationships, it is important to state that same-sex relationships are essential in the life of any priest. In many situations these relationships may deal with similar graces and problems as male-female relationships. Honest acceptance of sexual attraction and feelings of eroticism that may exist in any relationship is essential. 'Two people in a relationship, regardless of whether they are of the same or different sex, must feel something physical for one another', says Adolf Guggenbuhl-Craig, a Jungian analyst.[12] However, feelings constitute only a part of any friendship. The sexual aspect of any relationship is not the primary aspect. It is only one dimension of that friendship.

Many studies are being done today in the area of same-sex relationships, and it certainly seems as if this whole area of human relationships has finally come out of the dark.[13] In discussing homosexuality or heterosexuality, it is well to remember that most of us are neither exclusively homosexual nor heterosexual, but rather fall some where between the extremes of the scale.[14] For our purposes it is well to remember, when speaking of celibacy and intimacy, that same-sex relationships are called to respond to the same standards of morality as are heterosexual relationships and are, also, in many instances subject to the same problems. One must question if heterosexual or homosexual acts, if engaged in on a regular and consistent basis, are reconcilable with celibacy, and, certainly, the priest who is seeking an integration of all parts of his life must face with honesty the challenges involved in this integration. W Norman Pittenger tells us in *Making Sexuality Human* that sincerity, honesty, and integrity are the qualities one looks for in the sexual life of any person, whether that person be single, celibate, or married, male or female.[15]

Intimate friendships with other men, then, should be encouraged in the life of any priest as well as in seminary training. Priests, like all males, need other men who are close to them in order to validate their experiences of being men; to develop intimacy skills that surface in times of crises with women; to protect themselves against life's crises; to lessen dependencies on women; to minimise loneliness; and to serve as valuable resources in terms of re-affirming their sense of simply being alive.[16]

Relationships with Women

Heterosexual relationships certainly are as valuable as same-sex relationships. These opposite-sex relationships begin at conception when one is completely dependent on a member of the opposite sex for life, growth, and development. For any healthy priest, opposite-sex relationships should continue throughout life for, as Kenel tells us:

> Without the opportunity of learning to relate to the other half of the human race, some religious and clergy have been left in a state of immaturity that has diminished the quality of their own lives and has ultimately weakened the witness value of the celibacy that they have tried to preserve pristine and untarnished.[17]

A well-rounded personality demands the company of the opposite sex as a complement to one's life. Relationships with women call for different types of behaviour and call different complexes of emotions into action. These complexes of emotion are not present in same-sex relationships and, although this difference may be a factor of cultural conditioning, it is very real and will be the situation for some time to come.[18]

The priest who is working toward maturity and integration in his life needs to concentrate on blending male and female characteristics into his personality. The reconciliation of opposites, which women bring to men, is necessary for an inner wholeness to take place in one's personality. This bonding of opposites is essential in order for intimacy to be achieved and in order to proceed toward wholeness. The reconciliation of our *anima* and *animus* has been given much consideration by many psychologists in the last several years. The work done by Carl Jung has made all of us aware of the necessity of individuation in order to achieve integrity in our lives.[19]

Gustafson tells us that this meeting of opposites must occur in order for the possibility of love to break through. Having done much in this area of masculine–feminine polarities, she tells us that not only the work of Jung, but also the gnostic Gospel of Thomas, Hindu and Chinese literature, and Hebrew and Christian tradition all tell us of the power of this polarity.[20]

In addition, St Paul and the Gospel of John speak of this 'androgyny'. Both speak of it as a quality found in spiritual perfection. Men who can expose the tender and gentle sides of their personalities, as well as women who can develop the assertive and self-directed parts of theirs, are people who can grow through life's stages while finding faith, love, compassion, and hope. In this complementarity between the sexes we are brought to oneness. Androgyny shows us the imaginative and powerful wholeness beyond ourselves and brings us to be witnesses to that reality which we call God.[21]

Kilgore tells us that women give men a sense of gentleness, wholeness, balance, and a blending of the spiritual or mystical union of both men and women.[22] This blending is found in its finest form in opposite-sex relationships between mature men and women. It would be foolish today to assert that there are not men who display some otherwise feminine qualities as well as women who display some otherwise masculine attributes. Cultural factors are a major determinant of this. However, in the majority of relationships we find feminine qualities best personified in women and masculine qualities best personified in men.

In addition to inner wholeness men need women and close relationships with women inside and outside of marriage in order to free them from their mother complex. A man is not wholly free to be a man until he has expressed his feelings to another woman (not his mother) and confronted the *animus* in woman.[23] This, it seems, is a particular problem for some priests and seminarians as many of them seem to have chosen their career based on their mother's unfulfilled wishes. It is for this reason that we often see men leaving to get married or otherwise after their mother dies. In some men, the death of their mother is the only way to break the mother complex. Certainly, the 'father vacuum', well-described by Robert Bly[24] and many other current authors, should be considered as well. Its relationship to the mother-complex is a subject for further study.

The description of every type of intimate relationship between a man and a woman is unnecessary for the purposes of this chapter. However, we will specifically delve into close bonding between two people, one of whom is a priest and the other of whom is a woman. We will discuss some of the parameters, risks, joys, and problems that relationships might encounter.

Integrating Sexual Feelings and Responses

For the priest, before reaching the stage of integrating a love experience into his life, there are many questions that he must address to himself and his intimate friends. Most pronounced are those questions of sexual feelings. Goergen writes:

> Sexual feelings are present in many interpersonal relationships and should not be frightening. Sexlessness and coldness are not the measures of holiness. Friendship between the sexes involves sexual feelings, yet genitality does not become a primary mode of communication. A celibate person lives with sexual emotions. When he loves he feels the love. We are going to be excited about the loved one; we are going to be thinking about the loved one. Not all sexual feelings indicate love, but love usually involves sexual feelings. I do not mean simply affective sexuality but genital sexuality as well. Genitality is involved in a sexual response. Such genital excitement is healthy and need not be feared. It is part of the personal response of a sexual person to another sexual person for whom one cares deeply.
>
> Expressing heterosexual affection is not inappropriate as long as it is within the limits set by the relationship itself. Affection can be expressed in smiles, hugging, holding, kissing. Genital feelings may well be there. A mature person knows when he is communicating affection and when he is arousing genitality. Both dimensions of sexuality, affectivity as well as genitality, are involved. The celibate person is free to express the affection and is not frightened by the genital. Nor does he direct the relationship toward genitality.[25]

In dealing with genital and sexual feelings, it is most important that the priest today has a thorough understanding of sex. McGoey tells us:

> Sex is the material of celibacy, so the celibate must be thoroughly conversant with it, rather than morbidly intrigued by it. Only that celibate can remain celibate today who can live with sexual emotions ... When he first relates to a lovable and appealing member of the opposite sex the celibate must expect to feel like a person in love – distracted, excited, his thoughts continually moving to the loved one. However, none of these feelings need rob him of the judgment to know that loving is far more than emotional impact, which is only the barest beginning. With discipline he has the strength to move through feeling 'in love' to actually loving. To retreat from loving overtures as temptations, or occasions of sin, is to prevent the maturing growth and confirmation of celibacy itself. It is simply to refuse to develop the power to love required by celibate living, and to condemn oneself to an ineffectual ministry.[26]

Richard Gilmartin, who had been a consecrated celibate and is now a married man, relates that sexuality is not overwhelming or uncontrollable. Sexuality is no easier or more difficult to control in marriage than in religious life. Just because one is married and has a sexual relationship, it does not mean that others are not still attractive sexually.[27] It means only that one does not get genitally involved. Learning to deal with sexuality, then, is a part of maturity with which all human beings deal. Married people too must learn to deal with deep sexual feelings they may have for a person to whom they are not married. People fall in love several times throughout their lifetimes. This should not be a threat to marriage or to celibacy. Risks are present in all relationships of love. Kiesling tells us:

> As for the dangers to chastity and vocation, yes, they are present in human love between man and woman. They should be recognised and appropriately provided against, and they can be. Dangers exist also, of course, in the denial of affection.

> Dangers lurk likewise in preaching (one may become vain), in social action (one may neglect prayer), in teaching (one may become a manipulator), in administration (one may become ambitious for power), and even in prayer (one may become obsessed with method). If avoidance of danger is our criterion for what we choose or allow to happen in our lives, nothing will occur.[28]

Risk, then, is an essential part of maturing and growing in our relationships with others and with God. But sometimes when one risks, one fails, because chastity is not learned overnight. It is learned slowly by trial and error. We do not become perfectly chaste persons in an instant just as we do not become instantly perfect in any endeavour. Schneiders contends that '... the learning could be facilitated by an honest acceptance of the difficulty involved and by the early-acquired knowledge that everyone struggles with the same problems'.[29]

This conflict is being addressed in formation today more than ever before, as we have all come to a realisation that human persons are very much alike in so many ways. Learning to become human, if we are honest, is fraught with all kinds of questions, and learning to love is certainly not a path for one who can accept only perfection. Love comes only from a wisdom tested in reality. This wisdom develops from a combination of our integrity, our degree of curiosity and our imperfections. Perfectionists can never learn how to love; nor can they learn how to live.

When one encounters failure on the path to becoming fully human, what should be his outlook and determination? Goergen tells us:

> Not being perfect does not invalidate the striving after perfection. Striving for perfection means that we are not yet

> perfect. This is the eschatological tension in an individual's celibate life between the ideal of celibacy and his present growth. We must accept our humanity and be realistic about our expectations. At the same time we must not set aside our striving after the ideal. The ideal is still non-genital. The person learns each day that the celibate life is a beautiful life and that we have to continue to learn how to live it.[30]

This outlook, it seems, is a most biblical approach. In the Scriptures we always see the tension in that Jesus very much proclaims the ideal, while at the same time he very much loves and accepts the imperfect sinner. A brief saying from the Desert Fathers relates:

> And an old man said, 'Judge not him who is guilty of fornication, if thou are chaste: or thou thyself will offend a similar law. For He who said "Thou shalt not fornicate" said also "thou shalt not judge".'[31]

Always, the ideal that is to be proclaimed is that celibate love is not only possible, but also life-giving:

> Before undertaking the celibate life, a candidate must be sure of the same three things which assure a happy marriage. First, that he ... is certainly going to love personally and deeply. Second, that to do so successfully, he ... must have an appreciable emotional security, some adequacy as a person and a real awareness of manhood ... Third, that celibate love, like married love, is quite within the competence of a really good person and requires understanding, purpose and discipline.[32]

Pastoral Concern for Priestly Intimacy

Many of the dynamics of intimacy have already been discussed in Chapter Three. However, in the life of a priest there is some prerequisite knowledge which is essential in order that intimate relationships be successful and complementary to one's lifestyle. By the same token, there are problems to be examined which are peculiar to a priestly life. Some of these will be examined here.

One of the essentials in preparing for intimate relationships in a priest's life is an acceptance of the realisation that a priest may 'fall in love', and that this experience does not mean 'flight' either from the loved one or from the priesthood. Acceptance of this experience by peers is essential in order that the priest can grow in this experience and integrate it into his life. We must allow time and space for a priest to work with this powerful gift.

The acceptance and support by friends, mentors, and/or a spiritual director is essential in order that the priest not feel a need to be dishonest because of the suspicions of others. The priest should not be hiding his special friendship; nor should he flaunt it. Trusted, established friends with whom the priest can share are essential in this regard and, if they are genuine and honest, they will help him in dealing with a special relationship in his life.

Equally important in the life of a priest is that new intimate friends must be carefully selected. Each friend, in essence, becomes another self and comes to know and love all that occurs within his life. Aelred of Rievaulx writes: 'Your friend is the companion of your soul ... '[33] In terms of an intimate friendship, selectivity is an important area over which the priest has some control as a relationship develops. It seems to be essential, given all the knowledge that we have of human nature, that a priest will choose as an intimate friend someone who is equally committed and who has very strong values of fidelity to that commitment.[34] We find this commitment as a very powerful dynamic in the lives of many intimate friends who minister together today.

Generally speaking, relationships which are not deeply grounded in commitment, either to a religious way of life or to a marriage partner, can be very difficult to maintain as both people would not be holding onto similar values. This inequality in value systems makes for many difficulties in relationships between priests and women. Oftentimes a single person not bound by commitment will push for exclusivity, possessiveness, and marriage. In relationships such as these, one person is freer to think of a marriage commitment than is the other.

The questioning of value systems between people is a very delicate but essential part of the early stage of a relationship in which one comes to know what the other person is seeking in a friend or intimate. In the existing celibate structure, if one is seeking marriage or a life-long affair, it should be an immediate signal for non-involvement on the part of the priest (granted, this is easier said than done). Continual involvement in such a relationship will lead to the point where one party will manipulate the other and coerce the other into either marriage or a lifestyle of unauthentic living. It is essential that at the very beginning of a relationship good, honest communication be established between the two potential friends. If love is authentic, it will be recognised by truth. As the relationship matures, this communication should determine exactly what the direction of the friendship will be; what its tactual boundaries will be; and exactly how each person will be integrated into the other's life. Communication, **honest and thorough**, is the hallmark of any good relationship, most especially because we all are constantly changing, growing and maturing, and becoming more conscious and cognizant each day that we live.

Most authors who address intimacy in the life of a priest continually point to the necessity of prayer and a good spiritual director. These essentials have already been mentioned but a few more comments should be added here, as oftentimes their benefits have been overlooked. Karl Rahner, in his open letter to secular priests, says with regard to celibacy:

> Remember, this is a chapter of theology that cannot be dealt with by the lecturer's logic or widespread discussion or desultory talk at a meeting of parish priests. It is a part of a theology on its knees, at prayer. I hope there is still such a thing among us priests.[35]

Rahner makes an essential point here because, perhaps in the active life of a priest today, one may wonder where real prayer fits in. In sharing with many priests, it has become evident that the daily prayers of the Church or concentrated prayer time does not fit into too many lifestyles on an ongoing basis. This is extremely problematic, as the Christian community still has the expectation that the priest is a spiritual leader, and is somewhat 'in touch' with God by means of a prayer life. The demands of the apostolate are often so tiring that prayer may be relegated to a free moment before Mass or at the end of the day. Quality time before God is essential for all priests: time to listen; time to respond; time to feel deeply and integrate how God is working in one's life. Only a priest who is truly dedicated to a life of prayer can mould a profound love into a truly authentic celibate commitment.

Along with a life of deep prayer, a spiritual director is essential for a priest who is integrating an intimate friendship into his life. Time spent with a spiritual director on a regular basis enables one to look more objectively at the parameters of that relationship and be more aware of its dangers as well as its joys. A good spiritual director is essential in terms of helping one look at the obstacles to human growth as well as the opportunities for that growth.

Intimate Relationships: Difficulties and Decisions

With regard to intimate relationships, there are some pitfalls. Awareness of these problem areas is a first step in dealing with them. We will briefly discuss three of these problems: genitality, possessiveness, and the perceptions of other people.

Genitality is one pitfall which has already been discussed. However, at this point it is important because the way genitality is dealt with reflects future growth. Once genitality has been expressed between two people, it is difficult (but not impossible) to move back toward less physical modes of behaviour. With tremendous commitment, dedication, and perseverance of the two people involved, it can be done, and it can be the most humanly loving way of dealing with genitality.

Unfortunately, once two people reach the level of genitality, one of three possibilities frequently follows. Sometimes a priest who becomes genitally involved sees marriage as the only answer because he experiences the genital reality of the relationship to be overpowering and begins to think of celibacy as contrary to nature. A second option occurs when, for one or another reasons, a priest's desire to remain in the priesthood is extremely strong but also his desire to continue a genital relationship is equally strong. These two options will be discussed in subsequent chapters. A third possible outcome of a genital relationship is that of 'flight'. Often a priest will become frightened by genital involvement and will pull away from the relationship, as he sees no possibility of returning to less physical involvements. This is an unchristian way of reacting, as it does not allow those involved to grow and to move beyond the idea of intimacy being the same reality as genital sexuality.

The loving priest, on the road to Maslow's self-actualisation, knows that the challenge of intimacy in adult life can be faced and met. It involves tremendous perseverance, prayer, commitment, communication, and understanding on the part of both people involved. It is only possible for mature persons, and it is extremely demanding; but it is also a powerful witness to the determination that love is the most powerful force in the world. The self-emptying which this intimacy requires is a dynamic experience of the eschatological reality.

By accepting sexuality, yet suppressing genitality, two people are free to move on to a very powerful love. This celibate love is indeed sublimation, but sublimation gives direction to psychic energy and this energy becomes a life-giving force.[36] Sublimation of genital desires enables two close friends to move into an extremely powerful love. Redirection of this sexual energy into love of humanity and into action is most descriptive of authentic religious living.[37]

A second problem which seems to present itself in relationships between priests and women is that of possessiveness. In present day culture, men and women have different needs in terms of how close each wants to become. Often a priest will feel that a woman may want to control or dominate the relationship or vice versa.[38] Since men are culturally conditioned to independence while women are conditioned for relationships, this becomes problematic. A priest's training and background makes this all the more disconcerting. A great deal of patience and communication, as well as sensitivity, are required by both people to insure that both parties are coming from positions of equality and that neither is depending solely on the other for emotional fulfilment. The words of Kahlil Gibran (cited in Chapter Three) are most appropriate here.

A third problem is the perceptions of other people in the community, parish, rectory, etc. Since not all have made the paradigm shift from old ideas of priesthood to new ways of relational celibacy, it will be realistic to assume that suspicions, jealousies, and questions will, on occasion, be raised by some. Openness and honesty are the best prescriptions in this area. Admitting that a certain person is a very special friend and an attitude of friendliness toward all help to alleviate mistaken perceptions of others. It should be emphasised, however, that questions will arise and people will talk. The personalities of the two people involved have got to be strong enough to withstand the criticism, negative comments, jealousy, and gossip that may ensue.[39] The priest is a public figure and people will consider, rightly or wrongly, that they have ownership of him. Many fine priests that I have known have been hurt due to the consequences of jealousy.

There is no completely satisfactory answer to this problem, and any public figure will always be open to criticism in this area. Most priests are overly conscious of this, sometimes to the point of being neurotic. Prudence in this area is always necessary, but, nevertheless, one should be able to live one's own life without having to worry about everything that others may think. Perhaps the biblical adage that 'by their fruits you shall know them' is an appropriate attitude for a priest to adopt. People who are trusting of others are usually trustworthy people and being open about relationships helps others in their ability to trust.

In concluding this section, it would be well to state four modes of reacting vis-a-vis the need to integrate intimacy in the life of a celibate priest. All of these have been implied either directly or indirectly throughout this chapter.

The first way is **not** to integrate intimacy into one's life at all, choosing to remain instead on an intellectual level in all of one's relationships (Fr Matthew and Fr Smith). This cold, ineffective way of reacting is, as we have seen, completely opposed to Gospel values.

The second manner of dealing with intimacy in priestly life is to allow oneself to be moved from priestly commitment to the married state. This shift can and does happen and is determined by many factors such as self-concept, personality needs, upbringing, background, etc. This will be more fully discussed in the chapters on optional celibacy. At this stage of priestly ministry, however, that decision would preclude active Church ministry.

The third possibility of integrating intimacy into the life of a priest involves dismissing the value of celibacy and perhaps seeing disvalue in it, while still remaining in the priesthood. Although there is much discussion on the value of celibacy today, it is necessary to reaffirm the value of **commitment** made to God and community and question whether this mode of living is faithful to that commitment. This too will be discussed in the next chapters.

The fourth way is that of **integrating** intimate relationships into one's priestly life. Fr Mike, Fr Steve and Bishop Jim reflected these realities in their lives. To integrate this, one must be mature, responsible, growing in one's relationships with God and with others, moving toward self-actualisation, and committed to the value of celibacy. At the same time, one must be gentle with oneself, realising that relationships do not become perfectly integrated overnight and that the task of becoming celibate certainly involves more than not performing certain acts. Rather, becoming celibate is the creative task of a whole lifetime and is achieved in a most human manner by growing in love of God and others.

The Fruits of Successful Celibate Intimacy

Were intimacy to be healthily integrated into the life of the priest, this very powerful love of another human being (or human beings) can and does bring one through possible tumultuous times into a most dynamic love of God and of all humanity.

This creative love is reminiscent, for example, of the love that Dante had for Beatrice. His love of her in no way excluded passion, but neither did it lead to union with Beatrice, his beloved.[40] Deep relationships of celibate intimacy seem to drive persons to the brink of cosmic love. They bring one through the love of a certain person but, while still loving that person, they enable one to love all others as well as God. Dante's love for Beatrice was particularly reflective of this:

> No heart was ever so disposed to devotion
> and with more complete assent
> so readily to give itself up to God
> as I became at these words,
> and all my love was so set on Him
> that it eclipsed Beatrice in oblivion.
> This did not displease her; she smiled.[41]

For Dante, this love was the peak experience of his life as it became supremely redemptive and transformative. This is the type of relationship which is possible for those who love celibately: real sexual freedom combined with genuine intimacy.

Intimate relationships, if worked through honestly and genuinely, are transformative. They bring us through the specific love of one person, into a creative life-giving love for all humankind. Relationships which cause us to redirect our desire for unity with one bring us to an energised sense of the unity and oneness of all humanity. Through these relationships we find God. Karl Rahner confirms this in stating:

> The human person's first personal partner in terms of his categorical life, cannot be God, because a mediation is always needed. Because of the historicity and factitiousness of the human situation, then, the human person and the world must be the mediator.[42]

Through another person or persons, we find the power of the Incarnation, God taking on human flesh, and thus we are reminded of our connectedness to all of life.

Through relationships, we as autonomous persons are also empowered to bring God to others and come to a more powerful universal awareness. We are free to love all peoples because we have been freed from our fears of reaching out to others. The authentic love of one person, according to Rahner, opens us to love of all humanity. In terms of ministry, we become capable of offering ourselves to all women and men in an atmosphere of vulnerability, openness, and love, which includes an ability to risk. The experience gained in loving one person enables us to love others and, in fact, **empowers** us to love others, as one of love's strongest dynamism is the desire to share with others. Merton reminds us that:

> True happiness is found in unselfish love, a love which increases in proportion as it is shared. There is no end to the sharing of love, and, therefore, the potential happiness of such love is without limit. Infinite sharing is the law of God's inner life.[43]

Henri Nouwen in *Lifesigns* explains that 'this divine intimacy is neither possessive nor exclusive but opens our eyes to all people as brothers and sisters and frees our hands to work in solidarity with all of humanity, especially with those who are suffering'.[44]

M. Scott Peck describes this phenomena in more psychological terms in *The Road Less Travelled*. His analysis is valuable for the purpose of this book:

> What transpires then in the course of many years of loving, of extending our limits for our cathexes, is a gradual but progressive enlargement of the self, an incorporation within of the world without, and a growth, a stretching and a thinning of our ego boundaries. In this way the more and longer we extend ourselves, the more we love, the more blurred becomes the distinction between the self and the world. We become the distinction between the self and the world. We become identified with the world. And as our ego boundaries become blurred and thinned, we begin more and more to experience the same sort of feeling of ecstasy that we have when our ego boundaries partially collapse and we 'fall in love'.
>
> Only, instead of having merged temporarily and unrealistically with a single beloved object, we have merged realistically and permanently with much of the world. A 'mystical union' with the entire world may be established. The feeling of ecstasy or bliss associated with this union, while

> perhaps more gentle and less dramatic than that associated with falling in love, is nonetheless much more stable and lasting and ultimately satisfying. It is the difference between the peak experience, typified by falling in love, and what Abraham Maslow has referred to as the 'plateau experience'. The heights are not suddenly glimpsed and lost again; they are attained forever.[45]

Peck seems to reaffirm much of the work of Teilhard de Chardin, who tells us that 'a universal love is not only psychologically possible; it is the only complete and final way in which we are able to love'.[46]

However, it would be erroneous to leave the impression that a love like this is all 'plateau experience'. That would be a completely and totally unrealistic approach. Rather, genuine love empowers us to enter into all life, its pain and its joy, with a new understanding, compassion, perseverance, and realism. It gives one the ability to live through the difficulties of life, knowing that there is a power greater than ourselves who gives meaning to all of life.

Because a man has been so visibly touched by love in his priestly life, he can more energetically and enthusiastically share himself with others to whom he ministers, and he can bring the message of Jesus in a distinctly human way. Having been touched by love, one needs to share that love with all others, and so bringing God to others is a natural outpouring of one's reality. It is the nature of love to share. George Maloney in his final chapter of *Called to Intimacy*, entitled 'Releasing God's Presence in the World', tells us how love begets other loves:

> Through your deep, involving love shown toward one other person, be it God or a friend, you come to learn that true love cannot be turned inward in an exclusive way: it breaks out

> toward a larger community where you find your love growing as you assume responsibility for the happiness of your brothers and sisters. If your prayer is authentic and deeply transforming, if you truly are living in the presence of God's intimate, unselfish love for you, you will be turned toward others, especially those who have the greatest need, physically, psychically and spiritually.[47]

The intimate priest experiences ministry as an outpouring of the love he has been given. He can be most effective in loving the people he serves as he sees the connectedness of all other men, women and children and sees the world as a planetary family rather than an unconnected group of assorted persons. He sees the unity of all of life and love. This shift in perspective is perhaps a sign of the reign of God breaking into one's life and of coming to see life as a whole new reality and with a completely new awareness.

This priest is open to the prompting of the Spirit and thus is a leader in issues of peace, justice, and love for all. Any child being abused is his child. Any widow is his sister. Any person hungry is his brother or sister. Realistic responsibility for the people of God takes on new meaning as he works with other women and men in making the reign of God more of a **now** event in the life of others. Having been touched by God with love, he is empowered to touch all others and to work with all others in new and freeing ways. He is free to lead the people of God, and yet not control, as he knows that the Spirit is alive and present and works together with him and his people. The priest who has been affirmed in his identity as a loving person is free from the bonds of hierarchicalism and clericalism as well as the bonds of sexism, which we see so evident in our Church today. He is capable of working with and accepting the gifts of all women and men because he does not have to prove to anyone that he is 'somebody', for he **knows** who he is (see Erikson, Chapter Three). This priest is free to work with other men and women as peers because he has a keen awareness of the gifts that we bring to each other's life and a profound understanding of the fact that we need one another.

Such a priest values the dignity of all human persons and is interested in building up all peoples and most especially those most disadvantaged in the Church and the world. He brings to his ministry a depth of compassion which is evidenced in passion and caring for others. This 'compassion proceeds from a love of God and of neighbour which is a consuming fire while it moves one to relieve miseries of others'.[48] This compassion revolves around a sacrificial *kenosis* about which St Paul speaks:

> Your attitude must be that of Christ:
> Though he was in the form of God,
> he did not deem equality with God
> something to be grasped at.
> Rather, he emptied himself
> and took the form of a slave,
> being born in the likeness of men.
> He was known to be of human estate,
> and it was thus that he humbled himself,
> obediently accepting even death,
> death on a cross! (Ph 2:5-8)

This self-emptying is part and parcel of any intimate celibate relationship. The sacrifice that is required is not well-received in today's world. However, the end result of the sacrifice has a power and dynamism which cannot be explained; it can only be experienced in a mystical awareness of the Source of all love. The sacrifice which celibate loving requires transforms one's life into a graced event. As one matures in love, selfishness is replaced by self-giving. In this self-giving, one comes to touch the face of God.

I cannot tell you why, but I am quite sure that the old Jesuit, Fr Steve, had touched the face of God many times. I saw it in his ministry; I saw it in his compassion; I saw it in his gentleness; and I saw it in his love for all of humanity. He had obviously travelled this perilous and painful path of love only to find the mystery of God revealed to him through this 'powerful' experience of this woman in his life. At an advanced age he was peaceful, life-giving, generative, and full of wisdom. Undoubtedly, he had touched the face of God.

6

CELIBACY: A NECESSARY DISCIPLINE?

SATURDAY'S CHASTITY

That one lost rib
pains me
on celibate evenings
When even the breeze
seems godless.
Failing
in a restless attempt
to clothe
this naked knowledge,
I am exiled
from my paradise
by a flaming sword
of lonely fear
which forces
this clay vessel, unglazed,
to the edge –
and regretful smoke
in the abyss
pulls me down.
(Praise comes peacefully
while one is being fired.)
Just to be united
for a moment –
but the earth
is an altar for sacrifices
and the weak,
like ashes,

are scattered
by the hollow breeze
into the dark night.[1]

Albert Haase, OFM

Up until now we have stressed the need for intimacy in priestly life and have stated that intimacy when integrated with celibacy can bring out a very powerful love of God, love of another and love of all humanity.

Teilhard de Chardin points this out explicitly by recognising the dynamism of love:

> Love is in the process of undergoing a metamorphosis ... Some day, after mastering the winds, the waves, the tides, and gravity, we shall harness – for God – the energies of love. And then, for the second time in the history of the world, man will have discovered fire.[2]

Acknowledging the power of intimate celibate love is one half of the task of our book. Because we exist in a both/and reality, it is essential that we also look at the possibility of a completely intimate sexual love and the dynamism of that type of love in the lives of priests of the future. We turn now, in the next two chapters, to look at some life stories, some practical realities and some future possibilities for optional celibacy.

Fr David: Because I travel a great deal, I have had the privilege of meeting many fine priests throughout the country. One of these is a very dear friend whom I will call 'Fr David'. He serves as the pastor of a large suburban parish and also holds many important diocesan posts. In his early forties, he is well-respected and loved by many because of his easygoing collaborative style and his open, friendly ways. David is not a power-monger, not controlling or manipulative. He has a very accurate self-concept, a high degree of stability, maturity and spirituality. Above all, like most of the 'healthy' priests I know, he is light-hearted and he knows who he is. He ministers by sharing his gifts and talents and by recognising the dignity of all others who also have ministerial abilities to share. Fr David, one might say, is a role model for priests of the 1990s.

I first met David at a week-long national conference in San Francisco about eight years ago. At that time he was undergoing some personal difficulties which, during the course of the week, he shared with me. That sharing created a bond of trust, and since then we have become good friends. We see each other a few times a year at various conferences where we share lunch or dinner between sessions or enjoy the local sights in the free time. Once a year, right after the Christmas holidays, he visits in our home for a week of post-holiday 'rest and recreation'. Occasionally, we call or write each other, especially when some specific Church situation may require a second opinion. We highly value each other's thoughts on a variety of Church-related issues.

David is an extremely compassionate person. Compassion, or the lack thereof, is the first characteristic I note when I meet a new priest. Intuitively, it seems that I can tell within a few minutes if a person is compassionate. It is a character of the soul which is transmitted through the eyes and through one's whole demeanour. It tells me whether or not a person has enabled him/herself to love and to be loved. It is not a characteristic of perfect persons. It is a characteristic of good priests, of those who have struggled to integrate spirituality, emotional maturity, celibacy and intimacy. Meister Eckhart says, 'You may call God love, you may call God goodness. But the best name for God is compassion'.[3]

David's pastoral manner is one of collaborative ministry. He has initiated a team approach to ministry at his parish. The team includes one other priest, one religious woman, a layman, and a laywoman. Together the five of them assume responsibility for all the parish functions; they also make all major decisions and delegate responsibility for the parish ministries. This mutuality in ministry is based on the idea that whoever possesses the gifts to do certain ministries should use them. This relieves David of a lot of pressure, especially since he recognises that administration is not his most highly-developed talent. He frequently calls in experts from the parish to give input to the team before they make joint decisions.

David can work on team ministry without it being a threat to his authority because he has a high degree of self-esteem. He recognises that he has some of the gifts to share with his parish, but that he does not have all the wisdom needed to minister in his parish. He shares ministry.

On the diocesan level, David operates in a similar manner. This earns him much admiration from the laity as well as many priests. He reports, though, that some of his brother priests apparently feel that he has 'copped out' to lay demands. One of his close friends shared that some of the other priests feel that he is 'too controlled by women', 'not decisive enough', or 'too soft and compassionate'.

From my own experience, I wonder if these other priests might just be jealous of David and his popularity, although they probably would never admit it. However, regardless of these few disgruntled priests, he is greatly admired by friends, parishioners, and even the Bishop!

David has struggled and still struggles. That struggle is what makes him so splendidly human and capable of interaction with others. David is one who Maslow would describe as the self-actualised person. He is not afraid to admit his struggles in trying to be an authentic priest and an intimate, well-balanced man. He tries hard to lovingly live his vow of celibacy but he also recognises that he is human.

He has admitted to me that sometimes he finds celibacy next-to-impossible, for he shares a very close relationship with one particular woman in his life, a woman he has known since college and who has been very special to him ever since. For the sake of anonymity, I will call her 'Joan'. According to David, Joan helped him with his initial decision to enter the seminary (and to stay there!), and they have remained good friends ever since. They are mutually supportive and have seen each other through many crises. A highly intelligent and spiritual woman, Joan shares David's ministry, his life, and his spirituality. At times, because of David's respect for her logic and wisdom which often challenges his own point of view, she has influenced many of his decisions. They have a loving mutual relationship which, although sometimes painful and difficult, allows both of them to grow in love of God, self and others. The relationship has the characteristics of love, honesty, trust, care, and openness. It is powerfully sexual but is also respectful of commitments that David and Joan have made to their lifestyles.

David does not feel that his 'soul-friend' wants to manipulate him or in any way destroy his ministry, just as he does not desire to manipulate her or destroy her in any way. Rather, it seems that she tries to help him live life to the fullest in service to God and others. 'She energises me,'

David says, 'and she energises my ministry'.

I met Joan three years ago while visiting in David's parish. It was delightful to meet this woman whom I had heard so much about for so many years. I see in her so many of the characteristics that David had shared with me, and I recognise the power, peace, joy, and creativity that their relationship has brought to their lives. I am joyful for the two of them; I am also pained for them.

On many occasions, David has expressed to me his doubts about celibacy. Although committed to it, he has often questioned that commitment and wondered about its value in this day and age.

The charism of celibacy is a gift. After fifteen years of priesthood, David wonders if he has this gift. Perhaps more than ever, he recognises the goodness, beauty, and power of human sexuality, and he wonders just how the Church can put celibacy on a pedestal. Many times he has reiterated: 'Yes, celibacy has value, but so does committed sexuality'.

Having grown up in a very stable farm family, David often longs for the family ties of the past: the warmth of the fireside, the chatter of children, family games, the companionship of one special person for a lifetime, and the passion and fun of a sexual relationship. All these things he sees as good and desirable, and he wonders why they are not permitted him. I often try to listen to David's doubts and hurts, all the while trying to remind him that he may be a little unrealistic. After all, in today's American society, the fireside is all but gone, and the chatter of children is more like the clamour of hard rock to the point of bursting eardrums. Family games have pretty much been replaced by TV and Nintendo. Companionship has been destroyed by the economic system which encourages 'workaholism' and the need for two breadwinners in most families. I tease him and invite him to remember our chaotic household when he visits, with four teenagers on the scene! I remind him that the demands of life often take precedence over the passion and fun of a sexual relationship. All these arguments not withstanding, David still pines for family life, and, when we share together, I wonder if I am helping or hindering him by reflecting my own feelings. On one occasion, David related the pain of growing old without a life mate. It brought back the pain expressed in a recent movie:

> And yet, now that I am an old, old man, I must confess that of all the faces that appear to me out of the past, the one I see most clearly is that of the girl for whom I have never ceased to dream these many long years. She was the only earthly love of my life; yet I never knew or ever learned her name (*The Name of the Rose*).[4]

In my estimation, David is an exemplary priest, perhaps one of a handful of the finest priests that I will ever know. He has the vulnerability that allows all of us struggling human beings to identify with him. Henri Nouwen tells us we 'cannot be led out of the desert by someone who has never been there'.[5] David has been there. It is blatantly obvious by the way he prayerfully struggles to integrate intimacy as well as sexuality into his celibate lifestyle. He's on the same journey to God that each of us takes. That is why being with him is so very comfortable.

Priests like David are scarce and getting harder to find each day. I often wonder how long he can remain in the existing system with so little support. We need David and others like him, but is it fair or just to think that they should remain in a state of life that seems to be changing all around them? All the old supports are gone.

Celibacy, however, remains and the Church does not seem to be addressing the problem at all. 'There is, for example, no seminary in the United States, training priests, which has so much as a one semester course on celibacy or on the necessary correlative material of human sexual development,' writes Richard Sipe.[6] In addition, the topic is not open for discussion as some Church leaders consider the discussion 'systematic propaganda hostile to priestly celibacy'.[7]

David, like many other priests, is caught in a double bind, for if he leaves he will always be looking back over his shoulder and asking if he should have stayed. If he stays, he will always be wondering what it might have been like to have a wife, a family, and a complete sexual life. It is my hope for David that he will not attain the ripe old age of Fr Bill (Chapter One) and then ask himself, like Fr Bill, if he should have made other choices. This would be tragic for such a warm, loving human being. This would be tragic for *any* human being!

When I pray for David, I never know exactly what to pray for. Often I pray for the Latin-rite Church to change so that men like him will stay. After that I pray for David and Joan, that somehow, as they grow in love and intimacy, they will be able to continue to integrate their love for one another into valuable work for their community. Sometimes I pray that we will have a complete restructuring of this thing called 'priesthood' so that both men and women alike can serve side by side in a married or celibate lifestyle that will reflect the early Church.

Usually, I end up leaving it all in God's hands asking God to direct David and Joan as only God can. Since I powerfully believe and have faith in God's Providence, I trust that this will happen anyhow. But then, just in case, I always add a little prayer for our Church to wake up soon!

We desperately need priests like David: loving, compassionate, God-centred, whole. My years at the seminary showed me that the institution is not necessarily forming this type of priest today. Instead it seems to be focusing on liturgical form, correctness of dogma, administrative discipline, canonicity of law as well as oaths of fidelity and theological discipline. These things may have their place, but when we focus on the Jesus of the gospels, we seem to find a vastly different direction. We find most of Jesus' ministry reflective of Micah's magnanimous exhortation to live justly, love tenderly and walk humbly with our God (Mi 6:8).

David and the thousands of priests like him need the types of holy intimate friendships that he has. All the work done in previous chapters points to this reality. As David grows in love and intimacy with his special friend, he will undoubtedly come to question more and more if he can (or wants to) live out this celibate experience. The struggle he will face has been articulated by many as unjust, out of date, and reflective of a Church which refuses to give up power and control over the lives of her priests. The problem will be exacerbated as he quickly approaches mid-life and faces those challenges of growth and redirection. Should David, if he finds he cannot live a celibate life, have the option to marry and will this be positive for his ministry and for the Church?

This question has been re-articulated in many and various ways over the centuries. Since the mid-1960s we find the question recurring with phenomenal frequency. Various forums have addressed the topic of mandatory priestly celibacy. Prior to Vatican II, many voices were being raised in hopeful expectation of the change of celibacy regulations. George Frein in *Celibacy: the Necessary Option* highlights the two years between 1965 and 1967 when clerical celibacy was in open forum. His work shows strong support for optional celibacy in the Vatican II period.[8]

In 1975, the National Federation of Priests' Councils presented a resolution calling for the full utilisation of married priests. The Detroit Call to Action Conference, meeting in 1976 and representing '155 dioceses, including 110 bishops, called for the American bishops to petition Rome to change the present law on celibacy'.[9] In 1980, the South-east Asian bishops requested that the Vatican ordain married men.[10] At the 1990 Synod of Bishops Meeting, on the topic of priesthood, Bishop Lawrence Burke of Nassau advocated the ordaining of married men. In addition, many third world bishops also questioned celibacy in spite of a papal request prior to the synod that it not be discussed except to strengthen commitment.[11]

On 25 October, 1990, CBS news aired a report stating that 58% of American Catholics were in favour of optional celibacy, and 25% were opposed.[12] As we are frequently reminded, however, the Church is not a democracy, despite the fact that the Spirit of God always manifests Herself best in the *sensus fidelium*.

Most recently, Archbishop Rembert G. Weakland of Milwaukee, in a pastoral draft, wrote that he would seek papal clearance to ordain married men in an effort to ease the priest shortage.[13] Perhaps this first step by the prophetic Weakland will mark a breakthrough in this whole area.

Historical Perspectives of Celibacy

Let us take a look at some historical gleanings which shed some light on this topic. The following pages are not meant to be a complete historical overview on celibacy,[14] but rather to give some background information on this topic.

The progressive development of the discipline of celibacy for candidates seeking admission to priesthood has had a long history. Each succeeding era of the Church has made proclamations which carry its own theological values that underlie corresponding Church legislation. Historically, no one single factor was determinative in requiring ministers of sacred orders to embrace the celibacy which is presently mandated. In addition, no one could credibly maintain that celibacy was a requirement for ministerial priesthood in the first several centuries of the Church. There is no evidence in the teachings of Jesus that there is an essential connection between celibacy and the call to discipleship; in other words, Jesus did not mandate celibacy.

Cumulatively, several factors can be said to have influenced the Latin-rite Church to embrace celibacy. The primary value has consistently been the example of Christ himself, who was celibate throughout his life and who proposed celibacy as a free act of obedience to a special vocation, or as a spiritual gift for the sake of the reign of God (Mt 19:11-12). Yet, the first Pope was married and Jesus did not make celibacy a prerequisite of the 'official' Apostles, nor did the Apostles require it for those who presided over the first Christian communities (1 Tim 3:2-5, Tit 1:5-6). The ideal is proposed explicitly by St Paul (1 Cor 7:1, 8, 25-38), but this recommendation is made in his own name; he has no command from the Lord (1 Cor 7:25).[15]

Traditionally, the Fathers of the Church were firm in holding to the idea that one could not be compelled into virginity. Even one with as negative an attitude on sexuality as St Jerome writes to Eustochium that 'if this virginal life is forced it is *contra naturam*' (against nature).[16]

The first few centuries of the infant Church followed a domestic model. From the pastoral epistles of 1 Timothy 3:2-

5 and Titus 1:6, we learn that the preferred leader for the role of *episkopoi*, presbyter and deacon were those who were undoubtedly married family men.

Ecclesiastical legislation on celibacy for clerics began with a return to continence of widowers. Later, it was to be extended to those who were unmarried at the time of election to orders. Finally, in the west, it was extended to married men who were received into orders. At the beginning of the second millennium of the Church, this eventually led to legislation admitting the unmarried alone to reception of orders in the Church.[17]

With the development of the liturgy, the priest emerged as a cultic figure. The laity's role became restricted as the status of the clergy was elevated. Soon, rules of ritual purity were applicable to clerical ministers.[18] Old Testament instructions on ritual purity, Leviticus 15:16-18, Samuel 21, and the prevailing influences of the Greek philosophers, particularly that of the Stoics, with their hostility to everything that had to do with pleasure and passion, all contributed to the notion of cultic purity for priests.[19] Certainly the experiences of the Essenes and the Qumran communities also had their influence on ideas of ritualistic purity,[20] and made some contributions to ideas of celibacy.

Preferences for celibacy, as well as the ideas of cultic purity were reflected at the councils of this era in their legislation of continence. Edward Schillebeeckx relates that the reason behind laws of abstinence for married priests was ritual purity. The *lex continentiae* forbade priests from having sexual relations the night before they celebrated the Eucharist. This practice of celebrating eventually became a daily event, and therefore the ritual law of abstinence came to mean permanent celibacy.[21]

This cultic purity of Church ministers was reflected in

the Council of Elvira (305),[22] Ancyra (314),[23] and Neocaesarea (314-19).[24] Although these councils enacted legislation, they were only regional councils and did not receive far-reaching acceptance. For example, the Synod of Elvira forbade those who had received major orders to enter marriage or to continue a sexual relationship in an existing one. It forbade sexual intercourse to clergy (already married) as well as the begetting of children (a sure sign that intercourse had taken place). It did not, however, forbid or dissolve the marriage.[25] (This could be compared, in our day, to the recent pronouncement of the two officially married Catholic priests in Brazil who were told by the Vatican that they could remain married but could not cohabitate!) The Synod of Elvira was a small and individual synod of the Bishops of Granada and the surrounding districts. Although it did not receive far-reaching acceptance, its decrees were acknowledged in the west as being at least locally authoritative.[26]

Again, at the Ecumenical councils of Nicea (325) continence was proposed for the clergy. It was rejected because St Paphnutius, a much revered blind celibate and ascetic, protested it stating that it was too hard a burden, that marriage was a sacred and undefiled state, that it would promote danger to chastity, and that it was not respectful of the older tradition which stated only that clerics would not marry after ordination.[27]

Another Eastern Council held later that same century at Granges concerned itself with the holiness of Christian marriage and issued a formal condemnation of anyone who 'draws a distinction between a married and an unmarried priest, and says that it is not fitting to share in the oblation made by the former'.[28] The very fact that this statement needed to be made shows that there was a movement against marriage and for priestly celibacy.

'A certain disdain for ordinary human experiences'[29] was evidenced as bishops began to come from that group which had monastic training and a morality which reflected a preference for celibacy. It is here we see the power of the monastic lifestyle as the Church took charismatic celibacy, which had its place in monastic communities, and began to extend it to the whole clergy.[30]

The next six or seven hundred years finds the Church trying to set down rules and enforcing them for priests and often for deacons and subdeacons as well. Most especially, they tried to make marriage for priests, deacons and bishops unlawful in the Western Church.[31]

In 445, Pope Leo I placed a rather difficult pastoral demand upon priests: 'There is no need for them to leave their wives. They should consider themselves free from marriage, so that while marital love may remain, yet the business of the wedding feast may cease'.[32] (Again, we are reminded of the South American situation.)

Often there were inhuman measures imposed by some of the councils trying to enforce celibacy. Philip Kaufman gives us an example of this in the penalty of the 'enslavement of the offspring of clerics' (Council of Toledo in 655), a canon that was later incorporated into general law. Also there was a penalty of enslavement of priest's wives who had violated laws regarding celibacy.[33]

The Council of Trullo (692) gave final settlement to the question of continence for clerics in the east when it spoke of the marriage of the ordained presbyter and deacon to continue valid and firm, but not so for the bishop who had to put away his wife.[34]

Regional councils in the west co-operated with the papacy in making clerical celibacy obligatory. Yet the number of canons enacted at these regional councils indicates both the resistance that the policy of continence encountered and the efforts to impose the Roman discipline in their territory. With the barbarian invasions and the fall of the Roman Empire, the central authority of the state collapsed affecting the moral decline of both people and clergy.[35] During the ninth, tenth and eleventh centuries, there was widespread disregard of the laws; clerical concubinage and incontinence were rampant. Many priests led dissolute sexual lives.[36] It was only when a strong central authority gave backing to the legislation that the re-establishment of the discipline revived, as during the Carolingian Reform and the Reform of Pope Gregory VII (+1084). The revival of Monasticism at this time did point to the ideal of perfection, exemplified by the monks, as capable of being lived.

The Second Council of the Lateran (1139) made sacred orders a diriment impediment, an obstacle which automatically annuls a marriage.[37] It was here that the axe came down heavily. The marriages of subdeacons, deacons and priests were considered canonically null and void. Only those who had taken the vow of chastity, according to the Synod of Wincester, could be ordained.[38]

It is easily recognised that this was not adhered to. One hundred years later, in the Fourth Lateran Council, we find references to priests living in sin, married priests and abuses regarding priests' sons. These abuses lasted up until Reformation times and the Fifth Lateran Council (1512-1517) again makes similar references.[39]

The fight for celibacy went on however. Until the time of Alphonsus Liguori, we find that sexual intercourse, even married sexual intercourse, was thought to defile a man.[40]

Difficulties persisted for the secular clergy in acceptance of this discipline. The Council of Trent (1545-1563) upheld the traditional teaching and solemnly sanctioned celibacy for clerics in major orders in the Latin Church.[41] More importantly, Trent inaugurated a seminary system through which future clerics would receive a rigorous training beginning at youth and carried on over a long period of time under constant supervision and careful selection. Thus, candidates would be prepared to assume a complete dedication. The teachings of Trent were codified in the 1917 Code of Canon Law.[42]

Current Trends

Papal instructions on the value of celibacy have been given by every pope from Pope Pius X to the present. The significant contemporary reflection on celibacy as a value for clerics in the Latin Church is found in the documents of Vatican Council II: *Presbyterorum Ordinis* Art 16,[43] *Lumen Gentium* Art 42,[44] and the Encyclical Letter of Pope Paul VI *Sacerdotalis Caelibatus*, 24 June, 1967.[45] The 1967 Synod of Bishops theme of the Ministerial Priesthood resulted in the document *Ultimus Temporibus*, Part II, Article 4,[46] dealt with celibacy. An allocution of Pope John Paul II, *Novo Incipiente Nostro*, 6 April, 1979, was a letter to priests on Holy Thursday. This dealt with celibacy in Art 8.[47] The theological meaning gleaned from these recent teachings have been consistent in their treatment of celibacy.

Although the topic of celibacy was not one of the major themes of the Council and little was said officially on the subject, in all phases of the Council it was the topic of heated discussion. Some suggested a rejection of the general obligation to celibacy; some thought it appropriate in view of the shortage of priests to admit to the priesthood married men who had proven themselves in family life, at work, and in the life of the Church. Pope Paul VI, however, in a letter to the Council fathers, expressed his wish that this question of ecclesiastical celibacy be not publicly debated in the Council on account of the delicacy of the topic and the prudence required in its discussion. In this letter, he said that it was 'his purpose, in so far as in him lay, not only to maintain this ancient, sacred and providential law but also to strengthen its observance'.[48] Shortly after the conclusion of the Council, Pope Paul VI addressed his encyclical 'On Priestly Celibacy', already mentioned, to the Catholic world.

We have recently completed, on 28 October, 1990, another synod, the theme of which was 'The Formation of Priests in the Circumstances of Present Day'.[49] The synod addressed many topics, some of which were extremely challenging. The topic of celibacy, however, was not on the agenda to be discussed and was spoken about only in terms of reaffirmation of the centuries-old discipline.

One asks oneself: how can this be in light of so many questions on celibacy? It was only a month prior to this convening that the National Religious Vocation Conference meeting in San Mateo, California, issued a report called 'Awaken the Promise: Vocation Ministry in the United States'. This report called the Church requirement of celibacy the 'most significant element in not choosing an ordained or religious vocation.'[50] The report states that 'the number of men interested in becoming priests would quadruple if married men could be ordained'.[51] Report after report has told us the same thing. And yet, the Church refuses to look at this issue while many are being denied the celebration of Mass and reception of the Eucharist. The situation is untenable.

On this issue, Timothy Lynch, a priest and canonist, states:

> Today human motivation and practical expediency give rise to questions of the value of celibacy in a world that is experiencing a serious dearth of clergy. Research has shown that a celibate priesthood has been a major factor in the decline of vocations to the priesthood, as well as the major cause for defections numbering in the tens of thousands of priests who have left the ministry since the Council. A return to the Church at its beginning has been put forward as a solution to the crisis. This would again make celibacy optional and ordination of married men commonplace. Ministry would once again be redefined to meet the contemporary scene. The Church has had to redefine ministry repeatedly since the beginning. Legislation in the Church would, as in the past, follow this redefinition.[52]

Today many people are challenging the Church to relook at this discipline which is being viewed by many as outdated, repressive, dysfunctional, and dualistic. Over a century ago, Henry Lea wrote:

> The spirit of the age is not propitious for relentless discipline which will tolerate nothing but blind obedience, and the Church may find that only by yielding can it preserve its unity. The lesson of the sixteenth century should not be forgotten when unwisdom cost it nearly half its membership.[53]

How much more appropriate and prophetic are his words today!

7

CELIBACY: THE REALITIES AND IMPLICATIONS

The Priest: A Prayer on Sunday Night

Tonight, Lord, I am alone.
Little by little the sounds
died down in the church,
The people went away,
And I came home,
Alone.[1]

Michel Quoist

The short history of celibacy that has been given should be enough to enable us to make some comments and observations as well as ask some serious questions about the current discipline of mandating celibacy for Latin-rite priests. Why does the Church insist that the priest must come home alone?

One must question if our Church does not sometimes distort its logic in order to uphold laws which seem, for one reason or another, to be important. For example, the age-old argument against ordination of women is that Jesus did not call women to be among the 'official' (Church-decided official, as we know today from feminist scholars) Twelve, and, as a result, the Church does not think it appropriate for women to be priests. Jesus did, however, call married men, many of whom had families, to be apostles. The Church, however, reverses its logic in this situation and calls only celibate men. This is not consistent and trying to explain this reality is futile.

Despite the futility, there are many reasons today why we must look into this discipline and question its current validity. This is an obligation for all concerned Catholics. The *sensus fidelium* must speak to the institutional Church on this very critical issue.

The remainder of this chapter will be devoted to discussing seven historical realities with regard to celibacy and asking ourselves if all or any are valid today. If the underlying reasons for celibacy are no longer relevant, then perhaps it is time to change the discipline.

I. Celibacy: a man-made law: We know today that the law of celibacy is a Church-made law, and, therefore, it can be changed. The law was not based on ecclesiology, as the practice of the domestic Church was for the most part to have married men (and women) as leaders. The only ecclesiological basis for the mandating of celibacy was that Jesus was celibate (Jesus was also God and shared in divine qualities). Jesus never made celibacy a requirement.

Paul in 1 Corinthians 7 is not anti-marriage (7:5). He did not believe in celibacy for all (7:7), recommends it only because the time was short (he thought) before the second coming and the end of the world (7:29), and because he felt that celibacy would free people from worldly care (7:32).[2] Paul did not want to place restrictions on anyone (7:35) and therefore did not mandate celibacy in his teaching.

All the arguments are concerned with 'suitability' rather than necessity for ministry. In addition, Jesus did not link priestly life to consecrated celibacy.[3]

II. Ritual purity: We know that the laws of ritual purity, inherited from the ancients, the Stoics, the Essenes, the Qumran community, etc had much to do with the influence of a celibate lifestyle. Ritual purity was based on the notion that sex was unclean, and, therefore, anyone confecting the Eucharist should not be 'sullied' the night before the celebration. When eucharistic celebration came to be a daily event, the laws of ritual purity indicated that sexual expression would be permanently abandoned by the priest.

The ideas of ritual purity were also very much influenced by the body/soul dichotomy, by an unholistic and somewhat embarrassing view of sexuality, by the idea of living as pure spirits, and by the undercaste and negative views of woman which had come down through the ages. We will discuss these further, but it is important to state that, theologically, we hold none of these views today.

III. Negative theology of sexuality: Celibacy laws were effected by a negative view of marital sexuality which has been held down through the ages by many of the Fathers of the Church (Jerome, Gregory of Nyssa, Augustine, and even Aquinas).[4] Some of them, such as Cyril of Alexandria, St Athanasius, Eusebius of Caesaraea, and Theodoret saw in marriage a consequence of original sin.[5] Even the Protestant reformers such as Luther, Zwingli and Calvin held many of these comparably negative views.[6]

The negative views of marital sexuality have been somewhat and continue to be corrected in our written theology but are still held in our subconscious minds and still filter through much of modern teaching. It will take many decades of positive teaching on marriage and sexuality for the correction on marriage to become centre-stage. The spiritualistic-dualistic thought of Hellenistic Greece still follows us. As discussed in earlier chapters, this was not reflective of Old Testament thinking but did make its way into Christian thought and has been with us through the ages. Historical study in this area makes it quite clear why celibacy has been given so much primacy in our tradition. Certainly the negative views on sexuality are intertwined with the elevated views of celibacy, which will be discussed in the next section.

Many have written positive theologies of sexuality in recent years, and they have helped re-educate us in this area. James Nelson, however, has jumped light years ahead of many in writing about sexual theology. Nelson proposes the idea of shifting from theologies of sexuality to sexual theology. Sexual theology is a more holistic way of looking at our lives enmeshed in our human situation. It enables us to ask ourselves what our sexuality says about our perceptions of faith, our experience of God, our interpretation of scripture and tradition, and our way of living out the gospel. Because of the contemporary turn to human experience as a valid source of theological data, we can view sexual experience as giving us insights to theological perceptions which hold elements of sexual experience. Briefly, Nelson holds that:

> 1) Every sexual experience is perceived and conditioned through religious lenses.
> 2) There is a shift from understanding sexuality as detrimental or incidental to our experience of God to being essential in our understanding of God.
> 3) There is also a shift from understanding sexual sin as matter or wrong acts to understanding sexual sin as an alienation of intended sexuality.
> 4) Rather than seeing salvation as being opposed to our sexuality, we see that there is sexual salvation and sanctification.
> 5) There is a difference between act-centred sexual activity and

> relational sexual ethics.
> 6) Church is not an asexual but a sexual community.
> 7) Sexuality is not private, in the Victorian sense, but it is a personal phenomena and relates to our community activity.[7]

Perhaps the ability to look at sexuality in ways such as the above will be essential for us to make the paradigm shift from marital sexuality as still slightly tainted to marital sexuality as a God-given integral part of who we are.

Kosnik tells us that 'wholesome human sexuality is that which fosters a creative growth toward integration. Destructive sexuality results in personal frustration and interpersonal alienation'.[8] Again, we must ask if celibacy, imposed on our clerics, is fostering integration or frustration and alienation. The statistics that we have quoted in Chapter Four speak for themselves.

The above material is so relevant to Teilhardian theology and the whole creation-centred theology prevalent today.

> The prevailing view has been that the body ... is a fragment of the Universe, a piece completely detached from the rest and handed over to a spirit that informs it. In the future we shall have to say that the body is the very universality of thing ... My matter is not a part of the Universe that I possess *totaliter:* it is the **totality** of the Universe possessed by me *partiuliter*.[9]

IV. Elevated views of celibacy: An elevated view of celibacy is the next reality. It is connected to the previous one in the sense that the Church has always affirmed an either/or mentality. For example, the dualistic system we have has told us that either the body or the soul can be good, but both cannot have equal value. Either men or women can be more valued in our Church, but both can not have equal value. Either celibacy or married sexuality is good, but not both.

Our Church has not yet bought into a both/and mentality, where we can affirm both realities as being of equal value. For this reason we have seen many statements such as this, written as late as 1981:

> It is for this reason that the Church, throughout her history, has always defended the superiority of this charism to that of marriage, by reason of the wholly singular link which it has with the kingdom of God.[10]

What, one might ask, does this say about sexuality and marriage? The answer is crystal clear.

In 1954, Pope Pius XII wrote that 'according to the teachings of the Church, holy virginity surpasses marriage in excellence'.[11] Further on he writes: 'Let parents consider what a great honour it is to see their sons elevated to the priesthood ...'[12]

In 1967, Pope Paul VI called celibacy a 'brilliant jewel' and elsewhere exhorts 'he who accepts the priesthood be as pure as if he were in heaven'.[13] The language is beautiful and idealistic but one might question its relationship to a 1990s anthropology and psychology of human development.

Pope John Paul II says that 'virginity or celibacy by liberating the human heart in a unique way' is integrally connected to 'that pearl of great price which is preferred to every other value no matter how great and hence must be sought as the only definitive value'.[14]

What, we might ask, does it mean to be a definitive value? It means that it is the **most** complete value, that every other value is less complete or is defined in relationship to celibacy. Herein lies the problem. Until celibacy is accepted as being equal but not greater than married sexuality, we will continue to have this dichotomous structure, this dualistic system which says that no matter what we write about sexuality, celibacy is still preferred. Our Church, in an effort to address the problems and challenges of the twenty-first century, must correct this inferior view of marriage. This, in my opinion, will only happen when the married, who are fully functioning in their sexuality, are permitted to be ordained.

Most priest friends tell me they have tremendous difficulty seeing themselves placed on a pedestal because, in reality, they acknowledge that they have the same faults, failings and problems as many in their congregations. Most of these priests have tremendous unease with descriptions of celibacy as the 'bright pearl', or the 'finest ornament'. (For some, it is more like a crown of thorns!) The time for honesty has been thrust upon us, whether we like it or not.

'The Father does not say no to the prayers of his children',[15] Pope John Paul II has written in his opening remarks to the 1990 synod of Bishops. We in the Church recognise that the 'prayers of his children', our prayers, are for a both/and reality which would be reflective of the totality of our charisms as both celibate and sexually functioning persons.

V. Inequality and negative views of women: Priestly celibacy has inherently displayed negative and unequal views of woman and has fostered a tremendous fear for priests who become close to women. Our teachings through the ages, based on Greek philosophy, have taught that women were considered 'misbegotten males'[16] and temptresses to men. Many feminist scholars have done much fine work in this area, and volumes could be written about the Church's prohibition against women.[17] Although that is not the intent of this discussion, suffice it to say that the sexist dualism found throughout the ages in patriarchal systems and structures will probably be present in our subconscious theology for years to come. Males will be identified with mind and spirit; females with body and matter. The higher will control and suppress the lower until a mentality of equality is finally achieved. The question we must ask ourselves is how we will ever be able to envision the reign of God if this is not corrected in our thought?

The work done by Carol Gilligan[18] and others has enabled us to see the necessity for women's thought systems to be integrated with those of men. The most recent Synod of Bishops meeting in October of 1990 heard calls for women to become involved in teaching and other collaborative efforts at the level of seminary.[19] Women across the country are taking a wide variety of positions in Church and society. Current theology is being updated to reflect a more contemporary and holistic view of women as equal to men and as capable as men in terms of intelligence, achievements, etc. Our language is becoming more inclusive; our ministers are becoming more collaborative. Local bishops and our pope have written on the equality of women; the Church has confessed the sin of sexism.

All the interaction, writing and sharing between priests and women notwithstanding, women will not be accepted as equal within Church structures until they can be ordained alongside men. This is a reality the Church must face. If we do not, we will face the threat of losing whole generations of women who see themselves as equal to men in all other areas of their lives.

The very fact that the Church does not permit priests to marry (women) says volumes about women as well as about sexuality. Women are still seen by the Church as a temptation to men because of, among other things, the powerful attraction of their sexuality. Until our Church begins to see this powerful attraction as one of the dynamic gifts of God to create love rather then to defile men, nothing will really change in the Church's views of women.

VI. Apostolic availability: Availability for apostolic activity is a consideration which is still often mentioned today in discussions of the pros and cons of celibacy. Granted, one who does not have a wife and a family should have more time free for all people. Many of the papal documents of the last three popes have accentuated the freedom from 'worldly cares' or temporal affairs.[20]

Although family considerations are certainly important, this can be seen as a myopic view of the situation, since it does not take human motivational theory into account. The celibate person is often besieged with loneliness, lack of support, lack of belonging, etc and, therefore, frequently escapes to unrealistic and unhealthy modes of behaviour in order to make up for these powerful deprivations. Problematic areas are sometimes exacerbated by the unhealthy modes of behaviour (alcohol, power, control) which are often adopted. This person can be contrasted to the married man who, although busy, is often fulfilled by his marriage and family life. This fulfilment often supplies him with much more motivation and energy to serve others.

In addition, the assertion that a celibate priest is detached from the world and therefore has much more time and ability to be about God's business is one that can be critically questioned today. Today's priests, for the most part, do not live in a monastery. Their lives are in no way detached and, in fact, the more they are involved with God, the more they are involved with humanity. Their personal lives are also very much lived out in the world. Most of the priests I know are concerned about parish finances, their frantic schedules, their next car payment, who is going to take care of them when they retire, their pension, and many other worldly cares.

Spiritual liberty is almost impossible in this day and age. Freedom from material cares is not a reality for most priests, and celibacy, as we know it today, does not always set one free!

VII. Control: Finally, the Church of the past has used celibacy laws to control property, lives and money. The inability for property to be transferred to one's legal heirs has kept Church property in Church hands for many years. According to Schillebeeckx, this control of money and power may not have been the reason for celibacy in the first place; however, after the ritual law of abstinence became well-established, it began to function as a struggle for control, power and money.[21] One can see how it considerably increased the resources of the Church. After all, if one had no offspring then inheritance went back to the Church, no questions asked.

Richard McBrien tells us that, as result of the Gregorian Reform, simony, the buying and selling of Church benefices, was prohibited. In addition, celibacy was imposed in an effort to control the loss of property.[22] Due to the fact that many of the clergy belonged to the nobility or were of royal families, inheritance was an important issue. Who would inherit the property of these noble clerics? If there were to be no acknowledged offspring, there was no discussion of who received the property.[23] Celibacy then greatly increased the resources of Church in terms of money, land and investments.

The situation that existed in past Church history with

regard to property and money cannot be compared to the reality today. Religious order priests, generally speaking, do not have money with which to be concerned. Diocesan priests may or may not amass money. However, if they do, they may leave it to whomever they like, often times a relative or a charitable organisation.

The control of lives, however, is still an issue to be examined. Celibacy implies vows and/or promises of chastity and obedience. The Church can direct where a priest lives, how he lives, where he will minister, how he will be supported, and many other critical issues. Movement to optional celibacy would mean a restructuring of priorities which the Church would have to face. It seems that our Church has no intention of doing this in the very near future.

Summation

Celibacy is a Church-made law, not based in ecclesiology, for we know that most of the apostles were married men. Although Jesus was celibate, he did not make this a requirement of his call to ministry. Historically, celibacy is integrally involved with ideas of ritual purity, which inferred that sex was unclean, and, therefore, one confecting the Eucharist should abstain from sex on the night before the celebration. When celebration became a daily event, celibacy became the obvious mandate. Negative views of sexuality filter in and out of Church history, and we find the idea prevalent that even marital sexuality was tainted. Women, by virtue of the belief that they are the bearers of sexuality and the recipients of sexual relationships, are also looked upon with suspicion and fear. Further, the belief that marital sexuality and women by virtue of their connectedness to said sexuality are considered debased means celibacy is to be proclaimed as the definitive value toward which persons are to strive. A celibate priesthood, by virtue of it being only open to males and valued because of its sexual purity, puts both women and married life on lower planes. In addition, in times past when men lived together, celibacy provided for apostolic availability; men did not have to worry about worldly cares, giving the Church control of their property, money and lives.

Today, the values we proclaim which gave support for celibacy are for the most part no longer valid.

> 1) We know that neither Jesus Christ nor the early Church mandated celibacy. We know the Church can change the law if it no longer aids the Church's ministry.
> 2) We no longer uphold the ideas of ritual purity.
> 3) We have rewritten and are rewriting positive theologies of sexuality (although our mind-sets may not have caught up with the written word).
> 4) Most of us do not hold elevated views of celibacy, although Church doctrine is dichotomised.
> 5) We have proclaimed woman as equal, although many feel that this will not become a lived reality until our praxis changes (e.g., ordination of women). Sexism is called sinful.
> 6) Apostolic availability does not take human motivational theory and basic psychological principals into account. Therefore, it is a questionable practice (e.g., Protestant ministers).
> 7) Control, especially of lives, is probably the key issue here. The Church's inability to give up control (which does not mean giving up all forms of discipline) is a central issue. Control issues also effect all other areas.

The bottom line, then, is that the institutional Church need not be afraid to let the Spirit work. However, this seems to be the case. Our Church, in self-defence and in fear, still suffers from negative views of sexuality and of women.

The abject refusal to consider a married or a female clergy leaves our Church with unrealistic statements regarding celibacy and the unholistic view that celibacy is preferable over committed sexuality. Our Church's own psychosexual development, along with that of some of its clerics, has not progressed beyond an adolescent stage. Fear is paralysing. As a result, many decisions now being made are made out of a defensiveness and protectionism which inhibits the Spirit.

It is my personal conviction that until optional celibacy is accepted by the Church, it will be impossible for the Church to be the proclaimer of justice that she is called to be. Neither the equality of women nor a holistic life-giving approach to married sexuality will be truly accepted until priests can marry and women can be ordained. The signs and values involved in all these symbols are interconnected. Celibacy will only be accepted as valuable and powerful if it is chosen. Women will be accepted as equal when they can marry priests and when they can be priests. Married sexuality will be seen as equal to celibacy once priests can marry.

> By their symbols you shall know them.[24]

8

SIGNS OF THE TIMES

Tony entered the seminary soon after his 40th birthday, a handsome man, looking much younger than his years. I knew him only slightly in our first couple of years in class together, but then in the last two years, we became close. I thought I was kind of 'taking him under my maternal wing', so to speak, as I assumed he was a few years older than our oldest son. It came as a complete shock when this youthful-looking man told me he was 42 years old. From that day on, I chuckled to myself every time I ran into him.

Tony came from an Italian family in the west. He had decided to minister in the south as his family had moved there a few years before he entered the seminary. Before entering the seminary, he was an investment banker, successful but unfulfilled. He was capable, intelligent and had a very powerful need to minister and to serve other people. Tony, I had often thought during our seminary years, would make an outstanding priest.

While I was busy raising our four kids and working with my husband in our business, Tony was out there leading a carefree life. Had he been a customer, he would have been one of those people I never would have got too close to as his world had been a wild one. His life, he related, had been somewhat of an Augustinian experience, and in his twenties and thirties, he tried it all. He began this lifestyle in college, and it took a little less than twenty years for him to burn it out of his system. It was in his late thirties when he finally decided that his life was a waste of time.

Actually this *metanoia* experience began a few years earlier when he became restless and unhappy. He began to search for some answers. He went from church to an affirmation group to 'T' groups and back to different churches. Finally, he returned to the Catholic faith of his youth and he found this provided him with peace and contentment; more peace and contentment than he had known in years.

Through a series of events in his life he saw God working. First he made a Cursillo at his local parish. During this weekend he had a powerful mystical experience which haunted him for a couple of years. Next, his mother, with whom he was very close, died. This thrust him into utter depression for about a year. Finally one of his best friends, a woman who he had lived with in his twenties, committed suicide. He didn't know which way to turn. The only possibility was God. It was this series of events that led Tony to the seminary.

During those last couple of years at the seminary, Tony was a frequent visitor at our home. He'd stop by just for a cold drink and we'd spend a lot of time talking theology, changes and challenges in the Church, feminism, social justice, and all kinds of moral discussions, as moral theology was of interest to both of us. Occasionally he'd bring a friend or two and the debates would get heated. Tony was articulate and autonomous and he was constantly starting a new discussion with the words 'But what if...' We had a lot of theological debates during those years. We still do now that he is ordained.

Tony is now an active priest in a diocese, in a lovely wooded area outside a city. I see him every two or three months while I'm visiting my parents in the mountains or when he comes down south to visit. Occasionally, we do workshops together.

Tony is happy in his ministry now. Of course, as I always tell him, he's still on his honeymoon, but he is doing beautifully. He loves ministry; he loves people; he loves his life. In his parish, he is constantly sought out for counselling, for advice, for direction and for reconciliation. Word has gotten around the area that he is bright, sensible, spiritual, and that 'he's been there'. Tony has seen life and lived it to the extreme. This experience, although sometimes a source of regret, has provided him with powerful insights about the human spirit, about what's really important in life and about the 'dead-endedness' of some of our poor choices. Tony has a tremendous amount of wisdom. Because of his life experiences, he is well-qualified to give direction with compassion and love. Tony is not unremoved from or unacquainted with the evil of life or the restlessness which we seek to fulfil in many unredemptive ways.

Tony is often in my prayers and thoughts for many reasons. Most especially, he is in my thoughts because he has become an intimate friend and I care deeply about him. But more than that, I recognise that Tony has very deep affective needs with which he will soon have to deal. I recognise that he cannot be the 'dumping pot' forever. Soon he is going to need a whole battalion of support to keep him going. Every inlet needs an outlet. Every resource needs to be sourced. Everyone who loves deeply needs to be loved deeply. It is not inconceivable that soon after the honeymoon wears off, Tony will come to fall in love with a woman. In fact, I believe it's inevitable because of his tremendous needs for affirmation, support and love.

We have talked about this possibility many times and Tony does not find a love relationship to be problematic to his ministry. At mid-life, he is a completely sexually integrated man, with all the same hopes, longings, desires, dreams, fantasies, and passions that every other human being has.

When we talk about the realities of sexuality and his celibate commitment, Tony is pretty honest. He believes that the Church teaching needs to change; will change in the near future. 'It's only a matter of time,' he says.

He has carefully considered the risks of a sexual relationship with a woman and has come to the conviction that if it is life-giving and love-giving and committed, then it is 'of God'.

A recent conversation went like this:

'Just because the institutional Church is so unwhole in its approach to sexuality – it doesn't mean that we have to buy into the whole dysfunction does it, Donna? A sexual relationship between two caring, loving, committed adults is the most powerful way for us to experience God,' he says as my mind flies back to just a few days ago when I heard this same thing from a young deacon. As I look at him thoughtfully, he adds, 'This is something about which everyone of us must decide for oneself. Remember all that stuff we learned in moral (theology) ... sex is good, sex is holy – all that?' he questions. 'All those objective norms are important, but God also speaks to each one of us in the depth of our heart, in our experiences with others and through scriptures. It's just like the decision on birth control – everyone must come to his or her personal decision, no matter what *Humanae Vitae* says.' Tony and I have been through this birth control discussion *ad nauseam*, so I try to redirect the conversation.

'Okay, Tony,' I say, 'but what bothers me is that you would be living a double life. Remember all that stuff about being the person you say you are. I mean if you say you're celibate, then you're celibate right? Not that I think that being celibate is one millimetre more honourable than being married. In fact, sometimes when I think of the difficulties of family life, I definitely think that you have chosen the easier path. But wouldn't it bother you that you proclaim one thing and do another? Don't you think that's psychologically destructive?'

'Yes, Donna, you're probably right. It would mean hiding out, and secrecy and a very disjointed lifestyle. But every once in a while there is a very strong urge in me to fall in love and have a full sexual relationship. It's been a long time now ... I don't know if I even have this charism of celibacy. I've wanted to have it, have worked on it, and so far its okay, but I really don't know if I have the gift.'

As I sit with Tony, I feel so helpless. I feel pained for him. I feel mixed-up for him. We've had this conversation before, but not since he became a priest. It's different now and I cannot even counsel him on it because I feel too close to him and I feel his frustration.

He tries to close the conversation by saying, 'Look, Donna, I don't know about tomorrow. The bottom line is that the Church must change. Nothing is wrong with a sexual priesthood. We must come to that, and soon, before we become a counter-sign; a Church that proclaims one set of values and lives out another. That would be a real problem.'

As he speaks, my mind drifts to the reality that we as a Church **are** constantly proclaiming one set of values and living out of another. Take the equality issue, take the justice issue; take the women's issues. The 'celibate priesthood', I am afraid, is just another one of our 'disvalues' where we say one thing and do another. I think back to an article I recently read by Philip Keane: the 'forced choice of Catholicism's legislation can contribute to the clouding over of the gospel values which celibacy and virginity are supposed to proclaim'.[1]

Tony is right! The Church must change. Recent events have shown that there are more than a few priests leading a double life. The conversation I had with Tony is no longer unreflective of a lived reality. A couple of months ago I spent several hours in conversation with a middle-aged active Catholic priest whose seven year old daughter was recently, along with her mother, killed in a car accident. This man was overburdened with guilt that during his family's lifetime, he could not acknowledge them. These realities are not one in a hundred occurrences that are dug up for a scintillating television programme now and then. Many conversations with seminarians and priests have revealed that the lived acceptance level of lifetime celibacy has become extremely low. Tony's thinking, whether we like it or not, is not far left of centre anymore. I think it may be becoming the norm as the grass-roots priests are making up their own minds on this very important and vital issue. What is worse, it may be turning, like the birth control issue, to a 'non-issue', because people involved have become autonomous enough to look at the whole picture, and come to their own conclusions on the Church's refusal to change this disciplinary mandate. The Sipe report, taken alone, may be questioned. But what we know and read about the celibacy situation in Africa, South America, Mexico and European countries lends too much credibility to deny the existence of a problem with imposed celibacy any longer. It has become a disvalue for many.

Many see the Church's refusal to change as reflective of many of the things described in the last chapter: the Church's negative view of sexuality, negative view of women, desire to control priests lives, and the desire to control property. This should not come as shocking news to those of us who have heard the pleadings of optional celibacy for more than twenty-five years!

It has been said in canon law circles that the law changes slowly in order to catch up with praxis. In my sharings with priests, it seems to me that many today are making up their own minds about celibacy as well as other issues in the Church. They question the Church's judgment and discipline and recognise that they too, as a whole, should have a part in the decision making. The men who are choosing priesthood today are for the most part older than those of Vatican II days. They have been in the world longer and have been influenced by secular life and the media. Many of them have had sexual relationships with one or sometimes both sexes. They have come to their own determinations about the outcome of these relationships. Some of them have even come to powerful religious experiences as a result of their sexual relationships. Many of these men have seen enough of life to know that sexual relationships are good and life giving; women are also good and are to be treated like equals rather than approached as the 'devil's gateway' or the madonna/whores described by Sam Keen.[2] To deny the existence of these realities is to put on blinders.

Some of our priests have been given the gift of celibacy by which they will live out their sexuality. We support them in their powerful charism. Many others have not been given that gift. Priests of all ages, and especially those of a mystical bent find God in personal relationships, sometimes celibate, sometimes not. These relationships cause them to question their celibacy and to come to an integrated approach of following God as best they can in their lives. At the outset, they accept celibacy as a rider that goes with priesthood; as a necessary requirement. Then something or someone happens in their lives and they need to re-look at the whole issue because, in reality, it was never acceptable to them, never chosen by them in the first place. Rather, it was forced on them as a requirement. In this day and age, that just doesn't work.

Many consider the Church outdated and controlling; the institutional church, that is. The Church as the People of God is the Church which holds them fast, and the reason for their lifetimes of service. These men see a need for healthy relationships, a need to come to one's own mature decisions and a need to be treated with dignity and respect. They are making up their own minds about Church law and Church practice. This may be disconcerting to many of us but the reality cannot be denied.

These priests I speak about are not bad priests. They are, for the most part, good and dedicated priests who refuse to be victims of an outdated and unjust morality which dissects the human being into body and soul, with the body being evil and the soul being good. Being holistic and respectful of the gift of sexuality, they recognise that it is not a gift to be squandered. That recognition in itself presents a problem. For the dichotomous combination of being unable to live the vow of celibacy, being unable to make private commitments to and public acknowledgements of one's beloved, while at the same time preaching the necessity of integrity and commitments puts the priest in an impossible situation. Amidst all this, the last thing to be considered is the injustice to the woman who, if the situation becomes known, often ends up being deserted, rejected, discredited and alone. When this situation is repeated a few times in one's life, it begins to take on characterisitcs of a lifetime pattern of irresponsible sexuality in the life of an 'otherwise responsible person'.

We must begin to recognise that the stresses and strains of some institutional practices put impossible burdens on the lives of these men who have served us well. The fact that they have not been given the charism of celibacy, even though they have tried to live it should not turn us against them. Recent events in our Church have made us aware of the dichotomies of their sometimes disjointed lifestyles. In all justice, one must question if a lifetime of unrealistic demands has something to do with this dysfunction, for as we well know, priests are only human.

The priests I speak about are good priests; seekers, searchers, deep livers, prophets, and leaders who are active in life and in ministry. They have a great depth of spirituality, understanding and compassion. They also try to interpret how God is speaking to them through the people and events of their own lives, but sometimes the process can become clouded and there is no way out.

For priests and lay people alike, there comes a time in each life when one must make the adult choice to grow up and make one's own decisions. For some of us it comes at age 21; for others it comes after divorce; for some when one's parents die; for others at 45; and perhaps for some it never comes. But for most, when that time does come, we move out into the world with all the knowledge that our parents, teachers and, perhaps spouses, have given us. But we will know, each of us will know for ourselves when that time has arrived. Johanna Ohanneson relates: 'Each child will absorb and treasure the parents' legacy of love and wisdom, but in time the children will add that legacy to their own revelation of truth which they will have been given by the Spirit to share at their moment in history'.[3]

For many, including priests in the Church, that time is now. For more than twenty-five years, priests and lay people have tried to teach the Church about the question of celibacy. But the Church has not listened well. The *sensus fidelium* has not been heard. The Church needs to take a look at the world situation to realise that you can keep people 'in their place' for just so long. Priests are people too! Grown-up people, and they will not be treated like children. The Church has used tradition as a reason for not changing, a tradition shaped by sexism, bias and rejection of the real. That is no longer an acceptable reason. Ohanneson tells us that 'a sedated Church is deaf to the cries of its children. And in time it may roll over and smother the lives of its young'.[4]

More and more I am beginning to think that the critical press is right about the Church's abject refusal to face the issue of celibacy. Report after report (the Lilly report,[5] the Greely report,[6] the Sipe report,[7] 'Awaken the Promise'[8]) has come out pointing to celibacy as being one of the largest problems regarding the dearth of enrolments in seminaries.

Time and time again, the institutional Church reacts to these reports like an angry child. She pulls in her defences and just gets more stubborn in her refusal to face a problem. A perfect example is the 19 page report entitled the 'Formation of Priests in Circumstances of Present Day',[9] which is described as a practical guide for reflection and discussion in the synod hall. If this document is supposed to be a practical guide, it is difficult to understand why less than a handful of paragraphs, and small ones at that, even discuss celibacy and none of them speak of celibacy in relationship to a life of love. Obviously, the matter is closed but as Bishop Matthew Clark of Rochester, New York says: 'To declare a matter closed does not close the matter nor does it stop the questioning of the faithful'.[10]

It seems to me that we, as a Church, are not only dysfunctional in deleting this subject, but also that we must be blind not to recognise that the whole cosmos is becoming more unified, more together and more holistic while the Church hangs on to forms and disciplines that are unrealistic and far too rigid for most of her people including her priests. The forms of discipline as presently mandated speak to the human being in anthropological terms that are a dualistic phenomenon (body and soul) rather than an embodied person with needs, desires, wants, and aspirations.

It would be easy to suggest that if all priests who were opposed to celibacy were to leave tomorrow, it would bring the issue to a crisis point. One must ask himself if he contributes more to the problem by staying or leaving (a perennial question for feminists)!

But leaving is not realistic, not only for idealistic and theological reasons. There are also the problems of support, pensions, where to live, dissolving friendships, etc. etc.

Perhaps then, all one can do is stay, pray, try to remain faithful to God, oneself, others, live a holistic lifestyle, be honest, talk to one another, find support groups, take control of one's life, and encourage bishops in open frank dialogue. Easy advice, I suppose, as long as you don't have to live it.

As I sit writing the final touches to this book, I am overcome with the presence of the Transcendent. God is all over these North Carolina mountains – in the babbling bubbly brook, the verdancy of the trees and plants, in the majestic mountain tops which are in their late summer's glory and the crisp fresh air that defies the reality of our ecological crisis. I am powerfully aware of the Designer of the creation, of the fact that the atoms that are in the tree I lay next to this morning are also in my body and the bodies of all men and women. We are all one. That is not new age spirituality. It seems to me that our oneness is recognisable from natural law. All of nature strives to work inter-dependently with one another. **That is the law of nature**; to come together and create, whether that means to create together with our minds, or to birth together a child. No one of us is an island, as John Dunne tells us. No one of us is created to find meaning, hope, joy, or love alone. We need each other as much as the water I am listening to needs the rocks and the banks in order to babble.

It is my deepest prayer that the Church in the days to come will be released from the need to dominate people, the need to confine the Spirit and most epecially, the need to control the lives of our priests. Perhaps then she will be the *Gaudium et spes,* joy and hope, which reflects the light of the Creator to all peoples of the world.

CLOSING THOUGHTS

If a situation is born of obligation,
it deters freedom;
if a situation is born of choice,
it permits dignity.

Anonymous

It is my intention that this book be an affirmation to those who have been given the charism of celibacy. We are grateful for the very special form of love and witness that vowed celibate men and women have given to the world. Many have successfully integrated a celibate lifestyle with powerful loving relationships. They have shown the face of God in their ministry with and to others.

We also recognise, however, that the existing celibate reality has been the source of much pain, not only for those in the priesthood, but also for many who have felt called to ministry, yet have been excluded because they do not have the charism of celibacy.

While respecting the discipline of the Church, we also recognise a responsibility to let our voices be heard on this issue. Celibacy was not a condition of priesthood in the early Church, as most disciples were married, and Jesus did not make celibacy a prerequisite of ministry.

The anomaly of permitting married men of other faiths to Catholic priesthood while excluding Catholic priests who have married is contradictory. The recent situation, witnessed in Brazil, of admitting married men who abstain from a sexual relationship with their wives, is both an insult to women and degrading to the sacrament of marriage. Documented problems of priests leaving, Eucharisticless communities, the numbers and quality of seminary candidates, the disproportionate number of misogynists and ultra-conservatives, as well as the lack of prophetic leadership are all sources of concern to the Catholic faithful.[1] Report after report[2] has come out pointing to celibacy as being one of the largest problems relating to these realities.

Of particular concern is the age-old problem of extolling celibacy above marriage and the resulting disparagement of human sexuality as well as the implications regarding women. The theological and practical applications which celibacy held in former ages may not be relevant to a post-Vatican II Church.

It has been said in canon law circles that the law changes slowly in order to catch up with praxis. In my sharings with priests, it seems to me that many today are making up their own minds about celibacy as well as other issues in the Church.

Many in the Church are in favour of changing the laws of mandatory celibacy for priests. It is reasonable to assume that the whole structure of priesthood will see an overhaul within the next few decades and that the new structure will be faithful to the Church's teaching of equality for both men and women, to the form of the early Church, and to a married priesthood. Exactly how this will come about can only be imagined[3] but it is unrealistic to think that: 1) faithful men and women who feel the call to priesthood will participate in the existing Catholic Church as it is now structured, 2) the People of God will continue to support the present hierarchical structure, and 3) faithful Christian women and men will remain within a dysfunctional and sexist system such as we have now.

No one of us is perfect, no institution is perfect, and conversion continually calls us to re-examination and transformation of our lives and of our institutions. The signs of the times may be calling us to new ministerial forms, and perhaps back to many of the realities which existed in the early Christian communities. We encourage our Church to look to the *sensus fidelium* for discernment, as the Spirit instils the People of God with much wisdom. We encourage openness to the Spirit of God on this and other issues.

In the final analysis our credibility will be measured by our ability to be critical lovers of the very Church which has formed and nurtured us. This is an appropriate task for faithful Christian men and women, for if our Church is truly the People of God, then we, the people, have both the right and responsibility to help it come to new awarenesses, grow, change with the times, develop and be transformed.

Perhaps the challenge to the People of God who make up the institutional Church will be:

> To discover how to be truthful now ...
> To discover how to be living now ...
> To discover how to be loving now ...
> To discover how to be human now ... (W.H. Auden)[4]

It is my prayer that we will discover these values very soon because our Church holds a precious tradition of teaching which gives hope to the world. She is still home to millions, including me. And where does one go when one leaves home?

This book was written long before the recent sad events in the life of the Irish clergy. The timing of its publication in Ireland was beyond anyone's control and in my own view was an act of the Spirit. It is my deepest hope that it will be viewed as a compassionate plea for us to honestly look at the idealistic and unrealistic burdens we have placed on the lives of those who serve us and share our journey to God.

ABBREVIATIONS

DNT:

Xavier Léon-Dufour, *Dictionary of the New Testament*. Translated for the second revised French edition by Terrence Prendergast (San Francisco: Harper and Row, Publishers, 1980).

DTB:

John L. McKenzie, *Dictionary of the Bible* (New York: Macmillan Publishing Co. Inc., London: Collier Macmillan Publishers 1973).

JBC:

Brown, Raymond E., Joseph A. Fitzmeyer and Roland E. Murphy, eds., *The Jerome Biblical Commentary*. Vol. 1. *The Old Testament*; Vol. 2. *The New Testament and Topical Articles* (both bound in one book). (Englewood Cliffs, NJ: Prentice Hall, Inc., 1968).

NOTES

INTRODUCTION

1. Karl Rahner, 'Philosophy and Philosophising in Theology', in *Theological Investigations*, vol. 9, trans. Graham Harrison (New York: Herder and Herder, London: Darton Longman and Todd, 1972), 60-61.
2. James J McCartney,'Contemporary Controversies in Sexual Ethics: A Case Study in Post-Vatican II Moral Theology', in *Sexuality and Medicine*, vol. 2, ed. Earl E Shelp (n.p.: D Reidel Publishing Co., 1987), 219.
3. Many authors have made this statement.

CHAPTER ONE

1. Søren Kierkegaard, *Works of Love*, trans. Howard and Edna Hong (New York, Harper and Row, Publishers, Harper Torchbooks, 1962), 23-24.

CHAPTER TWO

1. Martin Buber, *I and Thou*, trans. Ronald Gregor Smith, 2d ed. (New York: Charles Scribner's Sons, 1958), 136. The exclusive language is not reflective

of the author's views. It is necessitated due to the exact quotation of original texts.

2. *Nelson's Expository Dictionary of the Old Testament*, 13th ed., s.v. 'chesed': defined as 'loving kindness; steadfast love; grace; mercy; faithfulness; goodness; devotion'. *Chesed* is more commonly written as *hesed.*

3. Earl F Palmer, *The Intimate Gospel: Studies in John* (Waco, TX: Word Books, 1978), 133-34.

4. Walter Brueggemann, *Tradition for Crisis: A Study in Hosea* (Richmond: John Knox Press, 1968), 71-79; James Luther Mays, *Hosea: A Commentary* (London: SCM Press Ltd., 1969), 7-15; Francis I. Andersen and David Noel Freedman, *Hosea: A New Translation with Introduction and Commentary*, The Anchor Bible, vol. 24 (Garden City, NY: Doubleday and Co., 1980), 115-22; *The Interpreters Dictionary of the Bible*, E – J, 1962 ed., s.v.'Hosea', 650-52. It should be noted that all biblical texts cited throughout will be from *The New American Bible*, St Joseph Edition (New York: Catholic Book Publishing Co., 1970).

5. Joseph Blenkinsopp, 'Deuteronomy', in *JBC* 1:6, 102.

6. John L McKenzie, 'The Gospel According to Matthew', in *JBC* 2:43, 101.

7. Edward F Campbell, Jr., *Ruth: A New Translation with Introduction, Notes, and Commentary*, The Anchor Bible, vol. 7 (Garden City, NY: Doubleday and Co., 1975), 28-32; and Geoffrey E Wood, 'Ruth, Lamentations', in *JBC*, 1:36, 605-9.

8. Kyle McCarter, Jr., *1 Samuel: A New Translation with Introduction, Notes and Commentary*, The Anchor Bible, vol. 8 (Garden City, NY: Doubleday and Co., 1980), 320-23, 332-45; and James C Turro '1 – 2 Samuel', in *JBC*, 1:9, 171-72, 174.

9. John A Sanford, *The Man Who Wrestled With God: Light From the Old Testament on the Psychology of Individuation* (New York: Paulist Press, 1974), 28-35; and G C Aalders, *Genesis: Vol 2*, trans. William Heynen, Bible Student's Commentary (Grand Rapids: Zondervan Publishing House, 1981), 112-16.

10. Brueggemann, 55-90; and Dennis J McCarthy, 'Hosea', in *JBC*, 1:15, 254-64.

11. Marvin H Pope, *Song of Songs: A New Translation with Introduction and Commentary*, The Anchor Bible, vol. 7c (Garden City, NY: Doubleday and Co., 1977), 199-205.

12. William Barclay, *The Letters of John and Jude*, rev. ed. (Philadelphia: The Westminster Press, 1976), 81-84, 96-101; and Bruce Vawter, 'Johannine Theology', in *JBC*, 2:80, 833.

13. Raymond E Brown, *The Epistles of John*, The Anchor Bible, vol. 30 (Garden City, NY: Doubleday and Co., Inc., 1982), 470.

14. Karl Rahner, 'Reflections on the Unity of the Love of Neighbour and the

Love of God', *Theological Investigations*, vol. 6, trans. Karl-H and Boniface Kruger (Baltimore: Helicon Press, London: Darton, Longman and Todd Ltd., 1969), 234; Thomas Barrosse, *Christianity: Mystery of Love: An Essay in Biblical Theology* (Notre Dame: Fides Publishers, Inc., 1964), 34; and Brown, *The Epistles of John*, 470.
15. Karl Barth, *The Epistle to the Romans*, trans. Edwyn C Hoskyns, 6th ed. (London: Oxford University Press), 492-97; Barrosse, 54; and Brown, *The Epistles of John*, 470.
16. Karl Rahner, *Grace in Freedom*, trans. Hilda Graef (New York: Herder and Herder), 218.
17. *DNT*, s.v. 'Love', 274.
18. *Ibid.*
19. William Barclay, *New Testament Words* (Philadelphia: The Westminster Press, 1974), 17-18.
20. *Ibid.*, 18.
21. *Ibid.*
22. *Ibid.*, 18-19.
23. *Ibid.*, 19.
24. *Ibid.*, 17-20.
25. Gerhard Kittel, ed., *Theological Dictionary of the New Testament*, trans. Geoffrey W Bromiley, 9 vols. (Grand Rapids: William B Eerdmans Publishing Co., 1964), 1:20-37; 9:116-30 and Barclay, *New Testament Words*, 20-23.
26. See *DTB*, s.v. 'Love', 520-23; *DNT*, s.v. 'Love', 274-76; Kittel, vol. 9:131; Rudolf Schnackenburg, *The Gospel According to St. John: Vol. 3*, trans. David Smith and G A Kon (New York: The Crossroad Publishing Co., 1982), 363 and Blenkinsopp, 'Deuteronomy', 107.
27. For information on Greek dualism, (sometimes, more correctly, called Platonic dualism), which has impoverished our theology of human sexuality, see James B Nelson, *Embodiment: An Approach to Sexuality and Christian Theology* (Minneapolis: Augsburg Publishing House, 1978), 45-46; Andre Guindon, *The Sexual Language: An Essay in Moral Theology* (Ottawa: The University of Ottawa Press, 1977) 63-64; Ignace Lepp, *The Psychology of Loving*, trans. Bernard B Gilligan (Baltimore: Helicon, 1963), 20-21. For negative views of women see Mary Jo Weaver, *New Catholic Women: A Contemporary Challenge to Traditional Authority* (San Francisco: Harper and Row, Publishers, 1985), 53-57; and Philip S Keane, *Sexual Morality: A Catholic Perspective* (New York: Paulist Press, 1977), 20-24. For 'misbegotten males' theory see Keane, 22 and Thomas Aquinas, *Sum. Th.* I, Q. 92, a.1.
28. Elizabeth A Clark, *Jerome, Chrysostom and Friends*, Studies in Women and Religion, vol. 2 (New York: The Edwin Mellen Press, 1979), 79.
29. Janie Gustafson, *Celibate Passion* (San Francisco: Harper and Row,

Publishers, 1978), 100.
30. *Ibid*.
31. Augustine, *Conf.* 4.4-6, trans. F J Sheed (New York: Sheed and Ward, 1942), 55-56.
32. Eugene Te Selle, 'Augustine As Client and as Theorist', *Journal for the Scientific Study of Religion* 25 (1986): 94.
33. Augustine, *Conf.* 1.1 as in *The Confessions of St. Augustine,* trans. Rex Warner (New York: The New American Library of World Literature, Inc., 1963), 17.
34. Jordan of Saxony, *To Heaven With Diana*, trans. Gerald Vann, (Chicago: Henry Regnery Co., 1965), letter 25.
35. Teresa of Avila, *Interior Castle*, trans. E Allison Peers, (Garden City, NY: Image Books, 1961).
36. John of the Cross, *Spiritual Canticle*, trans. E Allison Peers, (Garden City, NY: Doubleday, Image Books, 1961).
37. Gustafson, 101.
38. C F Kelley, *The Spirit of Love* (New York: Harper and Brothers Publishers, 1951), 239, note 70.
39. Gustafson, 101.
40. *Ibid*., 100.
41. Kenneth T Gallagher, *The Philosophy of Gabriel Marcel*, with foreword by Gabriel Marcel (New York: Fordham University Press, 1966), 70.
42. *Ibid*., 69.
43. Orlando Espin, 'The Concept of Incarnate Being in the Philosophy of Gabriel Marcel', (B.A. diss., St. Vincent de Paul Regional Seminary, 1968), 48.
44. Kenneth T Gallagher, 18-20.
45. *Ibid*., 13.
46. *Ibid*., 26.
47. *Ibid*.
48. *Ibid*.
49. *Ibid*., 28.
50. *Ibid*., 8.
51. Gabriel Marcel, *Metaphysical Journal*, trans. Bernard Wall (Chicago: Henry Regnery Co., A Gateway Edition, 1952), 147.
52. Kenneth T Gallagher, 8; we speak of this in Chapter Three.
53. Paul Tillich, *The Courage to Be* (New Haven: Yale University Press, 1952), 91.
54. Kenneth T Gallagher, 78.
55. Gabriel Marcel, *The Mystery of Being*, vol. 2, *Faith and Reality*, trans. G. S. Fraser (Chicago: Henry Regnery Co., 1951), 170.

56. Kenneth T. Gallagher, 79.
57. Marcel, *Metaphysical Journal*, 158. See also Kenneth T Gallagher, 79-81, for a fuller interpretation of the 'I–Thou' relationship and its connection to the theological virtue.
58. *Ibid.*, 95
59. Gabriel Marcel, *Les Coeur des Autres* (Paris: Librarie Grasset, 1921), 111.
60. Kenneth T Gallagher, 95.
61. Martin Buber, *Between Man and Man*, trans. Ronald Gregor Smith (New York: the Macmillan Co., 1972), 52.
62. Buber, *I and Thou*, 134-37. It is most interesting that Karl Barth, p. 495, makes the same connection using the 'I–Thou' relationship.
63. Martin Buber, *At the Turning* (New York: Martin Buber, 1952), 44.
64. *The Way of Response: Martin Buber: Selections from His Writings*, ed. Nahum N. Glatzer (New York: Schocken Books, 1966), 9-13.
65. Martin Buber, *Pointing the Way: Collected Essays*, trans. and ed. Maurice Friedman (London: Routledge and Kegan Paul, 1957), 225.
66. Martin Buber, 'Cheruth', an address given in Vienna in 1919, as quoted in Glatzer, 31-32.
67. Karl Rahner, *The Christian Commitment: Essays in Pastoral Theology*, trans. Cecily Hastings (New York: Sheed and Ward, 1963), 44-53.
68. Brian Grogan, 'Theological Trends: Is There Direct Experience of God?' *The Way* 22 (April 1982): 126. For a more thorough explanation see J Norman King, 'The Experience of God in the Theology of Karl Rahner', *Thought* 53 (June 1978): 174-202.
69. King, 184-200.
70. *Ibid.*, 180.
71. *Ibid.*
72. Karl Rahner, 'Theology of Freedom', in *Theological* , vol. 6, trans. Karl-H and Boniface Kruger (Baltimore: Helicon Press, London: Darton, Longman and Todd, 1969), 187.
73. *Ibid.*, 189-90. This translation as opposed to the one in footnote 16 adds more emphasis.
74. Rahner, 'Reflections on the Unity...', 242. This work gives a superb understanding of the unity and inseparability of human and divine love as well as self love as achieved through love of another.
75. Medard Kehl, 'Hans Urs von Balthasar: A Portrait', in *The von Balthasar Reader*, ed. Medard Kehl and Werner Loser, trans. Robert H Daly and Fred Lawrence (New York: A Crossroad Book, 1982), 3-22.
76. Hans Urs von Balthasar, *Love Alone*, trans. and ed. Alexander Dru (New York: Herder and Herder, 1969), 44.
77. *Ibid.*, 121-22.

78. *Ibid.*, 122.
79. *Ibid.*, 110.
80. *Ibid.*, 111.
81. Rahner, 'Reflections on the Unity...', 241.
82. King, 188.
83. Rahner, 'Reflections on the Unity...', 241.

CHAPTER THREE

1. Mary Rousseau and Charles Gallagher, *Sex is Holy* (Amity, NY: Amity House, 1986), 5.
2. *Ibid.*
3. Erik H Erikson, *Childhood and Society*, 2d ed. rev. (New York: W W Norton and Co., Inc., 1963), 263.
4. Elaine Hatfield, 'The Dangers of Intimacy', in *Communication, Intimacy and Close Relationships*, ed. Valerian J Derlega (Orlando, FL: Harcourt Brace Jovanovich, Publishers, 1984), 208.
5. Christopher Kiesling, *Celibacy, Prayer and Friendship, A Making-Sense-Out-of-Life Approach* (New York: Alba House, 1978), 74.
6. Harry Stack Sullivan, *The Interpersonal Theory of Psychiatry*, eds. Helen Swick Perry and Mary Ladd Gawal (New York: W. W. Norton and Co., Inc., 1953), 246. See pp. 263-96 where Sullivan distinguishes the 'lust need' from the 'intimacy need'.
7. Harry Stack Sullivan as cited in Rollo May, *Love and Will* (New York: Dell Publishing Co., W.W. Norton and Co., Inc., 1969), 82-83.
8. Evelyn Eaton Whitehead and James D. Whitehead, *Christian Life Patterns: The Psychological Challenges and Religious Invitations of Adult Life* (Garden City, NY: Image Books, Doubleday and Co., aainc., 1982), 66
9. Keith Clark, *An Experience of Celibacy: A Creative Reflection on Intimacy, Loneliness, Sexuality and Commitment* (Notre Dame: Ave Maria Press, 1982), 23.
10. *Ibid.*, 25.
11. Kahlil Gibran, *The Prophet*, (New York: Alfred A Knopf, Inc., 1969), 15-16. The feminist critique has made us particularly aware of this obliteration of one person by another. This is a common complaint in marriages and, in part, can be traced back to our Hebrew heritage in which women were considered chattel. See Mary Jo Weaver, p. 53-57.
12. 'Fecisti nos ad te; et inquietum est cor nostrum, donec requiscat in te'. Augustine *Conf.* 1:1 as in *The Confessions of St. Augustine*, trans. Rex Warner, 17.
13. See Buber, *I and Thou*; Buber, *Pointing the Way*; Buber, *Between Man and Man*; Marcel, *The Mystery of Being*, vol. 2., *Faith and Reality*; Marcel, *Being*

and Having; Gallagher, *The Philosophy of Gabriel Marcel;* and Joseph McCown, *Availability: Gabriel Marcel and the Phenomenology of Human Openness*, American Academy of Religion, Studies in Religion, no. 14 (Missoula, MO: Scholars Press, 1978).

14. Donald Goergen, *The Sexual Celibate* (New York: The Seabury Press, A Crossroads Book, 1974). In addition, Goergen has done a lecture series, *The Sexuality of the Celibate*, on tape (Boynton Beach, FL: St. Vincent de Paul Seminary, n.d.). These two sources are highly recommended as a realistic approach to celibate sexuality.

15. Mary Elizabeth Kenel, 'A Celibate's Sexuality and Intimacy', *Human Development* 7, no. 1 (Spring 1986): 14.

16. Sidney M Jourard as quoted by James E Kilgore, *The Intimate Man: Intimacy and Masculinity in the 80s* (Nashville: Abingdon Press, 1984), 26.

17. Kilgore, 27. Thomas Merton in *The Ascent to Truth* (New York: Harcourt, Brace and Co., 1951), 177, tells us that the first step to sanctity is 'self knowledge'.

18. Chantal as quoted in Kilgore, 47. This idea is affirmed in the work of Marcel. See also Eugene Kennedy in *The Heart of Loving* (Niles, IL: Argus Communications, 1973), 73-77, who speaks of the difficulties in coming to know oneself.

19. See Bernard Häring, *Free and Faithful in Christ: Moral Theology for Priests and Laity*, vol. 2, *The Truth Will Set You Free* (New York: The Seabury Press, A Crossroad Book, 1979), 81-83; Sidney M. Jourard, *The Transparent Self*, rev. ed. (New York: Van Nostrand Reinhold Co., 1971), 133-135; Buber, *Pointing the Way*, 225; Whitehead and Whitehead, 204-206; and Kenel, 14. This chapter will also discuss these values in the work of Maslow, Erikson and the Whiteheads.

20. Tim Timmons, *Loneliness Is Not a Disease* (Eugene, OR: Harvest House Publishers, 1981), 133.

21. H.F. Harlow, 'The Nature of Love', *American Psychologist* 13 (1958): 673-85; J Kagan, *Change and Continuity in Infancy* (New York: Wiley and Co., 1971); M H Hollander and A J Mercer, 'Wish to Be Held and Wish to Hold in Men and Women', *Archives of General Psychiatry* 33 (1976): 48-51; A F Silverman, M E Pressman and H W Bartel, 'Self-esteem and Tactile Communication', *Journal of Humanistic Psychology* 13 (1973): 73-77; W H Watson, 'The Meaning of Touch: Geriatric Nursing', *Journal of Communication* 25 (1975): 104-12; and Janet Macrae, *Therapeutic Touch: A Practical Guide* (New York: Alfred A Knopf, Inc., 1988).

22. Goergen, *The Sexual Celibate*, 91.

23. Ashley Montagu, *Touching – The Human Significance of the Skin* (New York: Harper and Row, Publishers, 1972), 273.

24. Goergen, *The Sexual Celibate*, 95.
25. William F Kraft,'Celibate Genitality', in *Celibate Loving*, ed. Mary Anne Huddleston (New York: Paulist Press, 1984), 74-75.
26. See Goergen, *The Sexual Celibate*, 178-208. See also Keith Clark, *Being Sexual ... and Celibate* (Notre Dame: Ave Maria Press, 1986), 21-30.
27. Ben Kimmerling, 'Friendship between Women and Priests', *The Furrow* 41, no. 10 (October 1990): 541-51. Kimmerling explains that celibate expression of love is an obligation for all. She speaks of the necessity of transforming twosomes into triangles (include community), into trinities of love. This is a superb article for priests and women who choose friendships with each other.
28. Abraham H Maslow, *Motivation and Personality*, 2d ed. (New York: Harper and Row, Publishers, 1970), 166, 185-86. For more information, see Maslow's chapter on 'Love in Self-Actualizing People', in the same book, 181-202.
29. *Ibid.*, 35-180.
30. *Ibid.*, 149-176.
31. *Ibid.*, 35-38.
32. *Ibid.*, 39-43.
33. *Ibid.*, 43.
34. *Ibid.*, 44.
35. *Ibid*. See also Rollo May, *Love And Will*, 145-52, who says that the avoidance of any close relationship brings one to the point of being out of touch with reality. It should be acknowledged that May has a concept of love as 'care'. His intertwining of love and will has many similarities to theological *agape*. Due to brevity, Rollo May's work could not be included, but his ideas are most valuable and form the background of much of this book. Additionally, May's work, like that of C S Lewis, (cf., *The Four Loves* [New York: Harcourt, Brace, Jovanovich, 1960]) and Erich Fromm, (cf., *The Art of Loving* [New York: Bantam Books, Harper and Row Publishers, Inc., 1956]) distinguishes different types of love relationships. The overlapping of all these types by different authors reinforces the difficulties in dissecting 'love'.
36. Maslow, *Motivation and Personality*, 44-45.
37. *Ibid.*, 187. Harry Stack Sullivan, in *The Interpersonal Theory of Psychiatry*, 246, concurs: '... interpersonal intimacy can consist of a great many things without genital contact; ...' Rollo May in *Love and Will*, p. 307, writes: 'for human beings, the more powerful need is not for sex, *per se*, but for relationship, intimacy, acceptance, and affirmation'.
38. Masow, *Motivation and Personality*, 45-46. Maslow alludes to theologians' discussion of pride and hubris as well as to other psychologists' work on

the concept of 'self'. With regard to this idea of self-esteem, perhaps a mention should be made of the 'instant' esteem that sometimes comes with ordination as opposed to the 'earned' esteem that comes from love and knowledge of achievement.

39. *Ibid.*, 46-47.

40. Erik H Erikson, *Identity: Youth and Crises* (London: Faber and Faber, 1968), 96-141. See chart on p. 94.

41. *Ibid.*, 135. This is another definition of intimacy which Erikson uses. The previous one used (from *Childhood and Society*, 263) is more descriptive.

42. Erikson, *Identity: Youth and Crises*, 135.

43. *Ibid.*, 135-36.

44. *Ibid.*, 136.

45. *Ibid.*

46. Erik H. Erikson, *Childhood and Society*, 263.

47. Erikson, *Childhood and Society*, 263-64.

48. Erikson, *Identity: Youth and Crises*, 137.

49. Erikson, *Childhood and Society*, 265-66.

50. Erikson, *Identity: Youth and Crises*, 137. In terms of pastoral ministry, of particular concern is the inability to develop a quality of 'care' since it is a gospel value that is called for in all ministry. With respect to this, an interesting relationship seems to exist between adult children of alcoholics and vocations to the religious life and priesthood. This relationship should be studied, as on one hand, ACOAs have usually been 'caretakers' in their families; but on the other hand, their difficult family experiences often make them feel incapable of caring for offspring on a steady basis. They sometimes choose the celibate lifestyle without ever facing their inability to develop the quality of 'care' (as well as their difficulties in developing the ability to trust). Many seminaries today are dealing with these realities by sending their men for professional help. This is a most positive step, but this professional help should also be integrated into the formation process. For introductory material to the 'adult-child/priest' see Janet Geringer Woititz, *Home Away From Home* (Pompano Beach, FL: Health Communications, Inc., 1987), 10-12. See also Sean Sammon, 'Understanding the Children of Alcoholic Parents', *Human Development* 8, no. 3 (Fall 1987): 28-35; and C Lawrence Miller, 'Treatment and Recovery of Alcoholics' Children', *Human Development* 8, no. 4 (Winter 1987): 31-32.

51. Erikson, *Identity: Youth and Crises*, 138.

52. *Ibid.*, 139.

53. Whitehead and Whitehead, 4.

54. *Ibid.*, 10-12.

55. *Ibid.*, 12. See also pp. 14-30 for development of this integration. This in-

cludes work on love as *agape* and *diakonia*, pp. 25-29.
56. *Ibid.*, 67.
57. *Ibid.* 67-68. This is related to the 'go-away closer' syndrome which is descriptive of the process of making intimate relationships. We fear, yet crave, intimacy because it makes such demands on our life. For more infomation, see David J Hassel, *Dark Intimacy: Hope for Those in Difficult Prayer Experiences* (New York: Paulist Press, 1986), 1-5.
58. Whitehead and Whitehead, 79-80.
59. *Ibid.*, 82. This is painfully evidenced in the lives of some priests.
60. *Ibid.*, 82-83.
61. *Ibid.*, 84-85.
62. *Ibid.*, 85.
63. Gerald G May, *Will and Spirit: A Contemplative Psychology* (San Francisco: Harper and Row, Publishers, 1982), 190, and Rollo May, *Love and Will*, 307. Although we have not delved into the work of these two in detail, their research has been used for much of our background.
64. Erich Fromm *The Art of Loving* (New York: Bantam Books, Harper and Row, Publishers, Inc., 1956), 8.
65. *Ibid.*, 15.
66. Edgar Jackson, *Understanding Loneliness* (Philadelphia: Fortress Press, 1980), 105.
67. See Jackson, 101-110 and Richard R. De Blassie, 'Intimacy in Pastoral Care', *Human Development* 7, no. 2 (Summer 1986): 27-31, for a fuller understanding of this Rollo May in *Love and Will* thoroughly describes the problems of 'sex' without intimacy.
68. Jourard, *The Transparent Self*, 7. Jourard agrees with Buber that self-disclosure is the apex of the'I–thou' relationship. It displays human functioning at the highest level (p. 6).
69. *Ibid.*, 32. See also Rollo May, 'Our Schizoid World', in *Love and Will*, 13-33.
70. Paul Tillich, *The Eternal Now* (New York: Charles Scribner's Sons, 1956), 17-18.
71. Henri Nouwen, *Reaching Out: The Three Movements of the Spiritual Life* (Garden City, NY: Doubleday and Co., Inc., 1975), 30.
72. Kennedy, *The Heart of Loving*, 21.
73. Margery Williams, *The Velveteen Rabbit* (New York: Avon Books, 1975), 12-13.
74. Eugene C Kennedy, *A Time for Love* (Garden City, NY: Doubleday and Co., Inc., 1970), 25.
75. Bernard J Bush, 'Celibacy, Affectivity and Friendship', *The Way Supplement* 47 (Summer 1983): 75.

76. *Presbyterorum Ordinis*, 12.
77. William McNamara, *Mystical Passion: Spirituality for a Bored Society* (New York: Paulist Press, 1977), 3.

CHAPTER FOUR

1. Joseph L Bernardin, 'I am Joseph, Your Brother', Homily for Evening Prayer upon taking up residence in the See of Chicago, 25 August 1982, 3-4. (Photocopy of text, given to author).
2. Edmund M Hussey, 'Needed: A Theology of Priesthood', Address presented at a conference titled 'U.S. Catholic Seminaries and Their Future', cosponsored by Foundations and Donors Interested in Catholic Activities and by the Lilly Endowment, Palm Beach, FL, 22 January 1988, as cited in *Origins* 17, no. 34 (4 February 1988): 577, 579-85.
3. M Eugene Boylan, *The Spiritual Life of the Priest* (Cork: The Mercier Press, 1962), 99. Translated means: Never one (male) alone with one (female)! Let your discourse be brief and tough ...
4. Boylan, 102.
5. *Ibid.*, 99.
6. See Manual Miguens, 'On Being a Christian and the Moral Life: Pauline Perspectives', *Principles of Catholic Moral Life*, ed. William E May (Chicago: Franciscan Herald Press, 1981), 89-110; Nelson, 84; Schnackenburg, *The Moral Teaching of the New Testament*, 245-54; and Charles E Curran *Directions in Fundamental Moral Theology*, (Notre Dame: University of Notre Dame Press, 1985), 51-52.
7. Paul E Dinter, 'Getting Some Respect', *Church* 3, no. 3 (Fall 1987): 5. For a fuller interpretation, see Mahoney, *The Making of Moral Theology*, 37-71.
8. See John H McGoey, *Dare I Love* (Huntington, IN: Our Sunday Visitor, Inc., 1974), 124-29. McGoey does an interesting treatment of how the past priestly 'image' dispensed celibates from many human problems. See also Archbishop Daniel Pilarczyk, 'The Changing Image of the Priest', *Origins* 16, no. 7 (3 July 1986): 140-41, who speaks of being a priest as the 'highest life a boy could aspire to'.
9. Joseph Blenkinsopp, *Celibacy, Ministry, Church* (New York: Herder and Herder, 1968), 18-26; and Henri Crouzel 'Celibacy and Ecclesiastical Continence in The Early Church: The Motives Involved', in *Priesthood and Celibacy*, ed. A M Charue and others (Milan: Editrice Ancora, n.d.), 451-502.
10. Weaver, 53-57; and Keane, 20-24.
11. McGoey, 3.
12. *Ibid.*, 95.
13. *Gaudium et Spes*, 4.
14. Thomas Kuhn, *The Structure of Scientific Revolutions* (Chicago: The Univ-

ersity of Chicago Press, 1962), 10-22, 77-90.
15. Marilyn Ferguson, *The Aquarian Conspiracy: Personal and Social Transformation in the 1980s* (Los Angeles: J.P. Tarcher, Inc., 1980), 26- 27.
16. Ernest E Larkin and Gerard T Broccolo, *Spiritual Renewal of the American Priesthood* (Washington, D.C.: Publications Office of the United States Catholic Conference, 1973), 16.
17. Sean D Sammon, *Growing Pains in Ministry* (Whitinsville, MA: Affirmation Books, 1983), 68. See Sammon's powerful chapter on 'The virtue of fidelity in an age of transition', 185-201. See also Rollo May, p. 13, who calls ours an era of 'radical transition'.
18. John Naisbitt, *Megatrends: Ten New Directions Transforming Our Lives* (New York: Warner Books, 1984), 279.
19. Norman Pittenger, *Process-Thought and Christian Faith.* (New York: Macmillan Co., 1969), 11-13. See also Eulalio R Baltazar, *God Within Process* (Paramus, NJ: Newman Press, 1970), 1-23. The ideas of process theology are well suited to self-actualisation theories upheld by A Maslow and C Rogers, as well as the works of Rollo May, *et al*. For discussion on this, see James J Gill, 'The Development of Persons', *Human Development* 2:29-39.
20. Secretariat, Bishops' Committee on Priestly Formation, National Conference of Catholic Bishops, *Spiritual Formation in the Catholic Seminary* (Washington, D.C.: United States Catholic Conference, 1984), 7.
21. *Ibid.*, 9.
22. Sammon, *Growing Pains in Ministry*, 69.
23. See, for example, Frank J McNulty, 'AUS Priest Addresses the Pope', in *Origins* 17, no. 15 (24 September 1987): 231-34. See also, Karl Rahner, *The Shape of the Church to Come*, trans. Edward Quinn (New York: Seabury Press, A Crossroad Book, 1974), 110.
24. A private document issued in 1982 by Seminary rectors, as quoted by Matthias Neuman in 'Living Celibately in Pastoral Ministry', *Human Development* 7, no. 3 (Fall 1986): 38.
25. Ferguson, 389. This is the same assertion the Whiteheads make about the struggle between isolation and intimacy which results in consistent strength for love and devotion.
26. This is a frequent assertion of Josef Fuchs, as expressed in lectures given at St Vincent de Paul Regional Seminary, Boynton Beach, FL, January – March, 1986.
27. The Bishops' Committee on Priestly Life and Ministry, 'Reflections on the Morale of Priests', in *Origins* 18, no. 31 (12 January 1989): 502, states: 'it has become axiomatic that having a sense of control over one's life, a sense of ownership and participation is basic to both morale and maturity'.
28. Bush, 76.

29. All the descriptions in this paragraph are supported by the following works: The Bishops' Committee on Priestly Life and Ministry, *A Reflection Guide on Human Sexuality and the Ordained Priesthood* (Washington, D.C.: National Conference of Catholic Bishops, 1983); The Bishops' Committee on Priestly Life and Ministry, 'Reflections on the Morale of Priests'; John Marshall, 'Strengths and Weaknesses of U.S. Seminaries', *Origins* 17, no. 30 (7 January 1988): 522-28; *The Priest and Stress* (Washington, D.C.: United States Catholic Conference, 1982), 1-13; J. Francis Stafford, 'The Mystery of the Priestly Vocation', *Origins* 18, no. 22 (10 November 1988): 351; Andrew A. Sorensen, *Alcoholic Priests: A Sociological Study* (New York: Seabury Press, A Crossroad Book, 1976) and McGoey, 95.

30. The Bishops' Committee on Priestly Life and Ministry, *The Health of American Catholic Priests: A Report and A Study* (Washington, D.C.: United States Catholic Conference, 1985), 4.

31. *Ibid.*, 5.

32. Martin C Devereaux, 'An Analysis of Individual Growth Among Priests in Ministry to Priests Program's Options, As Measured by the Personal Orientation Inventory' (Ph.D. diss. Nova University School of Professional Psychology, 1984), 56.

33. The Center for Human Development, *A Report on Phase One of the Ministry to Priests Program in the Archdiocese of Miami* (Washington, D.C.: Center for Human Development, 1981), 13-14.

34. *Ibid.*, 26. See also p. 62, which shows the capacity for 'I–Thou' relationships as problematic.

35. See Eugene C. Kennedy and Victor J. Heckler, *The Catholic Priest in the United States States: Psychological Investigations* (Washington, D.C.: Publications Office, United States Catholic Conference, 1972), 3-16, for an overview of their findings. One must keep in mind, however, that this study by Kennedy and Heckler is nineteen years old. See also Andrew M. Greeley *The Catholic Priest in the United States: Sociological Investigations* (Washington, D.C.: Publications Office, United States Catholic Conference, 1972).

36. The Center for Human Development, *A Report on Phase One...*, 13.

37. Devereaux, 11-36.

38. Kennedy and Heckler, 51-52.

39. Devereaux, 28.

40. E Kennedy, V Heckler, F Kobler, and R Walker, 'Clinical Assessment of a Profession: Roman Catholic Clergymen', *Journal of Clinical Psychology* 33 (1977): 120-28, as in Devereaux, 29-30.

41. *Ibid.*, as in Devereaux, 30

42. Johannes B. Metz, *Poverty of Spirit*, trans. John Drury (Paramus, NJ: Newman Press, 1968), 5-9.

43. Michael J Brickley, Address to the Ordination Class of 1972. The Jesuit School of Theology at Berkeley. (Photocopy of speech, given to author.)
44. Kenel, 14.
45. Sandra M Schneiders, *New Wineskins: Re-imagining Religious Life Today* (New York: Paulist Press, 1986), 221.
46. *Ibid.*, 221-23.
47. Bush, 74-75.
48. Frank J McNulty, 'The Tensions of Leadership: The Priest', *New Catholic World*, 223 (September/October 1980): 230. Emphasis is mine.
49. Richard Rohr, *The Price of Peoplehood,* lectures from a priests' retreat, cassette 923, St Anthony Messenger Tapes, 1979.
50. Helen Keller as quoted by Ken Druck and James C Simmons in *The Secrets Men Keep* (Garden City, NY: Doubleday and Co., Inc., 1985), 20.
51. Kiesling, 65-66.
52. Sidney J Harris, *The Authentic Person: Dealing With Dilemma* (Niles, IL: Argus Communications, 972), 40.
53. Michael J Scanlon. Commencement address given to the 1987 graduates of St Vincent de Paul Regional Seminary, Boynton Beach, FL, 13 May 1987.
54. Ida Friederike Gorres, *Is Celibacy Outdated?* trans. Barbara Waldstein Wartenberg (Westminster, MD: Newman Press, 1965), 94. See also Philip Rosato, 'Formation for Friendship', *The Way Supplement,* 56 (Summer 1986): 27, who speaks of this kenosis as a 'communion of suffering and joy'.
55. St John of the Cross, *Dark Night of The Soul*, trans. E. Allison Peers (Garden City, NY: Doubleday and Co. Inc., Image Books, 1959), 106.
56. Marc Oraison, *The Celibate Condition and Sex* (New York: Sheed and Ward, Inc., 1967), 91. Also, Gerald May, 190-91, says: 'Many very sexual, passionate, creative, spiritually mature people are celibate. And of course, many genitally active people are painfully uncreative'.
57. Kenneth Leech, *Soul Friend: The Practice of Christian Spirituality* (San Francisco: Harper and Row, Publishers, 1977), 112-13. Leech adds to our understanding of the integral relationship between spirituality and sexuality, pp. 112-16.
58. Karl Rahner, *Servants of the Lord,* trans. Richard Strachen (New York: Herder and Herder, 1968), 153.
59. *Ibid.*, 171.
60. Oraison, 92-100.
61. Martin W Pable, 'Psychology and Asceticism of Celibacy', in *Celibate Loving: Encounters in Three Dimensions*, ed. Mary Anne Huddleston (New York: Paulist Press, 1984), 14.
62. Maslow, *Motivation and Personality*, 107.
63. Pable, 23.

64. Henri Nouwen, 'From Resentment to Gratitude', an unpublished lecture. Cited in Pable, 23.
65. Leech, 112.
66. *Ibid.*,112-113.
67. Desmond F McGoldrick, *Living the Celibate Life: An Essay in the Higher Psychology of Faith* (New York: Vantage Press, 1970), 42-43.
68. McGoey, 97.
69. See Kimmerling on secrecy in relationships and invisible women, 546-51.
70. Rahner, *Servants of God*, 166.
71. Wendy M. Wright, 'Reflections on Spiritual Friendship Between Men and Women', *Weavings* 2, no. 4 (July/August 1987):23.

CHAPTER FIVE
1. McGoey, 96.
2. Druck and Simmons, *Secrets Men Keep*, 103-4.
3. Michael E McGill, *The McGill Report on Male Intimacy* (New York: Holt, Rinehart and Winston, Perennial Library, 1986), 157.
4. *Ibid.*, 181.
5. Druck and Simmons, 94-97.
6. Daniel J Levinson, *et al.*, *The Seasons of a Man's Life* (New York: Alfred A Knopf, 1985), 335. See Harry Stack Sullivan, 246-62 on the need for a boy to have a 'chum'.
7. Levinson, 25.
8. Letty Cottin Pogrebin, *Among Friends: Who We Like, Why We Like Them, and What We Do With Them* (New York: McGraw-Hill Book Co., 1987), describes many of these interesting studies throughout her work. See also Joseph H Pleck and Jack Sawyer, eds., *Men and Masculinity* (Englewood Cliffs: Prentice-Hall, Inc., 1974).
9. Kenneth R Mitchell, 'Priestly Celibacy from a Psychological Perspective', in *Celibate Loving: Encounters in Three Dimensions*, ed. Mary Anne Huddleston (New York: Paulist Press, 1984), 94.
10. *Ibid.*, 95-96.
11. Larkin and Broccolo, 28-30. All of Chapter 3, 'Personal Relationships and Spirituality', 25-38, is highly recommended.
12. Adolf Guggenbuhl-Craig, *Power in the Helping Professions* (New York: Spring Publications, 1971), 68.
13. Kiesling, 177, claims that 'one of the greatest challenges of the next decade will be integrating into Christian vowed celibate life people with acknowledged homosexual orientation'. Kiesling wrote this in the late seventies. Perhaps this specific integration will be the task of the next few decades as we have not yet properly addressed this issue in seminary training

or in the priesthood. On this topic, Thomas J Tyrell, in *Urgent Longings: Reflections on the Experience of Infatuation, Human Intimacy, and Contemplative Love* (Whitinsville, MA: Affirmation Books, 1980), has written a superb understanding of how young men in training form attachments to superiors. Because the paradigm of this experience will be carried into adult priesthood, it is highly recommended reading.

14. Alfred C Kinsey, Wardell B Pomeroy, and Clyde E Martin, *Sexual Behavior in the Human Male* (Philadelphia: WB Saunders Co., 1948), 636-55. See especially Figure 161, p. 638. See also Nicholas Berdyaev, *The Destiny of Man* (New York: Harper Torchbooks., 1960), 61-66. 'Man is not only a sexual but a bisexual being, combining the masculine and the feminine principle in himself in different proportions and often in fierce conflict ... It is only the union of these two principles that constitutes a complete human being'.

15. W Norman Pittenger, *Making Sexuality Human* (New York: The Pilgrim Press, 1979), 68.

16. Druck and Simmons, 104-6.

17. Kenel, 16. For a fuller understanding of women–men differences, see Carol Gilligan, *In a Different Voice: Psychological Theory and Women's Development* (Cambridge, MA: Harvard University Press, 1982).

18. Kiesling, 73.

19. Gustafson, 89. For a fuller understanding see C G Jung, *Two Essays in Analytical Psychology*, eds. Sir Herbert Read, Michael Fordham, and Gerhard Adler, trans. RFC Hull, 2d ed., Bollingen Series 20, *The Collected Works of C. G. Jung*, vol. 7 (New York: Pantheon Books), 173-241. Also see Robert A Johnson, *He: Understanding Masculine Psychology* (New York: Harper and Row Publishers, Perennial Libraray, 1977) and Robert A Johnson, *She: Understanding Feminine Psychology* (New York: Harper and Row Publishers, Perennial Library, 1977). Both works by Johnson interpret the psychological concepts of Jung and further our understanding of the individuation process.

20. Gustafson, 90-94.

21. William C McCready, 'Religion and the Life Cycle', in *Toward Vatican III*, ed., David Tracy with Hans Küng and Johann B Metz (New York: Concilium, Seabury Press, 1978), 279-80.

22. Kilgore, 113-120.

23. John Sanford and George Lough, *What Men Are Like* (Mahwah, NY: Paulist Press, 1988), 169.

24. Robert Bly, *Iron John: A Book About Men* (Reading, MA: Addison-Wesley Publishing Co., Inc., 1990).

25. Goergen, 183.

26. McGoey, 112-13.

27. Richard Gilmartin, 'Coping with Humanity', in *Coping: Issues of Emotional Living in an Age of Stress for Clergy and Religious,* The First Psychotheological Symposium (Whitinsville, MA: Affirmation Books, 1979), 51-52.
28. Kiesling, 175-76.
29. Schneiders, *New Wineskins: Re-imagining Religious Life Today*, 213. See also Fran Ferder and John Heagle, *Partnership: Women and Men in Ministry* (Notre Dame: Ave Maria Press, 1989), on chastity as the fundamental stance of our hearts, 180-81.
30. Goergen, 187.
31. Helen Waddell, ed., *The Desert Fathers* (London: Constable and Co., 1960), 136.
32. McGoey, 100.
33. Aelred of Rievaulx, *Spiritual Friendship*, trans. Mary Eugenia Laker (Washington, D.C.: Cistercian Publications, Consortium Press, 1974), 92-93.
34. Keane, 297-98.
35. Rahner, *Servants of the Lord*, 167.
36. Kiesling, 66.
37. Kenel, 18.
38. 'Love does not dominate, it cultivates', Goethe, as quoted by Kilgore, 53.
39. Kimmerling, 541-51.
40. Rachel Gosmer, *Gender and God: Love and Desire in Christian Spirituality* (n.p.: Cowley Publications, 1986), 96-97. See 78-97 for a fuller description of this relationship.
41. Dante, *Paradise*, canto X, lines 55-61 as cited in Gustafson, 97.
42. Rahner, *Reflections on the Unity ...* , 241.
43. Thomas Merton, *No Man is an Island* (New York: Harcourt, Brace, Jovanovich, Dell Publishing Co., 1955), 25.
44. Henri J M Nouwen, *Lifesigns: Intimacy, Fecundity, and Ecstasy in Christian Perspective* (Garden City, NY: Doubleday and Co., Inc., 1986), 52.
45. M. Scott Peck, *The Road Less Traveled: A New Psychology of Love, Traditional Values and Spiritual Growth* (New York: Simon and Schuster, a Touchstone Book, 1978), 95.
46. Pierre Teilhard de Chardin, *The Phenomenon of Man* , trans. Bernard Wall (New York: Harper and Brothers Publishers, 1959), 266.
47. George A Maloney, *Called to Intimacy: Living in the Indwelling Presence* (New York: Alba House, 1983), 160.
48. Matthew Fox, *A Spirituality Named Compassion and the Healing of the Global Village, Humpty Dumpty and Us* (Minneapolis: Winston Press, 1979), 22.

CHAPTER SIX

1. Albert Haase as in Joan Ohanneson, *And They Felt No Shame: Christians Reclaim Their Sexuality* (Minneapolis: Winston Press, 1989), 88-89.
2. Pierre Teilhard de Chardin, 'L'Evolution de la Chasteté', quoted in Claude Cuenot, *Telihard de Chardin: A Biographical Study* (Baltimore: Helicon Press, 1965), 28-29.
3. Matthew Fox, *Meditations with* Meister Eckhart (Santa Fe, NM: Bear and Co., 1982), 111.
4. Jean-Jacques Annaud, dir., *The Name of the Rose* (n.p., Neve Constantin Film Productions, 1986).
5. Nouwen, *Lifesigns* ... 52.
6. A W Richard Sipe, *A Secret World: Sexuality and the Search for Celibacy* (New York: Brunner/Mazel, Publishers, 1990), 278.
7. Agostino Bono, 'Synod of Bishops Reaffirms Traditional Priestly Practices', *Catholic News Service* as printed in *Florida Catholic*, 2 November 1990, 18.
8. George Frein, ed. *Celibacy : The Necessary Option* (New York: Herder and Herder, 1968), 7-17.
9. Ohanneson, 112.
10. Joseph A Tetlow, 'The Second-Half Generation', *New Catholic World* 223 (September/October 1980): 197.
11. Bono, 18.
12. CBS News, 25 October 1990.
13. Lynda Richardson, 'Bishop Backs Ordaining Married Men', *Washington Post*, 10 January 1991.
14. Henry Lea, *History of Sacerdotal Celibacy in the Christian Church* (New York: Russel and Russel, 1957), gives a very inclusive history up until 100 years ago. See also Richard Sipe for some interesting observations.
15. Timothy Lynch, 'Celibacy and the Clerical State', (unpublished paper submitted for JCL, Catholic University, 1987), 1-2.
16. Jerome, *To Eustochium 20, Corpus Scriptorum Ecclesiasticorum Latinorum* 54 as cited by John T. Noonan, 'Celibacy in the Fathers of the Church', in *Celibacy: The Necessary Option*, ed. George Frein, 151.
17. Timothy Lynch, 2-3.
18. John E Lynch, 'Marriage and Celibacy of the Clergy, the Discipline of the Western Church: An Historical – Canonical Synopsis', *The Jurist* 32 (1972), 21-22.
19. Timothy Lynch, 3-4.
20. Richard J Devine, *Holy Virginity: A Study of the New Testament on Virginity and Celibacy* (Rome: Typis Pontificiae Universitatis, 1964), 44-61.
21. Edward Schillebeeckx, *Ministry: Leadership in the Community of Jesus*

Christ (New York: Crossroad Publishing, 1981), 85-86.
22. Council of Elvira, Canon 33, E Hispano, *Concilos Visigoticos*, (Barcelona 1963), 7. This date is disputed. Samuel Laeuchli in *Power and Sexuality: The Emergence of Canon Law at the Synod of Elvira* (Philadelphia: Temple University Press, 1972), 95, places the date at 309.
23. Council of Ancyra, Canon 10, 67, in *The Seven Ecumenical Councils*, ed. Henry R. Percival (Grand Rapids, MI: W.B. Eerdmans Publishing Co., n.d.).
24. Council of Neocaesarea, Canon 1, 79, in *The Seven Ecumenical Councils*, ed. Henry R. Percival (Grand Rapids, MI: W.B. Eerdmans Publishing Co., n.d.).
25. Laeuchli, 95.
26. Michael Pfliegler, 'Celibacy' in *Life in the Spirit*, ed. Hans Küng (New York: Sheed and Ward, 1967), 128-29.
27. *Ibid.*, 130.
28. Socrates, *Hist. Eccles.* I.2 as quoted in David O'Neill, *Priestly Celibacy and Maturity* (New York: Sheed and Ward, 1965), 14.
29. Richard McBrien, *Catholicism: Study Edition* (San Francisco: Harper and Row, Publishers, 1981), 613.
30. Hans Küng, 'Hans Küng Writes the Pope About Celibacy', *National Catholic Reporter*, 16 May 1980, 15-16.
31. Ohanneson, 92.
32. Pfliegler, 132.
33. Philip S Kaufman, 'An Immoral Morality?' *Commonweal* (12 September 1980), 496 as in Ohanneson, 93.
34. Council of Trullo, Canon 13, 371, as in *The Seven Ecumenical Councils*, ed. Henry R. Percival (Grand Rapids, MI: W.B. Eerdmans Publishing Co., n.d.).
35. Timothy Lynch, 4.
36. O'Neill, 14-15.
37. Timothy Lynch, 4-5.
38. Pfliegler, 138.
39. O'Neill, 16.
40. Pfliegler, 147.
41. Council of Trent, Session XXIV C.9-10, de Matrimonio Joseph Alberigo, *et al*, *Conciliorum Oecumenicorum Decreta* (Freiberg: Herder, 1962), 731.
42. *Codex Iuris Canonici*, Canon 132.1.
43. Decree on the Ministry and Life of Priests, *Presbyterorum Ordinis* (7 December 1965), *A.A.S* 58 (1966), 991-1024.
44. Dogmatic Constitution on the Church, *Lumen Gentium* (21 November 1964) *AAS* 57 (1965), 5-71.
45. Pope Paul VI, Encyclical Letter on Priestly Celibacy, *Sacerdotali Caelibatuss* (24 June 1967), *AAS.* 59 (1967), 657-97.

46. Synod of Bishops, on the Ministerial Priesthood, *Ultimis Temporibus* (30 November 1967), *AAS*. 63 (1971), 898-942.
47. Pope John Paul II, Letter to Priests, *Novo Incipiente Nostro* (6 April 1979), *AA.S* 71 (1979), 393-417.
48. Pope Paul VI to Vatican II (10 October 1965), Concilium Vaticanum Secundum, *Acta et Document*, Vol. IV, Part I, 40.
49. See *Origins*, Vol. 20: no. 18 (11 October 1990) through Vol. 20: no. 22 (8 November 1990).
50. 'Celibacy Key Factor for Young Adults', *National Catholic Reporter*, 21 September 1990, 4.
51. *Ibid*.
52. Timothy Lynch, 12.
53. Lea, 576.

CHAPTER SEVEN

1. Michel Quoist, *Prayers* , trans. Agnes M. Forsyth and Anne Marie de Commaille (Kansas City: Sheed and Ward, 1963), 65.
2. Anthony Kosnik, *Human Sexuality: New Directions in American Catholic Thought* (New York: Paulist Press, 1977), 26.
3. Pierre Hermand, *The Priest: Celibate or Married* (Baltimore: Helicon, 1965), 76.
4. McBrien, 534-35. McBrien mentions the latter three. Jerome's ideas have been documented previously.
5. Hermand, 91-92. See 89-102 for more information.
6. McBrien, 535.
7. James B. Nelson, *The Intimate Connection: Male Sexuality, Masculine Spirituality* (Philadelphia: The Westminster Press, 1988), 115-32.
8. Kosnik, 86.
9. Pierre Teilhard de Chardin, *Science and Christianity* (New York: Harper and Row, 1968), 12-13.
10. Pope John Paul II, *Apostolic Exhortation: The Role of the Christian Family in the Modern World* (Boston: Daughters of St Paul, 1982), 29-30.
11. Pope Pius XII, 'Encyclical Letter of His Holiness Pius XII on Holy Virginity', in *Selected Documents of His Holiness, Pius XII* (Washington, DC: National Catholic Welfare Conference 1954), 8.
12. *Ibid*., 24.
13. Pope Paul VI, *Sacerdotalis Caelibatus*, no. 39.
14. Pope John Paul II, *Apostolic Exhortation: The Role of the Christian Family* ... 29.
15. Pope John Paul II, 'Homily Opening 1990 Synod of Bishops', in *Origins* 20, no. 18 (11 October 1990), 284.

16. See ft. 27, Ch. Two.
17. See, for example, Weaver, 53-57; Sipe, 17-51; Maria Riley, *Transforming Feminism* (Kansas City: Sheed and Ward, 1989); Elisabeth Schüssler Fiorenza, *Bread Not Stone: The Challenge of Feminist Biblical Interpretation* (Boston: Beacon Press, 1984;) Sandra M Schneiders, *Beyond Patching: Faith and Feminism in the Catholic Church* (New York: Paulist Press, 1991) and Riane Eisler, *The Chalice and the Blade: Our History, Our Future* (San Francisco: Harper and Row, Publishers, 1987).
18. Carol Gilligan, already cited.
19. James Hickey, 'The Laity's Role in Priestly Formation', in *Origins* 20, no. 20 (25 October 1990): 323; Henri Goudreault, 'Corresponsibility of Priests and Laity', in *Origins* 20, no. 20 (25 October 1990): 330; and Albert De Courtnay, 'Roles for Women in Priestly Formation', in *Origins* 20, no. 20 (25 October 1990); 332.
20. Hermand, 73-75.
21. Schillebeeckx, 89.
22. McBrien, 621.
23. Schillebeeckx, 89.
24. Ohanneson, 90.

CHAPTER EIGHT

1. Philip Keane, 'The Meaning and Functioning of Sexuality in the Lives of Celibates and Virgins,' *Review for Religious* 34 (1975): 313.
2. See Sam Keen, *Fire in the Belly*.
3. Ohanneson, 117.
4. *Ibid*., 116.
5. James L Franklin, 'Contemporary Studies on the Priest Shortage'.
6. Andrew Greeley, *The Catholic Priest in the United States: Sociological Investigations*.
7. Richard Sipe, *A Secret World: Sexuality and the Search for Celibacy*.
8. 'Awaken the Promise: Vocations Ministry in the United States.'
9. Synod of Bishops, 'Formation of Priests in the Circumstances of Present Day', in *Origins* 20, no. 10 (2 August 1990): 149, 151-168.
10. Matthew Clark, 'On Hearing the Wisdom of the People', in *Origins* 20, no. 28 (20 December 1990): 452.

CLOSING THOUGHTS

1. Paul Wilkes, 'The Hands That Would Shape Our Souls' in *Atlantic Monthly*, December 1990, 59-88.
2. See for example, 'Awaken the Promise: Vocation Ministry in the United States', address presented at the National Religious Vocations Conference,

San Mateo, CA (6-10 September 1990) , as cited in *National Catholic Reporter*, 21 September 1990; James L. Franklin, 'Contemporary Studies on the Priest Shortage', in *Progressions: A Lilly Endowment Occasional Report* 1, no. 2 (June 1990): 7-10; Dean R. Hoge, 'Carrying Out Ministry in a Priest Shortage', lecture given at the Future of the American Church Conference, Washington DC, 29 September 1990; Dean Hoge, *Future of Catholic Leadership: Response to the Priest Shortage* (Kansas City: Sheed and Ward, 1987); and Richard A. Schoenheer *et al*., 'The Catholic Priest in the US: Demographic Investigations', as cited in *Catholic News Service*, 17 July 1990, 1.

3. See the creative work of Joseph F. Girzone, *The Shepherd* (New York: Macmillan Publishing Co., 1990).

4. W H Auden, 'For the Time Being', in *Collected Poems*, ed. Edward Mendelson (New York: Random House, 1976), 285-86.

BIBLIOGRAPHY

Aalders, G Ch. *Genesis: Vol 2*. Translated by William Heynen. Bible Student's Commentary. Grand Rapids: Zondervan Publishing House, 1981.

Aelred of Rievaulx. *Spiritual Friendship*. Translated by Mary Eugene Laker. Washington, D.C.: Cistercian Publications, Consortium Press, 1974.

Andersen, Francis I, and David Noel Freedman. *Hosea: A New Translation with Introduction and Commentary*. The Anchor Bible. Vol. 24. Garden City, NY: Doubleday and Co., Inc., 1980.

Annaud, Jean-Jacques, director. *The Name of the Rose*. N.p.: Neve Constantin Film Productions, 1986.

Aquinas, St Thomas. *Summa Theologica*. Pt I; Pt II-II.

Arbuckle, Gerald. 'Seminary Formation as a Pilgrimage'. *Human Development* 7, no. 1 (Spring 1986): 27-33.

Au, Wilkie'. Particular Friendships Revisited'. *Human Development* 7, no. 1 (Spring 1986): 34-38.

Auden, WH. 'For the Time Being'. *Collected Poems*. Edited by Edward Mendelson. New York: Random House, 1976.

Audet, Jean Paul. *Structures of Christian Priesthood*. Translated by Rosemary Sheed. New York: The Macmillan Co., 1967.

Augustine, *Christian Doctrine*. As cited in *Sum. Th.* II-II.

— *The City of God*, VII-XVI. Translated by Gerald G. Walsh and Grace Monahan.

— *The Fathers of the Church*. Vol. 14. New York: The Fathers of the Church, 1952.

— *Confessions*. Translated by F J Sheed. New York: Sheed and Ward, 1942.

— *The Confessions of St Augustine*. Translated by Rex Warner. New York: The New American Library of World Literature, Inc., 1963.

— *The Trinity*. Translated by Stephen McKenna, *The Fathers of the Church*. Vol. 45. Washington, D.C.: The Catholic University of America Press, 1963.

'Awaken the Promise: Vocation Ministry in the United States'. Religious Vocations Conference, San Mateo, CA. September 6-10, 1990 as reported in *National Catholic Reporter*, 21 September 1990.

Baltazar, Eulalio R. *God Within Process*. Paramus, NJ: Newman Press, 1970.

Balthazar, Hans Urs von. *Love Alone*. Translated and edited by Alexander Dru. New York: Herder and Herder, 1969.

Barclay, William. *The Gospel of John*. Vol. 2. Rev. ed. Philadelphia: The Westminster Press, 1975,

— *The Letters of John and Jude* . Rev.ed. Philadelphia: The Westminster Press, 1976

— *New Testament Words*. Philadelphia: The Westminster Press, 1974.

Barrosse, Thomas. *Christianity: Mystery of Love: An Essay in Bibilical Theology*. Notre Dame: Fides Publishers, Inc., 1964.

Barth, Karl. *The Epistle to the Romans*. Translated by Edwyn C Hoskyns. 6th ed. London: Oxford University Press, 1965.

Berdyaev, Nicholas. *The Destiny of Man*. New York: Harper Torchbooks, 1960.

Bernardin, Joseph L. 'I am Joseph, Your Brother'. Homily for evening prayer upon taking residency in the See of Chicago. 25 Aug 1982. Photocopy of text, given to author.

Bernard. *Opera* 7. Edited by J Leclercq and H Rochais. Rome: Editiones Cistercienses, 1963. Cited in Jean Leclercq. *Monks and Love in Twelfth-Century France*. Oxford: Clarendon Press, 1979.

Bernard. *The Works of Bernard of Clairvaux: Treatises* 2. Vol. 5. Translated by Jean Leclercq and Henri Rochais. Cistercian Fathers Series, no. 13. Rome: Editiones Cistercienses, Washington, D.C.: Consortium Press, 1974.

Bilotta, Vincent M. *Sexual Emergence as an Access to the Spiritual Life*. Spiritual Health Series, no. 2. Whitinsville, MA: Affirmation Books, 1981.

Bishops' Committee on Priestly Formation, The. *The Program of Continuing Education of Priests*. Washington D.C.: National Conference of Catholic Bishops, 1972.

Bishops' Committee on Priestly Formation, The. *Spiritual Formation in The Catholic Seminary*. Washington, D.C.: National Conference of Catholic Bishops, 1984.

Bishops' Committee on Priestly Life and Ministry, The. *A Reflection Guide on Human Sexuality and the Ordained Priesthood*. Washington, D.C.: National Conference of Catholic Bishops, 1983.

Bishops' Committee on Priestly Life and Ministry, The. 'Reflections on the Morale of Priests'. *Origins* 18, no. 31 (12 January 1989): 497, 499-505.

Bishops' Committee on Priestly Life and Ministry, The. *The Health of American Catholic Priests: A Report and A Study*. Washington, D.C.: United States Catholic Conference, 1985.

Bishops' Committee on Priestly Life and Ministry, The. *The Priest and Stress*. Washington, D.C.: United States Catholic Conference, 1982.

Blenkinsopp, Joseph. *Celibacy, Ministry, Church*. New York: Herder and Herder, 1968; 'Deuteronomy'. *JBC* 1:6, 101-122.

Bly, Robert. *Iron John: A Book About Men*. Reading, MA: Addison-Wesley Publishing Co. Inc., 1990.

Bono, Agostino. 'Synod of Bishops Reaffirms Traditional Priestly Practices'. *Catholic News Service* as printed in *Florida Catholic*, 2 November 1990, 18.

Borders, William. 'Archbishop Borders' Pastoral Letter: Human Sexuality'. *Origins* 16 (30 April 1987): 807-15.

Boylan, M Eugene. *The Spiritual Life of the Priest*. Cork: The Mercier Press, 1962.

Brickley, Michael J. Address to the Ordination Class of 1972. The Jesuit School of Theology. Photocopy of speech, given to author.

Brown, Raymond E. *The Epistles of John*. The Anchor Bible. Vol. 30. Garden City, NY: Doubleday and Co., 1982; *The Gospel According to John* (13-21). The Anchor Bible Vol. 9A. Garden City, NY: Doubleday and Co., Inc., 1970.

Brown, Raymond E, Joseph A Fitzmyer, and Roland E. Murphy. *Jerome Biblical Commentary*. Vol. 1. *7 e Old Testament;* Vol. 2. *The New Testament and Topical Articles* (both bound in one book). Englewood Cliffs, NJ: Prentice-Hall, Inc., 1968.

Brueggemann, Walter. *Tradition for Crises: A Study in Hosea*. Richmond John Knox Press, 1968.

Buber, Martin. *At The Turning*. New York: Martin Buber, 1952.

— *Between Man and Man*. Translated by Ronald Gregor Smith. New York: The Macmillan Co., 1972.

— 'Cheruth'. An address, given in Vienna in 1919. Quoted in Nahum Glatzer, ed. *The Way of Response: Martin Buber: Selections from His Writings.*

— *I and Thou*. Translated by Ronald Gregor Smith. 2d ed. New York: Charles Scribner's Sons, 1958;

— *Pointing the Way: Collected Essays*. Translated and edited by Maurice Friedman. London: Rutledge and Kegan Paul, 1957.

Bultmann, Rudolf. *The Gospel of John: A Commentary*. Translated and edited by GR Beasley-Murray with RWN Hoare and JK Riches. Philadelphia: The Westminster Press, 1976.

Burke, Eugene P. 'St Jerome as a Spiritual Director'. In *A Monument to Saint Jerome: Essays on Some Aspects of His Life, Works and Influence*. Edited by Francis X Murphy. New York: Sheed and Ward, 1952.

Bush, Bernard J. 'Celibacy, Affectivity and Friendship'. *The Way Supplement* 47 (Summer 1983): 72-79.

Buttrick, George A, ed. *The Interpreter's Bible*. Vol. 7. New York: Abingdon Press, 1951.

— ed. *The Interpreter's Dictionary of the Bible*. E-J. New York: Abingdon Press, 1962.

CBS News Report. Aired 25 October 1990.

Cahill, Lisa Sowle. *Between the Sexes: Foundations for a Christian Ethics of Sexuality*. Philadelphia: Fortress Press, 1985.

Campbell, Edward F. Jr. *Ruth: A New Translation with Introduction, Notes and Commentary*. The Anchor Bible Vol. 7. Garden City, NY: Doubleday and Co., Inc., 1975.

Capps, Walter Holden, and Wendy M. Wright, eds. *Silent Fire: An Ivitation to Western Mysticism*. San Francisco: Harper and Row, Publishers, 1978.

Cardman, Francine. 'Singleness and Spirituality'. *Spirituality Today* 35, no. 4 (Winter 1983): 304-18.

Carr, Ann. 'Theology and Experience in the Thought of Karl Rahner'. *Journal of Religion* 53 (July 1973): 359-76.

Carson, D.A. 'Matthew'. In *The Expositor's Bible Commentary*. Vol. 8. Edited by Frank E. Gaebelein. 12 vols. Grand Rapids: Zondervan Publishing House, 1984.

Catholic Theological Society of America. Anthony Kosnik, Chairperson. *Human Sexuality: New Directions in American Catholic Thought*. New York: Paulist Press, 1977.

Catholic Trends 19, no. 1 (12 November 1988).

'Celibacy Key Factor For Young Adults'. *National Catholic Reporter*, 21 September 1990, 4.

Center for Human Development. *A Report on Phase One of the Ministry to Priests Program in the Archdiocese of Miami*. Washington, D.C.: Center for Human Development, 1981.

Charue, AM, P Chauchard, H Crouzel, G Cruchon, A de Bouis, J Folliet, J Guitton, P Hacker, L Hodl, H Hoffner, H Jedin, J Kosnetter, L Legrand, L Leloir, M Marini, JP Massaut, Nedoncelle, G Rambaldi, AM Stickler, F van Steenberghen, and J Coppens. *Priesthood and Celibacy*. Milan, Editrice Ancora, n.d. [post Vat. II].

Chauchard, Paul. *Our Need of Love*. Translated by Una Morrissy. New York: P.J. Kennedy and Sons, 1968.

Clark, Elizabeth A. *Jerome, Chrysostom, and Friends*. Studies in Women and Religion. Vol. 2. New York: The Edwin Mellen Press, 1979.

Clark, Matthew, 'On Hearing the Wisdom of the People', *Origins* 20 (20 December 1990): 445, 227, 453.

Clark, Keith. *Being Sexual ... and Celibate*. Notre Dame: Ave Maria Press, 1986.

— *An Experience of Celibacy: A Creative Reflection on Intimacy, Loneliness, Sexuality and Commitment*. Notre Dame: Ave Maria Press, 1982.

Codex Iuris Canonici (1918), Canon 132.1.

Coleman, John. 'Choosing a Metaphor for Ordained Ministry Today'.

Origins 20, no. 37 (21 February 1991): 601-9.

Conner, Paul M. *Celibate Love*. Huntington, IN: Our Sunday Visitor, Inc., 1979.

Conway, Jim. *Men in Mid-Life Crises*. Elgin, IL: David C Cook Publishing Co., 1978.

Council of Ancyra. Canon 10, 67. *The Seven Ecumenical Councils*. A Select Library of Nicene and Post-Nicene Fathers, Vol. 14. Edited by Henry R Percival. Grand Rapids, MI: W B Eerdmans Publishing Co., n.d.

Council of Elvira. Canon 33. E Hispano. *Concilos Visigoticos*. Barcelona, 1963.

Council of Neocaesarea. Canon 1, 79. *The Seven Ecumenical Councils*. A Select Library of Nicene and Post-Nicene Fathers, Vol. 14. Edited by Henry R Percival. Grand Rapids, MI: W B Eerdmans Publishing Co., n.d.

Council of Trent. Session XXIV C 9-10, de Matrimonio Joseph Alberigo, *et al. Conciliorum Oecumenicorum Decreta*. Frieburg: Herder, 1962.

Council of Trullo. Canon 13, 371. *The Seven Ecumenical Councils*. A Select Library of Nicene and Post-Nicene Fathers. Vol. 14. Edited by Henry R Percival. Grand Rapids, MI: W B Eerdmans Publishing Co., n.d.

Crouzel, Henri. 'Celibacy and Ecclesiastical Continence in the Early Church: The Motives Involved'. *Priesthood and Celibacy*, ed., AM Charue, *et al.*, 451-502. Milan: Editrice Ancora, n.d. [post Vat. II].

Cuenot, Claude. *Teilhard de Chardin: A Biographical Study*. Baltimore: Helicon Press, 1965.

Curran, Charles E. *Directions in Fundamental and Moral Theology*. Notre Dame: University of Notre Dame Press, 1985.

Dante. Cited by Thomas Merton. *Disputed Questions*. New York: Farrar, Straus and Cudahy, 1960.

— *Paradise*, X. 55-61. Cited by Janie Gustafson. *Celibate Passion*. San Francisco: Harper and Row, Publishers, 1978.

DeBlassie, Richard R. 'Intimacy in Pastoral Care'. *Human Development* 7, no. 2 (Summer 1986): 27-31.

deCastillejo, Irene Claremont. *Knowing Woman: A Feminine Psychology*. New York: Harper and Row, Publishers, 1973.

Decourtray, Albert. 'Roles for Women in Priestly Formation'. *Origins* 20, no. 20 (25 October 1990): 332.

Derlega, Valerian J, ed. *Communication, Intimacy and Close Relationships*. Orlando, FL: Harcourt Brace Jovanovich, Publishers, 1984.

Devereaux, Martin. 'An Analysis of Individual Growth Among Priests in Ministry To Priests Programs Options, As Measured by the Personal Orientation Inventory'. Ph.D. diss. Nova University School of Professional Psychology, 1984.

DeVine, Richard J. *Holy Virginity: A Study of the New Testament Teaching on Virginity and Celibacy*. Rome: Typis Ponticiae University, 1964.

Dictionary of the Bible. 1973 ed. S.v. 'Love', by John L. McKenzie.

Dictionary of the New Testament. 1980 ed. S.v. 'Love', by Xavier Leon-Dufour.

Dictionary of Theology. 1981 ed. S.v. 'Love', by Karl Rahner and Herbert Vorgrimler.

Dinter, Paul E. 'Getting Some Respect'. *Church* 3, no. 3 (Fall 1987): 3-7.

Dodd, CH. *Gospel and Law: The Relation of Faith and Ethics in Early Christianity*. New York: Columbia University Press, 1963.

Donnelly, Dody H. *Radical Love: An Approach to Sexual Spirituality*. Minneapolis: Winston Press, Inc., 1984.

Drilling, Peter J. 'Fellow Pilgrim and Pastoral Leader: Spirituality for the Secular Priest'. *Spirituality Today* 35 (Winter 83): 319-335.

Druck, Ken, and James Simmons. *The Secrets Men Keep*. Garden City, NY: Doubleday and Co., Inc., 1985.

Dunne, John S. *The Reasons of the Heart*. New York: Macmillan Publishing Co., Inc., 1978.

Durkin, Mary G. *Feast of Love: Pope John Paul II on Human Intimacy*. Chicago: Loyola University Press, 1983.

Eisler, Riane. *The Chalice and the Blade: Our History, Our Future*. San Francisco: Harper and Row, Publishers, 1987.

Erikson, Erik H. *Childhood and Society*. 2nd ed., rev. New York: W W Norton and Co., Inc., 1963.

— *Identity: Youth and Crises*. London: Faber and Faber, 1968.

— *Insight and Responsibility: Lectures on the Ethical Implications of Psychoanalytic Insight*. New York: W W Norton and Co., Inc., 1964.

Espin, Orlando. 'The Concept of Incarnate Being in the Philosophy of Gabriel Marcel'. BA Thesis, St. Vincent de Paul Regional Seminary, 1968.

Evans, GR. *The Mind of St. Bernard of Clairvaux* . Oxford: Clarendon Press, 1983.

Ferguson, Marilyn. *The Aquarian Conspiracy: Personal and Social Transformation in the 1980s*. Los Angeles: J.P. Tarcher, Inc., 1980.

Fiorenza, Elisabeth Schüssler. *Bread Not Stone: The Challenge of Feminist Biblical Interpretation*. Boston: Beacon Press, 1984.

Fitzmeyer, Joseph A. 'The Letter to the Romans'. *JBC* 2:53, 291-331.

Flannery, Austin, gen. ed. *Vatican Council II: The Conciliar and Post Conciliar Documents*. Boston: Daughters of St Paul, 1980.

Florida Bishops. 'Heritage of Love'. *Origins* 17 (21 January 1988): 552-3.

Forrest, Tom, ed. *'Be Holy!' God's First Call to Priests Today*. South Bend:

Greenlawn Press, 1987.

Fourez, Gerard. *A Light Grasp on Life: An Essay on the Evangelical Life and Celibacy*. Abingdon, n.p., 1973. Cited by Bernard Bush, 'Celibacy, Affectivity and Friendship'. *The Way Supplement* 47 (Summer, 1983): 72-79.

Fowler, James W. *Stages of Faith. The Psychology of Human Development and the Quest for Meaning*. San Francisco: Harper and Row, Publishers, 1981.

Fox, Matthew. *Meditations with Meister Eckhart*. Santa Fe, NM: Bear and Co., 1982.

— *A Spirituality Named Compassion And the Healing of the Global Village, Humpty Dumpty and Us*. Minneapolis: Winston Press, 1979.

Francis de Sales. *Introduction to A Devout Life*. Ratisbon and Rome: Frederick Pustet and Co., n.d.

— *Treatise on the Love of God*. Translated by Henry Benedict Mackey. Library of St. Francis de Sales. Vol. 2. London: Burns, Oates and Washbourne, Ltd., [1884].

Frankl, Victor E. *Man's Search for Meaning: An Introduction to Logotherapy*. Rev. ed. New York: Washington Square Press, Pocket Books, 1963.

Franklin, James L. 'Contemporary Studies on the Priest Shortage'. *Progressions*. A Lilly Endowment Occasional Report: 1, no. 2 (June 1990): 7-10.

Frein, George, ed. *Celibacy: The Necessary Option*. New York: Herder and Herder, 1968.

Fromm, Erich. *The Art of Loving*. New York: Bantam Books, Harper and Row, Publishers, Inc., 1956.

Fuchs, Josef. *Christian Ethics in a Secular Arena*. Translated by Bernard Hoose and Brian McNeil. Washington, D.C.: Georgetown University Press, 1984.

— Class Lectures given at St Vincent de Paul Regional Seminary. Boynton Beach, FL, January – March 1986

Gaebelein, Frank E. *The Expositor's Bible Commentary*. Vol. 8. New York: Abingdon Press, 1984.

— *The Expositor's Bible Commentary*. Vol. 10. Grand Rapids: Zondervan Publishing House, 1976.

Gallagher, Charles A, and Thomas L. Vandenberg. *The Celibacy Myth: Loving for Life*. New York: The Crossroad Publishing Co., 1987.

Gallagher, Kenneth T. *The Philosophy of Gabriel Marcel*. Foreword by Garbriel Marcel. New York: Fordham University Press, 1966.

Gibran, Kahlil. *The Prophet*. New York: Alfred A Knopf, Inc., 1969.

Gill, James J. 'The Development of Persons'. *Human Development* 2: 29-39.

Gilligan, Carol. *In a Different Voice: Psychological Theory and Women's Dev-*

elopment. Cambridge, MA: Harvard University Press, 1982.

Gilmartin, Richard J. 'Coping with Humanity'. *Coping: Issues of Emotional Living In an Age of Stress For Clergy and Religious*, by the First Boston Psychotheological Symposium, 37-56. Whitinsville, MA: Affirmation Books, 1976.

Girzone, Joseph F. *The Shepherd.* New York: MacMillan Publishing Co., 1990.

Glatzger, Nahum N, ed. *The Way of Response: Martin Buber: Selections from His Writings.* New York: Schocken Books, 1976.

Goergen, Donald. *The Power of Love: Christian Spirituality and Theology*. Chicago: The Thomas More Press, 1979.

— *The Sexual Celibate.* New York: The Seabury Press, A Crossroads Book, 1974.

— *The Sexuality of the Celibate*. Lecture series on tape. Boynton Beach, FL: St Vincent de Paul Regional Seminary, n.d.

Goerres, Ida Friederike. *Is Celibacy Outdated?* Translated by Barbara Waldstein-Wartenberg. Westminster, MD: Newman Press, 1965.

Gosmer, Rachel. *Gender and God: Love and Desire in Christian Spirituality*. N.p., Cowley Publications, 1986.

Goudreault, Henri. 'Corresponsibility of Priests and Laity'. *Origins* 20, no. 20 (25 October 1990): 329-330.

Greeley, Andrew. *The Catholic Priest in the United States: Sociological Investigations*. Washington, D.C.: Publications Office, United States Catholic Conference, 1972.

Grogan, Brian. 'Theological Trends: Is There Direct Experience of God? *The Way* 22 (April 1982): 122-33.

Guggenbuhl-Craig, Adolf. *Power in the Helping Professions*. New York: Spring Publications, 1971.

Guindon, Andre. *The Sexual Language: An Essay in Moral Theology*. Ottawa: The University of Ottawa Press, 1977.

Gula, Richard M. *What Are They Saying About Moral Norms?* New York: Paulist Press, 1982.

Gutierrez, Gustavo. *We Drink From Our Own Wells: The Spiritual Journey of a People*. Translated by Matthew J O'Connell. Maryknoll NY: Orbis Books, 1984.

Gustafson, Janie. *Celibate Passion*. San Francisco: Harper and Row, Publishers, 1978.

Hanigan, James P. *What Are They Saying About Sexual Morality?* New York: Paulist Press, 1982.

Häring, Bernard. *Free and Faithful in Christ: Moral Theology for Priests and Laity*, Vol. 2. *The Truth Will Set You Free.* New York: The Seabury Press,

A Crossroad Book 1979.

Harlow, Harry F. 'The Nature of Love'. *American Psychologist* 13 (1958): 673-85.

Harnan, Nicholas. *A Spirituality of the Heart.* Spiritual Health Series, no. 7. Whitinsville, MA: Affirmation Books, 1982.

Harris, Sydney J. *The Authentic Person: Dealing With Dilemma* . Niles, IL: Argus Communications, 1972.

Harrison, Everett F 'Romans'. *In The Expositor's Bible Commentary.* Vol. 10. Edited by Frank E Gaebelein. 12 vols. Grand Rapids: Zondervan Publishing House, 1976.

Hassel, David J. *Dark Intimacy: Hope for Those in Difficult Prayer-Experiences.* New York: Paulist Press, 1986.

Hatfield, Elaine. 'The Dangers of Intimacy'. In *Communication, Intimacy and Close Relationships,* ed. Valerian J Derlega, 207-20. Orlando, FL: Harcourt Brace Jovanovich, Publishers, 1984.

Heris, Charles V. *Spirituality of Love.* Translated by David Martin. St Louis: B. Herder Book Co., 1965.

Hermand, Pierre. *The Priest: Celibate or Married.* Baltimore: Helicon, 1965.

Hickey, James. 'The Laity's Role in Priestly Formation'. *Origins* 20, no. 20 (25 October 1990): 322-23.

Hoge, Dean R. 'Carrying Out Ministry in a Priest Shortage'. Lecture given at the Future of the American Church Conference, Washington DC, 29 September 1990.

— 'The Future of Catholic Leadership: Responses to the Priest Shortage'. Kansas City: Sheed and Ward, 1987.

Hollander, MH, and AJ Mercer. 'Wish to Be Held and Wish to Hold in Men and Women'. *Archives of General Psychiatry* 33 (1976): 48-51.

Hollaway, Ida Nelle. *Loneliness: The Untapped Resource.* Nashville: The Boardman Press, 1982.

Holley, Bobbie Lee. *Person to Person*. Austin, TX: Sweet Publishing Co., 1969.

Huddleston, Mary Anne, ed. *Celibate Loving: Encounters in Three Dimensions.* New York: Paulist Press, 1984.

Hussey, M Edmund. 'Needed: A Theology of Priesthood'. *Origins* 17 (4 February 1988): 577-83.

Interpreter's Dictionary of the Bible. E-J. Edited by George A. Buttrick. New York: Abingdon Press, 1962.

Jackson, Edgar N. *Understanding Loneliness.* Philadelphia: Fortress Press, 1980.

Jerome. Letter 45; Letter 65. *Corpus Scriptorum Ecclesiasticorum Latinorum*. Cited in Elizabeth A. Clark. *Jerome, Chrysostom, and Friends*. Studies in

Women and Religion. Vol. 2. New York: The Edwin Mellen Press, 1979.
— *The Letters of Saint Jerome*. Vol. 1. Translated by Charles Christopher Mierow. Ancient Christian Writers, no. 33 Westminster, MD: The Newman Press, 1963.
— *To Eustochium 20. Corpus Scriptorum Ecclesiasticorum Latinorum*, 54. Cited by John T Noonan in 'Celibacy in the Fathers of the Church'. In *Celibacy: The Necessary Option*, ed. George Frein, 151. New York: Herder and Herder, 1968.
John of the Cross. *Dark Night of the Soul*. Translated by E Allison Peers. Garden City, NY: Doubleday and Co., Inc., Image Books, 1959.
— *Spiritual Canticle*. Translated by E Allison Peers. Garden City, N Y: Doubleday, Image Books, 1961.
John Paul II. *Apostolic Exhortation: The Role of the Christian Family in the Modern World (Familiaris Consortio)*. Boston: Daughters of St Paul, 1982.
— 'Homily Opening 1990 Synod of Bishops'. *Origins* 20, no.18 (11 October 1990): 281, 283-84.
— Letter to Priests, '*Novo Incipiente Nostro*', (6 April 1979). *Acta Apostolicae Sedis* 71 (1979): 393-417.
— *Physics, Philosophy and Theology: A Common Quest for Understanding*. Notre Dame: University of Notre Dame Press [1988]. Cited in *Catholic Trends* 19, no. 1 (12 November 1988): 1.
Johnson, Robert A. *He: Understanding Masculine Psychology*. New York: Harper and Row, Publishers, Perennial Library, 1977.
— *She. Understanding Feminine Psychology*. New York: Harper and Row, Publishers, Perennial Library, 1977.
Johnson, Sherman. 'The Gospel According to St. Matthew'. In *The Interpreter's Bible*, Vol. 7. Edited by George A Buttrick. 12 vols. New York: Abingdon Press, 1951.
Jordan of Saxony. *To Heaven With Diana*. Translated by Gerald Vann. Chicago: Henry Regnery Co., 1965.
Jourard, Sidney M. *The Transparent Self*. Rev. ed. New York: Van Nostrand Reinhold Co., 1971.
Judd, Mary. *Love and Lifestyles: Building Relationships in a Changing Society*. Winona, MN: St. Mary's Press, Christian Brothers' Publications, 1981.
Jung, C.G. *Two Essays on Analytical Psychology*. Edited by Sir Herbert Read, Michael Fordham, and Gerhard Adler. Translated by RFC Hull, 2d ed. Bollingen Series 20. New York: Pantheon Books, 1966.

Keane, Philip, 'The Meaning and Functioning of Sexuality of Sexuality in the Lives of Celibates and Virgins', *Review for Religious* 34, (1975), 312-17.

Kagan, J. *Change and Continuity in Infancy*. New York: Wiley and Co., 1971.

Kaufman, Philip S. 'An Immoral Morality?' *Commonweal*, 12 September 1980, 496 as in Ohanneson, 93.

Keane, Philip S. *Sexual Morality: A Catholic Perspective*. New York: Paulist Press, 1977.

Keen, Sam. *Fire in the Belly: On Being A Man*. New York: Bantam Books, 1991.

Kehl, Medard. 'Hans Urs von Balthasar: A Portrait'. In *The von Balthasar Reader*. Edited by Medard Kehl and Werner Loser. Translated by Robert J. Daly and Fred Lawrence. New York: A Crossroad Book, 1982.

Keller, Helen. Quoted by Ken Druck and James C Simmons, in *The Secrets Men Keep*. Garden City, NY: Doubleday and Co., Inc., 1985.

Kelley, CF. *The Spirit of Love*. New York: Harper and Brothers Publishers, 1951.

Kenel, Mary Elizabeth. 'A Celibate's Sexuality and Intimacy'. *Human Development* 7, no. 1 (Spring 1986): 14-19.

Kennedy, Eugene. *The Heart of Loving*. Niles, IL: Argus Communications, 1973.

— *A Time For Being Human*. Garden City, NY: Doubleday and Co., Inc., Image Books, 1987.

— *A Time For Love*. Garden City, NY: Doubleday and Co., Inc., 1970.

Kennedy, Eugene C, and Victor S. Heckler. *The Catholic Priest in the United States: Psychological Investigations*. Washington, D.C.: Publications Office, United States Catholic Conference, 1972.

Kennedy, E, V Heckler, F Kobler, and R Walker. 'Clinical Assessment of a Profession: Roman Catholic Clergyman'. *Journal of Clinical Psychology* 33 (1977): 120-28. Cited in Martin Devereaux. 'An Analysis of Individual Growth Among Priests in Ministry To Priests Programs Options, As Measured by the Personal Orientation Inventory'. Ph.D. diss. Nova University School of Professional Psychology, 1984.

Kierkegaard, Søren. Translated by Howard and Edna Hong. *Works of Love*. New York: Harper and Row, Publishers, Harper Torchbooks, 1962.

Kiesling, Christopher. *Celibacy, Prayer and Friendship: A Making-Sense-Out-of-Life Approach*. New York: Alba House, 1978.

Kilgore, James E. *The Intimate Man: Intimacy and Masculinity in the 80s*. Nashville: Abingdon Press, 1984.

Kimmerling, Ben. 'Friendship between Women and Priests'. *The Furrow* 41, no. 10 (October 1990): 541-51.

King, J Norman. 'The Experience of God in The Theology of Karl Rahner'. *Thought* 53 (June 1978): 174-202.

Kinsey, Alfred C, Wardell B. Pomeroy, and Clyde E. Martin. *Sexual Behavior in the Human Male*. Philadelphia: W.B. Saunders Co., 1948.

Kittel, Gerhard, ed. *Theological Dictionary of the New Testament*. Vols. 1 and 9. Translated by Geoffrey W Bromiley. 9 vols. Grand Rapids: William B. Eerdmans Publishing Co., 1964.

Knight, David. *The Good News about Sex*. N.p.: St Anthony Messenger Press, 1979.

Kosnik, Anthony. *Human Sexuality: New Directions in American Catholic Thought*. New York: Paulist Press, 1977.

Kraft, William. 'Celibate Genitality'. In *Celibate Loving*, ed., Mary Anne Huddleston, 69-90. New York: Paulist Press, 1984.

Kuhn, Thomas S. *The Structure of Scientific Revolutions*. Chicago: The University of Chicago Press, 1962.

Küng, Hans. 'Hans Küng Writes the Pope About Celibacy'. *National Catholic Reporter*, 16 May 1980, 15-16.

— ed. *Life in the Spirit*. New York: Sheed and Ward, 1967.

Laeuchli, Samuel. *Power and Sexuality: The Emergence of Canon Law at the Synod of Elvira*. Philadelphia: Temple University Press, 1972.

Larkin, Ernest E, and Gerard T Broccolo. *Spiritual Renewal of the American Priesthood*. Washington, D.C.: Publications Office of the United States Catholic Conference, 1973.

Lea, Henry. *History of Sacerdotal Celibacy in the Christian Church*. New York: Russel and Russel, 1957.

Leclercq, Jean. *Bernard of Clairvaux and the Cistercian Spirit*. Translated by Claire Lavoie. Cistercian Studies Series, no. 16. Kalamazoo, MI: Cistercian Publications, 1976.

— *Monks and Love in Twelfth-Century France*. Oxford: Clarendon Press, 1979.

Leech, Kenneth. *Soul Friend: The Practice of Christian Spirituality*. San Francisco: Harper and Row, Publishers, 1977.

Lepp, Ignace. *The Psychology of Loving*. Translated by Bernard B Gilligan. Baltimore: Helicon, 1963.

Levinson, Daniel J, with Charlotte. Darrow, Edward B. Klein, Maria H. Levinson, and Braxton McKee. *The Seasons of a Man's Life*. New York: Alfred A. Knopf, 1985.

Lewis, C.S. *The Four Loves*. New York: Harcourt Brace Jovanovich, Publishers, 1960.

Liebescheutz, JHWG *Antioch: City and Imperial Administration in the Later Roman Empire*. Oxford: Clarendon Press, 1972. Cited by Elizabeth A. Clark, in *Jerome, Chrysostom, and Friends*. Studies in Women and Religion. Vol. 2. New York: The Edwin Mellen Press, 1979.

Linn, Matthew, and Dennis Linn. *Healing Life's Hurts: Healing Memories Through Five Stages of Forgiveness*. New York: Paulist Press, 1978.

Loftus, John Allan. *The Integration of Psychology and Religion:-An Uneasy Alliance*. Spiritual Health Series, no. 4. Whitinsville, MA: Affirmation Books, 1981.

Lonergan, Bernard JF *Insight: A Study of Human* Understanding. Rev. student ed. New York: Philosophical Library, 1958.

— *Method in Theology*. New York: Herder and Herder, 1972.

Lukas, Mary, and Ellen Lukas. *Teilhard. The Man, The Priest, The Scientst*. Garden City, NY: Doubleday and Co., 1977.

Lynch, John E 'Marriage and the Celibacy of the Clergy, The Discipline of the Western Church: An Historical-Canonical Synopsis'. *The Jurist* 32 (1972): 1114-38.

Lynch, Timothy. 'Celibacy and the Clerical State'. An unpublished paper submitted for JCL degree at Catholic University, Washington, DC, 1987.

Macrae, Janet. *Therapeutic Touch: A Practical Guide*. New York: Alfred A. Knopf, Inc., 1988.

Mahoney, John. *The Making of Moral Theology: A Study of the Roman Catholic Tradition*. Oxford: Clarendon Press, 1987.

Mally, Edward J. 'The Gospel According to Mark'. *JBC* 2:42, 21-61.

Maloney, George A. *Called to Intimacy: Living In the Indwelling Presence*. New York: Alba House, 1983.

Mann, CS *Mark: A New Translation with Introduction and Commentary*. The Anchor Bible. Vol. 27. Garden City, NY: Doubleday and Co., Inc., 1986.

Marcel, Gabriel. *Being and Having*. London: Collins, The Fontana Library, 1965.

— *Creative Fidelity*. Translated by Robert Rosthal. New York: The Noonday Press, Farrar, Straus and Giroux, 1964.

— *Les Coeur des Autres*. Paris: Librarie Grasset, 1921.

— *Metaphysical Journal*. Translated by Bernard Wall. Chicago: Henry Regnery Co., A Gateway Edition, 1952.

— *The Mystery of Being*. Vol. 2. *Faith and Reality*. Translated by G.S. Fraser. Chicago: Henry Regnery Co., 1951.

Marshall, John. 'Strengths and Weaknesses of U.S. Seminaries. *Origins* 17, no. 30 (7 January 1988): 522-8.

Maslow, Abraham H *The Farther Reaches of Human Nature*. New York: The Viking Press, 1971.

— *Motivation and Personality*. 2d ed. New York: Harper and Row, Publishers, 1970.

— *Religions, Values, and Peak Experiences*. Colombus: Ohio State University Press, 1964.

— *Toward A Psychology of Being*. Princeton: D. Van Nostrand Co., Inc., 1962.

May, Gerald G. *Will and Spirit: A Contemplative Psychology*. San Francisco: Harper and Row, Publishers, 1982.

May, Rollo. *Love and Will*. New York: Dell Publishing Co., WW Norton and Co., Inc., 1969.

— *Man's Search for Himself*. New York: WW Norton and Co., Inc., 1953.

May, William E., ed. *Principles of Catholic Moral Life*. Chicago: Franciscan Herald Press, 1981.

Mays, James Luther. *Hosea: A Commentary*. London: SCM Press Ltd., 1969.

McBrien, Richard. *Catholiicism: Study Edition*. San Francisco: Harper and Row, Publishers, 1981.

McCarter, P Kyle Jr. I *Samuel: A New Translation with Introduction Notes and Commentary*. The Anchor Bible. Vol. 8. Garden City, NY: Doubleday and Co., Inc., 1980.

McCarthy, Dennis J. 'Hosea'. *JBC* 1:15, 253-64.

McCartney, James J. 'Contemporary Controversies in Sexual Ethics: A Case Study in Post-Vatican II Moral Theology'. In *Sexuality and Medicine*. Vol. 2. Edited by Earl E. Shelp. N.p.: D. Reidel Publishing Co., 1987.

McCool, Gerald, ed. *A Rahner Reader*. New York: The Crossroad Publishing Co., 1984.

McCown, Joseph. *Gabriel Marcel and the Phenomenology of Human Openness*. American Academy of Religion, Studies in Religion, no. 14. Missoula, MO: Scholars Press, 1978.

McCready, William C. 'Religion and the Life Cycle'. In *Toward Vatican III*, ed., David Tracy with Hans Küng and Johann B. Metz, 272-81. New York: Concilium, The Seabury Press, 1978.

McGill, Michael E *The McGill Report on Male Intimacy*. New York: Holt, Rhinehart and Winston, Perennial Library, 1986.

McGoey, John H. *Dare I Love*. Huntington, IN: Our Sunday Visitor, Inc., 1974.

McGoldrick, Desmond F. *Living the Celibate Life: An Essay in the Higher Psychology of Faith*. New York: Vantage Press, Inc., 1970.

McKenzie, John L. 'The Gospel According to Matthew'. *JBC* 2:43, 62-114.

McNamara, Marie Aquinas. *Friends and Friendship for Saint Augustine*. New York: Alba House – St Paul Publications, 1964.

McNamara, William. *Christian Mysticism: A Psycho-theology*. Chicago: Franciscan Herald Press, 1981.

— *Earthy Mysticism: Contemplation and the Life of Passionate Presence*. New York: The Crossroad Publishing Co., 1983.

— *Mystical Passion: Spirituality for a Bored Society*. New York: Paulist Press, 1977.

McNulty, Frank. 'The Tensions of Leadership: The Priest'. *New Catholic World* 223 (Sept/Oct 1980):228-31.

— 'AUS Priest Addresses the Pope'. *Origins* 17, no. 15 (24 September 1987): 231-4.

Meehan, Francis X. *A Contemporary Social Spirituality*. Maryknoll, NY: Orbis Books, 1982.

Menges, Robert J., and James E. Dittes. *Psychological Studies of Clergymen: Abstracts of Research*. New York: Thomas Nelson and Sons, 1965.

Merton, Thomas. *The Ascent to Truth*. New York: Harcourt, Brace and Co., 1951.

— *Disputed Questions*. New York: Farrar, Straus and Cudahy, 1960.

— *No Man Is An Island*. New York: Harcourt Brace Jovanovich, Publishers, 1955.

— *Thomas Merton on St. Bernard*. Cistercian Studies Series, no. 9. Kalamazoo, MI: Cistercian Publications, 1980.

Metz, Johannes Baptist. *Poverty of Spirit*. Translated by John Drury. Paramus, NJ: Newman Press, 1968.

Miguens, Manuel. 'On Being a Christian and the Moral Life: Pauline Perspectives'. In *Principles of Catholic Moral Life*. ed., William E. May, 89-110. Chicago: Franciscan Herald Press, 1981.

Miller, C. Lawrence. 'Treatment and Recovery of Alcoholics' Children'. *Human Development* 8, no. 4 (Winter 1987): 31-32.

Mitchell, Kenneth R. 'Priestly Celibacy from a Psychological Perspective'. In *Celibate Loving*, ed., Mary Anne Huddleston, 91-108. New York: Paulist Press, 1984.

Montagu, Ashley. *Touching – The Human Significance of the Skin*. New York: Harper and Row, Publishers, 172.

Moustakas, Clark E. *Loneliness*. New York: Prentice-Hall, Inc., 1961.

Murphy, Francis X., ed. *A Monument to Saint Jerome: Essays on Some Aspects of His Life, Works and Influence*. New York: Sheed and Ward, 1952.

Naisbitt, John. *Megatrends: Ten New Directions Transforming Our Lives*. New York: Warner Books, 1984.

Nelson, James B. *Embodiment: An Approach to Sexuality and Christian Theology*. Minneapolis: Augsburg Publishing House, 1978.

— *The Intimate Connection: Male Sexuality, Masculine Spirituality*. Philadelphia: The Westminster Press, 1988.

Nelson's Expository Dictionary of the Old Testament. Edited by Merrill F. Unger and William White. Nashville: Thomas Nelson Publishers, 1980.

Neuman, Matthias. 'Living Celibately in Pastoral Ministry'. *Human Development* 7, no. 3 (Fall 1986): 38-40.

New American Bible. St. Joseph Edition. New York: Catholic Book Publishing Co., 1970.

Noonan, John T. 'Celibacy in the Fathers of the Church'. *In Celibacy: the Necessary Option*, ed. George Frein, 138-51. New York: Herder and Herder, 1968.

Nouwen, Henri JM. *Clowning in Rome: Reflections on Solitude, Celibacy, Prayer and Contemplation* Garden City, NY: Image Books, 1979.

— *Intimacy: Essays in Pastoral Psychology*. San Francisco: Harper and Row, Publishers, 1969.

— *Lifesigns: Intimacy, Fecundity, and Ecstacy in Christian Perspective.* Garden City, NY: Doubleday and Co., Inc., 1986.

— *The Living Reminder. Service and Prayer in Memory of Jesus Christ.*, New York: The Seabury Press, 1981.

— *Reaching Out: The Three Movements of the Spiritual Life*. Garden City, NY: Doubleday and Co., Inc., 1975.

— *The Way of the Heart.* New York: Ballantine Books, 1981.

— *The Wounded Healer*. Garden City, NY: Doubleday and Co., Inc., 1972.

O'Connell, Timothy E. *Principles for a Catholic Morality*. San Francisco: Harper and Row, Publishers, 1976.

Oden, Thomas. *Game Free: The Meaning of Intimacy*. New York: Harper and Row, Publishers, 1974.

Ó Fiaich, Tomas Cardinal, Kevin McNamara, Joseph Cunnane, and Thomas Morris. *Love Is For Life.* A Pastoral Letter Issued on Behalf of the Irish Hierarchy. Dublin: Veritas Publications, 1985.

Ohanneson, Joan. *And They Felt No Shame: Christians Reclaim Their Sexuality.* Minneapolis: Winston Press, 1983.

O'Meara, Thomas Franklin. *Theology of Ministry.* Ramsey, NJ: Paulist Press, 1983.

O'Neill, David. *Priestly Celibacy and Maturity.* New York: Sheed and Ward, 1965.

Oriason, Marc. Translated by Leonard Mayhew. New York: Sheed and Ward, Inc., 1967.

Origins. Vol. 20: no. 18 through no. 22 (11 October 1990 through 8 November 1990).

Pable, Martin W. 'Psychology and Asceticism of Celibacy'. In *Celibate Loving: Encounters in Three Dimensions*, ed. Mary Anne Huddleston, 11-28. New York: Paulist Press, 1984.

Palmer, Earl F. *The Intimate Gospel: Studies in John*. Waco, TX: Word Books, 1978.

— *Love Has its Reasons: An Inquiry into New Testament Love*. Waco, TX: Word Books, 1977.

Paul VI. Encyclical Letter on Priestly Celibacy, *Sacerdotalis Caelibatus* (24 June 1967). *Acta Apostolicae Sedis* 59 (1967): 657-97.

— Pope Paul VI to Vatican II (10 October 1965). *Concilium Vaticanum Secundum. Acta et Documenta* Vol. 12, Part I, 40.

Peck, M. Scott. *The Different Drum: Community Making and Peace*. New York: Simon and Schuster, 1987.

— *The Road Less Traveled: A New Psychology of Love, Traditional Values and Spiritual Growth*. New York: Simon and Schuster, A Touchstone Book, 1978.

Pennington, M. Basil. 'Two Treatises on Love'. *Saint Bernard of Clairvaux: Studies Commemorating the Eight Centenary of His Canonization*. Edited by M. Basil Pennington. Cistercian Studies Series, no. 28. Kalamazoo, MI: Cistercian Publications, 1977.

Pflieger, Michael. 'Celibacy'. In *Life in the Spirit*, ed. Hans Küng, 109-57. New York: Sheed and Ward, 1967.

Phillips, John. 'Bright Darkness: A Pastoral Reflection on Suffering'. Masters Thesis, St Vincent de Paul Regional Seminary, April 1986.

Pilarczyk, Daniel. 'The Changing Image of the Priest'. *Origins* 16, no 7 (3 July 1986): 137, 139-146.

Pittenger, Norman. *Loving Says It All*. New York: The Pilgrim Press, 1978.

— *Making Sexuality Human*. New York: The Pilgrim Press, 1979.

— *Process-Thought and Christian Faith*. New York: The Macmillan Co., 1968.

Pius XII. 'Encyclical Letter of His Holiness Pius XII on Holy Virginity'. *Selected Documents of His Holiness, Pius XII*. Washington DC: National Catholic Welfare Conference, 1954.

Pleck, Joseph H., and Jack Sawyer, eds. *Men and Masculinity*. Englewood Cliffs, NJ: Prentice-Hall, Inc., 1974.

Pogrebin, Letty Cottin. *Among Friends: Who We Like, Why We Like Them, and What We Do With Them*. New York: McGraw-Hill Book Company, 1987.

Polcino, Anna, ed. *Intimacy: Issues of Emotional Living in an Age of Stress for Clergy and Religious*. Whitinsville, MA: Affirmation Books, 1978.

Polcino, Anna. *Loneliness. The Genesis of Solitude, Friendship, and Contemplation*. Spiritual Health Series, no. 1. Whitinsville, MA: Affirmation Books, 1979.

Pope, Marvin H. *Song of Songs: A New Translation with Introduction and Commentary*. The Anchor Bible. Vol. 7c. Garden City, NY: Doubleday and Co., 1977.

Powell, John. *The Christian Vision: The Truth That Sets Us Free*. Allen, TX: Argus Communications, 1984.

— *Why Am I Afraid To Love?* Allen, TX: Argus Communications, 1982.

— *The Secret of Staying in Love.* Allen, TX: Argus Communications, 1974.

Quoist, Michel. *Prayers*. Translated by Agnes M. Forsyth and Anne Marie de Commaille. Kansas City: Sheed and Ward, 1963.

Raguin, Yves. *Celibacy for Our Times.* Translated by Mary Humbert Kennedy. Publication of the Religious Experience Series. Vol. 7. St Meinrad, IN: Abbey Press, 1974.

Rahner, Karl. *The Christian Commitment: Essays in Pastoral Theology.* Translated by Cecily Hastings. New York: Sheed and Ward, 1963.

— 'From Resentment to Gratitude'. An unpublished lecture. Cited in Martin Pable, 'Psychology and Asceticism of Celibacy'. In *Celibate Loving: Encounters in Three Dimensions,* ed. Mary Anne Huddleston, 11-28. New York: Paulist Press, 1984.

— *Grace In Freedom.* Translated by Hilda Graef. New York: Herder and Herder, 1969.

— 'Philosophy and Philosophising in Theology'. In *Theological Investigations.* Vol. 9. Translated by Graham Harrison. New York: Herder and Herder, London: Darton Longman and Todd, 1972.

— 'Reflections on the Unity of the Love of Neighbor and the Love of God'. *Theological Investigations*. Vol. 6. Translated by Karl-H. and Boniface Kruger. Baltimore: Helicon Press, London: Darton, Longman and Todd, 1969.

— *Servants of the Lord*. Translated by Richard Strachan. New York: Herder and Herder, 1968.

— *The Shape of the Church to Come*. Translated by Edward Quinn. New York: Seabury Press, A Crossroad Book, 1974.

— 'Theology of Freedom'. In *Theological Investigations*. Vol. 6. Translated by Karl-H. and Boniface Kruger. Baltimore: Helicon Press, London: Darton, Longman and Todd, 1969.

Ratzmann, George. 'The Contemporary Exacerbation of Loneliness and its Spiritual Effects on the Lives and Ministries of Priests'. Masters Thesis, St Vincent de Paul Regional Seminary, April, 1986.

Richardson, Lynda. 'Bishop Backs Ordaining Married Men'. *Washington Post,* 10 January 1991.

Riley, Maria. *Transforming Feminism.* Kansas City: Sheed and Ward, 1989.

Rilke, Rainer Maria. *Letters to a Young Poet*. Translated by Stephen Mitchell. New York: Random House, 1984.

Rogers, Carl R. *Counseling and Psychotherapy: Newer Concepts in Practice.* Boston: Houghton Mifflin Co., 1942.

— *On Becoming A Person: A Therapist's View of Psychotherapy.* Boston:

Houghton Mifflin Co., 1961.

Rohr, Richard. *The Price of Peoplehood.* Lectures from a priest's retreat. Cassette 923, St Anthony Messenger Tapes, 1979.

Rosato, Philip. 'Formation for Friendship'. *The Way Supplement* 56 (Summer 1986): 16-28.

Rousseau, Mary, and Charles Gallagher. *Sex is Holy*. Amity, NY: Amity House, 1986.

Sammon, Sean D. *Growing Pains in Ministry*. Whitinsville, MA: Affirmation Books, 1983.

— 'Understanding the Children of Alcoholic Parents'. *Human Development* 8, no. 3 (Fall 1987): 28-35.

Sanford, John A *The Invisible Partners: How the Male and Female in Each of Us Affects our Relationships.* New York: Paulist Press, 1980.

— *The Man Who Wrestled with God: Light From the Old Testament on the Psychology of Individuation.* New York: Paulist Press, 1974.

— *Ministry Burnout.* New York: Paulist Press,1982.

Sanford, John A. and George Lough. *What Men Are Like.* Mahwah, NY: Paulist Press, 1988.

Scanlon, Michael. J. Commencement Address given to the 1987 graduates of St Vincent de Paul Regional Seminary. Boynton Beach, FL, 13 May 1987.

Schillebeeckx, Edward. *Ministry: Leadership in the Community of Jesus Christ.* New York: Crossroad Publishing, 1981.

Schnackenburg, Rudolf. *The Gospel according to St. John: Vol.* 3. Translated by David Smith and G.A. Kon. New York: The Crossroad Publishing Co., Inc., 1982.

— *The Moral Teaching of the New Testament.* Translated by J. Holand-Smith and W.J. O'Hara. 2d rev. ed. New York: Herder and Herder, 1965.

Schneiders, Sandra M. *New Wineskins: Re-imagining Religious Life Today*. New York: Paulist Press 1986.

— *Beyond Patching: Faith and Feminism in the Catholic Church.* New York: Paulist Press, 1991.

Schoenheer, Richard A. et al. 'The Catholic Priest in the U.S.: Demographic Investigations'. Cited in *Catholic News Service*, 17 July 1990, 1.

Schulte, James H. 'Roman Catholic Views on Sexuality'. In *Religion and Sexuality*. Judaic-Christian Viewpoints in the U.S.A. Monograph no. 1., ed. John M. Holland. San Francisco: The Association of Sexologists, 1981.

Shea, John. 'Doing Ministerial Theology Today'. In *Toward Vatican III*, ed. David Tracy, Hans Küng, and Johann B. Metz, 188-95. New York: The

Seabury Press, 1978.

Sheehy, Gail. *Passages: Predictable Crises of Adult Life.* New York: E. P. Dutton & Co., Inc., 1974.

Silverman, A.F., M.E. Pressman, and H.W. Bartel. 'Self-esteem and Tactile Communication'. *Journal of Humanistic Psychology* 13 (1973): 73-77.

Simons, Joseph, and Jeanne Reidy. *The Risk of Loving.* New York: Herder and Herder, 1968.

Sipe, Richard. *A Secret World: Sexuality and the Search for Celibacy.* New York: Brunner/Mazel, Publishers, 1990.

Smart, J.D. 'Hosea'. In *The Interpreter's Dictionary of the Bible,* E-J. Edited by George A. Buttrick. New York: Abingdon Press, 1962.

Socrates. *Hist. Eccles.* I, 2. Cited by David O'Neill. *Priestly Celibacy and Maturity.* New York: Sheed and Ward, 1965.

Sorensen, Andrew A. *Alcholic Priests: A Sociological Study.* New York: The Seabury Press, A Crossroad Book, 1976.

Spicq, Ceslaus. *Agape in the New Testament.* Vol. 1: *Agape in the Synoptic Gospels.* Translated by Marie Aquinas McNamara and Mary Honoria Richter. St Louis: B. Herder Book Co., 1963.

Stafford, J. Francis. 'The Mystery of the Priestly Vocation'. *Origins* 18, no. 22 (10 November 1988): 349, 351-60.

Steinmann, Jean. *Saint Jerome.* Translated by Ronald Matthews. London: Geoffrey Chapman, 1959.

Sullivan, Harry Stack. *The Interpersonal Theory of Psychiatry.* Edited by Helen Swick Perry and Mary Ladd Gawal. New York: W. W. Norton and Co., Inc., 1953.

— Cited in Rollo May. *Love and Will.* New York: Dell Publishing Co., WW. Norton and Co., Inc., 1969.

Sullivan, Teresa A. 'Numbering Our Days Aright: Human Longevity and the Problem of Intimacy'. In *Toward Vatican III,* ed. David Tracy, Hans Küng, and Johannn B. Metz, 282-94. New York: The Seabury Press, 1978.

Synod of Bishops. *The Ministerial Priesthood and Justice in the World.* Washington, D.C.: United States Catholic Conference, 1982.

— On the Ministerial Priesthood, *Ultimus Temporibus* (30 November 1967). *Acta Apostolicae Sedis* 63 (1971): 898-942.

Tanner, Ira J. *Loneliness: The Fear of Love.* New York: Harper and Row, Publishers, 1973.

Teilhard de Chardin, Pierre. 'L'Evolution de la Chastete'. Quoted in Claude Cuenot. *Teilhard de Chardin: A Biographical Study.* Baltimore: Helicon Press, 1965.

— *The Phenomenon of Man*. Translated by Bernard Wall. New York: Harper and Brothers, 1959.

— *Science and Christianity*. New York: Harper and Row, 1968.

— *Toward the Future* . Translated by Rene Hague. New York: Harcourt Brace Jovanovich, Publishers, 1975.

Teresa of Avila. *Interior Castle*. Translated by E. Allison Peers. Garden City, NY: Image Books, 1961.

— *The Way of Perfection*. Translated and edited by E. Allison Peers. Garden City, NY: Doubleday and Co., Image Books, 1964.

TeSelle, Eugene. 'Augustine As Client and as Theorist'. *Journal for the Scientific Study of Religion* 25, no. 1 (1986): 92-101.

Texas Bishops. 'Texas Bishop's Statement on Sexuality'. *Origins* 17, no. 31 (14 January 1988): 541-44.

Tetlow, Joseph A. 'The Second-Half Generation'. *New Catholic World* 223 (September/October 1980): 196-200.

Thils, Gustave. *The Diocesan Priest*. Translated by Albert J. LaMothe, Jr. London: Geoffrey Chapman, Ltd., 1965.

Thompson, William M. *The Jesus Debate: A Survey and Synthesis*. New York: Paulist Press, 1985.

Tillich, Paul. *The Courage to Be*. New Haven: Yale University Press, 1952.

— *The Eternal Now*. New York: Charles Scribner's Sons, 1956.

— *Theology of Culture*. Oxford: Oxford University Press, Inc., 1959.

Timmons, Tim. *Loneliness Is Not a Disease*. Eugene, OR: Harvest House Publishers, 1981.

Tracy, David with Hans Küng, and Johann B. Metz, eds. *Toward Vatican III*. New York: Concilium, The Seabury Press, 1978.

Turro, James C. '1-2 Samuel'. *JBC* 1:9, 163-178.

Tyrrell, Thomas J. *Urgent Longings: Reflections on The Experience of Infatuation, Human Intimacy, and Contemplative Love*. Whitinsville, MA: Affirmation Books, 1980.

Unger, Merril F., and William White Jr. *Nelson's Expository Dictionary of the Old Testament*. Nashville: Thomas Nelson Publishers, 1980.

van Kaam, Adrian. *The Mystery of Transforming Love*. Denville, NJ: Dimension Books, 1981.

— *Spirituality and the Gentle Life*. Denville, NJ: Dimension Books, Inc., 1974.

van Kaam, Adrian, Bert van Croonenburg, and Susan Annette Muto. *The Emergent Self*. Vol. 1. Wilkes-Barre, PA: Dimension Books, Inc., 1968.

Vanier, Jean. *Be Not Afraid*. New York: Paulist Press, 1975.

— *Man and Woman He Made Them*. Mahwah, NJ: Paulist Press, 1985.

Vatican Council II. Decree on the Ministry and Life of Priests, *Prebyterorum Ordinis* (7 December 1965). *Acta Apostolicae Sedis* 58 (1966): 991-1024.

— Dogmatic Constitution on the Church, *Lumen Gentium* (21 November 1964). *Acta Apostolicae Sedis* 57 (1966): 5-71.

— Pastoral Constitution on the Church in theModern World, *Gaudium et Spes* (7 December 1965). *Vatican Council II: The Conciliar and Post Conciliar Documents*, ed. Austin Flannery, 903-1001. Boston: Daughters of St Paul, 1975.

Vatican Synod Secretariat, 'Formation of Priests in Circumstances of the Present Day', *Origins* 20, no. 10 (2 August 1990): 149, 151-168

Vawter, Bruce. 'The Gospel According to John'. *JBC* 2:63, 414-466.

— 'Johannine Theology'. *JBC* 2:80, 828-839.

Viscott, David. *Risking*. New York: Simon and Schuster, Inc., 1977; Pocket Books, 1979.

Waddell, Helen, ed. *The Desert Fathers*. London: Constable and Co., 1960.

Watson, W.H. 'The Meaning of Touch: Geriatric Nursing'. *Journal of Communication* 25 (1975): 104-12.

Weaver, Mary Jo. *New Catholic Women: A Contemporary Challenge to Traditional Religious Authority*. San Francisco: Harper and Row, Publishers, 1985.

Whitehead, Evelyn Eaton, and James D. Whitehead. *Christian Life Patterns: The Psychological Challenges and Religious Invitations of Adult Life*. Garden City, NY: Image Books, Doubleday and Co., Inc., 1982.

Wicks, Robert J. *Christian Introspection: Self-Ministry through Self-Understanding*. New York: The Crossroad Publishing Co., 1983.

Wiesen, David S. *St. Jerome as a Satirist: A Study in Christian Latin Thought and Letters*. Ithica, NY: Cornell University Press, 1964.

Wilkes, Paul. 'The Hands That Would Shape Our Souls'. *Atlantic Monthly*, December 1990, 59-88.

Williams, Margery. *The Velveteen Rabbit*. New York: Avon Books,1975.

Woititz, Janet Geringer. *Home Away From Home*. Pompano Beach, FL: Health Communications, Inc., 1987.

Wood, Geoffrey E. 'Ruth, Lamentations'. *JBC* 1:36, 603-13.

Wright, Wendy M. 'Reflections on Spiritual Friendship Between Men and Women'. *Weavings* 2, no. 4 (July/August 1987): 13-23.

More Interesting Titles

CONTEMPORARY THEOLOGIANS
JAMES J. BACIK

Contemporary Theologians is intended for all those who want to participate more fully in the great conversation about the religious concerns which tug at the mind and heart. James Bacik discusses the work of 20 theologians and the first grouping contains the three giants of Catholic systematic theology – Karl Rahner, Bernard Lonergan and Yves Congar. They are followed by four more systematic theologians who have worked out of the broad Catholic tradition, Hans Urs von Balthasar, Edward Schillebeeckx, John Macquarrie and Hans Kung. Next comes Karl Barth and Paul Tillich, two influential Protestant theologians. Reinhold Niebuhr and John Courtney Murray are then linked together as public theologians. They are followed by four political and liberation theologians, Johann Metz, Gustavo Gutierrez, Rosemary Ruether and Martin Luther King. The next grouping consists of authors who are not professional theologians but excercised great influence on religious thought: Alfred North Whitehead, Jacques Maritain and Teilhard de Chardin. Finally, Martin Buber and Mohandis Gandhi, influential thinkers who represent religious traditions other than Christianity, complete the list.

'This insightful introduction to some of the major theologians of the twentieth century captures the thrust of their thought and presents it in a readable and engaging fashion.'

–John Shea

RETROSPECT:

The Origins of Catholic Beliefs and Practices

JOHN DEEDY

For generations Catholics lived by the assurance that theirs was a church that had never changed and never would change. It was a proud boast and a perpetual consolation. At the same time it was an assurance that did not always bear close scrutinizing as in several areas — among them slavery, usury, church and state, and salvation outside the church — church teaching has taken on different contexts, if nothing more.

Did the church change? Yes and no.

The church does not change in essentials. It changes all the time, however, in incidentals. The church's story takes fascinating, colourful and surprising turns. The purpose of this book is to trace those turns as it explores aspects of church history. The author looks at the origins and evolution of many of those practices which are part and parcel of modern Catholicism. Was celibacy always a requirement of priests? Was the mass always the carefully structured liturgical ceremony it is today? Have devotional practices like novanas, the rosary and the stations of the cross always been part of the Catholic experience?

RETROSPECT: The origins of Catholic Beliefs and Practices examines subjects such as The Mass, Indulgences, Miracles, Marriage, Divorce and Annulment, Celibacy, Papal Infallibility and many others.

Body-Mind Meditation
A Gateway to Spirituality

Louis Hughes, OP

You can take this book as your guide for a fascinating journey that need not take you beyond your own hall door. For it is an inward journey, and it will take you no further than God who, for those who want him as a friend, lives within. On the way to God-awareness, you will be invited to experience deep relaxation of body and mind.

Body-Mind Meditation can help you become a more integrated balanced person. It is an especially helpful approach to meditation if the pace of life is too fast for you, or if you find yourself frequently tense or exhausted.

An Easy Guide to Meditation

Roy Eugene Davis

Meditation is the natural process to use to release tension, reduce stress, increase awareness, concentrate more effectively and be open to life. In this book you will learn how to meditate correctly for inner growth and spiritual awareness. Specific guidelines are provided to assist the beginner as well as the more advanced meditator. Here are proven techniques used by accomplished meditators for years: *prayer, mantra, sound–light contemplation, ways to expand consciousness and to experience transcendence.*

PETER CALVAY HERMIT

Rayner Torkington

This is a fast moving and fascinating story of a young priest in search of holiness and of the hermit who helps him. The principles of Christian Spirituality are pinpointed with a ruthless accuracy that challenges the integrity of the reader, and dares him to abandon himself to the only One who can radically make him new. The author not only shows how prayer is the principal means of doing this, but he details a 'Blue Print' for prayer for the beginner, and outlines and explains the most ancient Christian prayer tradition, while maintaining the same compelling style throughout.

Over 34,000 copies of this bestseller have been sold.

PETER CALVAY PROPHET

Rayner Torkington

This book is first and foremost a brilliant exposition of the inner meaning of prayer and of the profound truths that underlie the spiritual life. Here at last is a voice that speaks with authority and consumate clarity amidst so much contemporary confusion, of the only One who makes all things new and of how to receive Him.